Problems of Biblical Theology in the
Twentieth Century

Problems of Biblical Theology in the Twentieth Century

Henning Graf Reventlow

Fortress Press   Philadelphia

Translated by John Bowden from the German
Hauptprobleme der Biblischen Theologie im 20. Jahrhundert,
Ertrage der Forschung 203,
published by Wissenschaftliche Buchgesellschaft, Darmstadt 1983.

© Wissenschaftliche Buchgesellschaft, Darmstadt 1983

Translation © John Bowden 1986

First Fortress Press edition 1986

Library of Congress Cataloging-in-Publication Data

Reventlow, Henning, Graf.
  Problems of Biblical theology in the twentieth
century.

  Translation of: Hauptprobleme der Biblischen
Theologie im 20. Jahrhundert.
  Includes bibliographical references.
  1. Bible—Theology—History—20th century.
2. Bible. N.T.—Relation to the Old Testament.
I. Title.
BS543.R4813 1986   220.6′09′04   84–4722
  ISBN 0–8006–1935–8

2558C86   Printed in the United Kingdom   1–1935

Contents

Preface

This is the sequel to my *Problems of Old Testament Theology in the Twentieth Century*, the English translation of which appeared in 1985. That volume already anticipated the theme of 'salvation history' (cf. Chapter III, 4); here all the other areas of more recent scholarly discussion are covered which have to do with the relationship between the two Testaments. Thus the scope is rather wider than that of the most recent debate over the possibility of recovering a 'biblical theology' (which is dealt with in the last section of the present book).

The problems discussed in this wider area have in no way been made obsolete by the latest approaches. Most of these problem areas involve perspectives and touch on elements of truth which need to be thought about further if contemporary biblical scholarship is to press forward and find new answers to probably the most difficult and controversial set of tasks with which it has ever been faced. A 'biblical theology' has yet to be written. The way towards it is not only one of high hopes; it is also beset by a good deal of scepticism. It will only prove viable if premature solutions are rejected and all perspectives are considered comprehensively and with the necessary methodological care. 'Biblical theology' is in the widest sense of the term an exegetical, hermeneutical and systematic discipline. It must be continued with, despite all the justifiable hesitations over some of the answers which have already been given. For its concern is to present to Christian faith an account of how far and why the *whole* of the Bible, Old Testament and New, has come down to us as Holy Scripture. Biblical scholarship cannot refuse the church an answer to this question. We shall have to see as we go on how far it can derive help from systematic theology and other disciplines. But in the first place, this is its own specific task.

I must also thank my co-workers most warmly for their help in preparing this book. Hans-Joachim Güttler, Hannelore Hollstein, Christine Latuner, Gudrun Müller and Ulrike Liebau have helped me over it with extreme conscientiousness. Friedbert Fellert has checked the translation meticulously. I am grateful to Ute Portmann for her careful preparation of the manuscript and to all those of the two publishing staffs involved in its production.

Here too, my concern has been to give the reader as much information as possible about the discussion in specific areas. Because of the care necessary in such a survey, I have not included works to which I had no access. This English edition is enlarged and corrected; I have added details of further material which has since come to my attention. I am again grateful to Drs L.W.Nijendijk of Utrecht for help in securing some Dutch publications for me, and to Dean B.Harvey of Kilkenny, Ireland, for sending me a copy of *The Loom of God*, of which he is co-author.

Bochum
15 March 1982/30 September 1985

Abbreviations

AAS	*Acta apostolicae sedis*
ACJD	Abhandlungen zum christlich-jüdischen Dialog
AEcR	*American Ecclesiastical Review*
AGSU	Arbeiten zur Geschichte des Spätjudentums und Urchristentums
AnBib	*Analecta Biblica*
AnGr	*Analecta Gregoriana*
Anton	*Antonianum*
APPR	Abhandlungen zur Philosophie, Psychologie und Sociologie der Religion
ASNU	Acta seminarii neotestamentici Upsaliensis
AT	Altes Testament
ATANT	Abhandlungen zur Theologie des Alten und Neuen Testaments
ATD	Das Alte Testament Deutsch
ATh	*Année Théologique*
ATR	*Anglican Theological Review*
AUSS	*Andrews University Seminary Studies*
AVTRW	Aufsätze und Vorträge zur Theologie und Religionswissenschaft
AzTh	Arbeiten zur Theologie
BCES	*Bulletin du comité des études, compagnie de Saint Sulpice*
BenM	*Benediktinische Monatsschrift*
BETL	Bibliotheca ephemeridum theologicarum Lovaniensium
BEvTh	Beiträge zur evangelischen Theologie
BFCT	Beiträge zur Förderung christlicher Theologie
BHT	Beiträge zur historischen Theologie

Bib	*Biblica*
BiBe	Biblische Beiträge
BiblThom	Bibliotheque Thomiste
Bijdr	*Bijdragen. Tijdschrift voor philosphie en theologie*
BiKi	*Bibel und Kirche*
BiLe	*Bibel und Leben*
BiLi	*Bible und Liturgie*
BiTod	*Bible Today*
BJRL	*Bulletin of the John Rylands Library*
BK	Biblischer Kommentar
Bl	*Blackfriars*
BR	*Biblical Research*
BS	*Bibliotheca sacra*
BSt	Biblische Studien
BT.D	Bibliotheque de théologie 1 sér. Théologie dogmatique
BTS	Biblisch-theologische Studien
BTZ	*Berliner Theologische Zeitschrift*
BVC	*Bible et Vie Chretienne*
BWANT	Beiträge zur Wissenschaft vom Alten und Neuen Testament
BZ	*Biblische Zeitschrift*
BZAW	Beihefte zur Zeitschrift für die alttestamentliche Wissenschaft
CaC	*Christianity and Crisis*
Cath (M)	*Catholica (Münster)*
CBQ	*Catholic Biblical Quarterly*
CCen	*Christian Century*
CD	see *KD*
CFi	*Cogitatio fidei*
CHB	*Cambridge History of the Bible*
CivCatt	*Civiltà cattolica*
CiW	*Christ in der Welt*
CJT	*Canadian Journal of Theology*
CleR	*Clergy Review*
CMind	*Catholic Mind*
Com	*Commentary*
Conc	*Concilium*
ConQ	*Congregational Quarterly*
CQR	*Church Quarterly Review*

CSion	*Cahiers sioniens*
CSS	Cursus scripturae sacrae
CThM	Calwer theologische Monographien
CTJ	*Calvin Theological Journal*
CTM	*Concordia Theological Monthly*
CTom	*Ciencia Tomista*
CV	*Communio viatorum*
DBS	*Dictionnaire de la Bible. Supplement*
DtPfrBl	*Deutsches Pfarrerblatt*
dtv	*Deutscher Taschenbuchverlag*
Dü	*Der Überblick*
DublRe	*Dublin Review*
DunR	*Dunwoodie Review*
DViv	*Dieu vivant*
EdF	Erträge der Forschung
EE	*Estudios ecclesiásticos*
EeV	*Esprit et vie*
EHK	*Eine heilige Kirche*
EHS.T	Europäische Hochschulschriften, R.23, Theologie
EK	*Evangelische Kommentare*
EKK.V	*Evangelisch-katholischer Kommentar zum Neuen Testamentum – Vorarbeiten*
EnchB	*Enchiridion biblicum*
ER	*Ecumenical Review*
ErJb	*Eranos Jahrbuch*
ESt	Eichstätter Studien
EstB	*Estudios biblicos*
ET	English Translation
EtJ	Études juives
ETL	*Ephemerides theologicae Lovanienses*
ETR	*Études Théologiques et Religieuses*
ETS	Erfurter theologische Studien
EvMis	*Evangelische Mission*
EvQ	*Evangelical Quarterly*
EvTh	*Evangelische Theologie*
ExpT	*Expository Times*
EZS	Evangelische Zeitstimmen
FAB	*Für Arbeit und Besinnung*
FDV	Franz Delitzsch Vorlesungen
FolLov	Folia Lovaniensia

FRLANT	Forschungen zur Religion und Literatur des Alten und Neuen Testaments
FrRu	*Freiburger Rundbrief*
FS	Festschrift
FÜI	*Friede Über Israel*
FV	*Foi et vie*
FzB	Forschungen zur Bibel
FZTP	*Freiburger Zeitschrift für Philosophie und Theologie*
GNT	*Grundrisse zum Neuen Testament*
GPM	*Göttinger Predigtmeditationen*
GTT	*Gereformeerd theologisch Tijdschrift*
GWU	*Geschichte in Wissenschaft und Unterricht*
HBT	*Horizons in Biblical Theology*
HDB	*Harvard Divinity Bulletin*
HerKorr	*Herder-Korrespondenz*
HeyJ	*Heythrop Journal*
HNT	Handbuch zum Neuen Testament
HTh.S	*History and Theory.* Supplement
HTR	*Harvard Theological Review*
HTS	*Hervormde Teologiese Studies*
HUCA	*Hebrew Union College Annual*
IDB	*Interpreter's Dictionary of the Bible*
IDB.S	*Interpreter's Dictionary of the Bible. Supplementary Volume*
IKaZ	*Internationale Katholische Zeitschrift*
IluCle	*Ilustración del clero*
Imm	*Immanuel*
Int	*Interpretation*
Iren	*Irénikon*
IRM	*International Review of Mission*
ITQ	*Irish Theological Quarterly*
JAAR	*Journal of the American Academy of Religion*
JBL	*Journal of Biblical Literature*
JBR	*Journal of Bible and Religion*
JChS	*Journal of Church and State*
Jdm	*Judaism*
JEM	*Jahrbuch evangelischer Mission*
JES	*Journal of Ecumenical Studies*
JETS	*Journal of the Evangelical Theological Society*

JJS	*Journal of Jewish Studies*
JR	*Journal of Religion*
JSJ	*Journal of the Study of Judaism in the Persian, Hellenistic and Roman Period*
JSOT	*Journal for the Study of the Old Testament*
JSOT.S	*Journal for the Study of the Old Testament, Supplement*
JTS	*Journal of Theological Studies*
Jud	*Judaica*
KatBl	*Katechetische Blätter*
KBRS	*Kirchenblatt für die reformierte Schweiz*
KD/CD	Karl Barth, *Kirchliche Dogmatik/Church Dogmatics*
KeTh	*Kerk en theologie*
KiZ	*Kirche in der Zeit*
KJ	*Kirchliches Jahrbuch*
KKTS	Konfessionskundliche und kontroverstheologische Studien
KT	Kaiser-Traktate
KuD	*Kerygma und Dogma*
KuM	*Kerygma und Mythos*
KVR	Kleine Vandenhoeck-Reihe
LebZeug	*Lebendiges Zeugnis*
LeDiv	Lectio Divina
LM	*Lutherische Monatshefte*
LMJ (B)	*Lutherische Missions-Jahrbuch für die Jahre*
LoS	*Life of the Spirit*
LQHR	*London Quarterly and Holborn Review*
LR	*Lutherische Rundschau*
LTK	*Lexikon für Theologie und Kirche*
LTK.E	*Lexikon für Theologie und Kirche. Ergänzungsheft*
Lum	*Lumen*
LuthQ	*Lutheran Quarterly*
LV(L)	*Lumière et Vie*
MCom	*Miscelanea Comillas*
MD	*Maison-Dieu*
MenJ	*Menorah Journal*
MHP	Miscellanea historiae pontifici
MPT	*Monatsschrift für Pastoraltheologie*

MSR	*Mélanges de science religieuse*
MTS	Marburger Theologische Studien
MTZ	*Münchener theologische Zeitschrift*
MySal	*Mysterium Salutis*
NCW	New Catholic World
NF	Neue Folge
NGTT	*Nederduits gereformeerde teologiese tydskrif*
NKS	*Nederlands(che) katholieke stemmen*
NRT	*Nouvelle revue théologique*
NS	New Series
NStB	Neukirchener Studienbücher
NT	New Testament
NT	*Novum Testamentum*
NT.S	*Novum Testamentum.* Supplement
NTA	Neutestamentliche Abhandlungen
NTS	*New Testament Studies*
NTT	*Norsk Teologisk Tidsskrift*
NTWSA	*Nieuw testamentiese werkgemeenschap in Suid-Afrika*
NZST	*Neue Zeitschrift für systematische Theologie*
OBMRL	*Occasional Bulletin of the Missionary Research Library*
OBO	Orbis biblicus et orientalis
Orien	*Orientierung*
OS	*Oudtestamentische Studien*
OT	Old Testament
OTL	Old Testament Library
OTWSA	Ou testamentiese werkgemeenskap in Suid-Afrika
OTWSA.P	*Papers read at OTSWA*
PalCl	*Palestra del Clero*
PBL	*Pastoralblätter für Homiletik, Katechetik und Seelsorge*
PCB	*Peake's Commentary on the Bible*
PCTSA	*Proceedings of Annual Meeting. Catholic Theological Society of America*
PRSt	*Perspectives in Religious Studies*
PT	*Pastoraltheologie*
QD	Quaestiones Disputatae
RB	*Revue Biblique*

RDT	*Revue diocesaine de Tournai*
RelLife	*Religion in Life*
RET	*Revista Espanola de teologia*
RExp	*Review and Expositor*
RF	*Razón y Fé*
RFF	*Rundbrief zur Förderung der Freundschaft zwischen dem alten und dem neuen Gottesvolk im Geiste der beiden Testamente*
RGG	*Die Religion in Geschichte und Gegenwart*
RHPR	*Revue d'histoire et de Philosophie religieuses*
RKZ	*Reformierte Kirchenzeitung*
RoMo	Rowohlts Monographien
RPS	Religious Perspectives Series
RSR	*Recherches de science religieuse*
RThom	*Revue Thomiste*
RTP	*Revue de théologie et de philosophie*
RTR	*Reformed Theological Review*
SANT	Studien zum Alten und Neuen Testament
SBEsp	*Semana biblica española*
SBKAB	Studien und Berichte der katholischen Akademie in Bayern
SBS	Stuttgarter Bibelstudien
SBT	*Studia Biblica et Theologica*
ScC	*Scuola Cattolica*
ScEs	*Science et esprit*
SEA	*Schriftenreihe der evangelischen Akademie*
SEÅ	*Svensk exegetisk årsbok*
SJK	Schriften zur Judentumskunde
SJT	*Scottish Journal of Theology*
STAEKU	Schriftenreihe des theologischen Ausschusses der evangelischen Kirche der Union
StZ	*Stimme der Zeit*
StEnc	*Study Encounter*
StTh	*Studia Theologica*
STU	*Schweizerische theologische Umschau*
SVT	Supplements to *Vetus Testamentum*
SvTK	*Svensk Teologisk kvartalskrift*
SWJT	*Southwestern Journal of Theology*
TA	Theologische Arbeiten
TAik	*Teologinen aikakauskirja*

TB	Theologische Bücherei
TDNT	*Theological Dictionary of the New Testament* (ET of *TWNT*)
TGW	*Tydskriv vir geesteswetenshappe*
ThD	*Theology Digest*
ThExH	Theologische Existenz Heute
ThBeitr	Theologische Beiträge
ThBer	Theologische Berichte
Theol	*Theology*
ThF	*Theologische Forschung*
ThG (B)	*Theologie der Gegenwart* (Bergen)
ThGl	*Theologie und Glaube*
THK	Theologischer Handkommentar zum Neuen Testament
ThMed	*Theologische Meditation*
ThQ	*Theologische Quartalschrift*
ThStKr	Theologische Studien und Kritiken
ThTo	*Theology Today*
ThV	*Theologische Versuche*
TLZ	*Theologische Literaturzeitung*
TP	*Theologie und Philosophie*
TPQ	*Theologisch-praktische Quartalschrift*
TQ	*Theologische Quartalschrift*
TRE	*Theologische Realenzyklopädie*
TS	*Theological Studies*
TS(B)	Theologische Studien, ed. K. Barth
TS(I)	*Terra Santa*
TSFBull	*Theological Students Fellowship Bulletin*
TTK	*Tidsskrift for Teologie og Kirke*
TU	Texte und Untersuchungen zur Geschichte der altchristlichen Literatur
TTZ	*Trierer Theologische Zeitschrift*
TWNT	*Theologische Wörterbuch zum Neuen Testament*
TynB	*Tyndale Bulletin*
TZ	*Theologische Zeitschrift*
US	*Una Sancta*
USQR	*Union Seminary Quarterly Review*
UTB	Uni-Taschenbücher
UUA	*Uppsala Universitets Årsskrift*
VC	*Verbum Caro*

VD	*Verbum Domini*
VF	*Verkündigung und Forschung*
VieI	*Vie Intellectuelle*
VoxEv	*Vox evangelica*
VoxTh	*Vox theologica*
VS	*Vie spirituelle*
VT	*Vetus Testamentum*
WdF	Wege der Forschung
WiWei	*Wissenschaft und Weisheit*
WPKG	*Wissenschaft und Praxis in Kirche und Gesellschaft*
WTJ	*Westminster Theological Journal*
WuD	*Wort und Dienst*
WUNT	Wissenschaftliche Untersuchungen zum Neuen Testament
WuW	*Wort und Wahrheit*
WV	*Worldview*
ZAW	*Zeitschrift für die alttestamentliche Wissenschaft*
ZdZ	*Zeichen der Zeit*
ZKT	*Zeitschrift für Katholische Theologie*
ZNW	*Zeitschrift für die Neutestamentliche Wissenschaft*
ZRGG	*Zeitschrift für Religions- und Geistesgeschichte*
ZTK	*Zeitschrift für Theologie und Kirche*
ZTK.B	*Zeitschrift für Theologie und Kirche.* Beiheft
ZW	*Zeitwende*

I

The Anglo-Saxon 'Biblical Theology Movement'

Not only in Germany, but also in Great Britain and America – though after some delay – the altered intellectual climate resulted in the revival of a direct interest in the Bible on the part of Christian believers. This movement, which began shortly before and during the Second World War in Great Britain, combined a concern for a commitment in faith to the Bible on the part of believers with a marked interest in all its aspects, so that the question of the theological significance of the Old Testament and its relationship to the New played a major part in the discussion. Great Britain had not experienced any politically motivated attacks on the Old Testament; nevertheless, estimation of it among church people and the general public had sunk for the moment to an all-time low (thus in the Lower House of the Canterbury Convocation of 1940 a motion was introduced to replace Old Testament texts with readings from non-biblical literature in the lectionary, cf. *Church Times*, 19 January 1940, and in August 1962 the correspondence columns of *The Times* still contained a lively dispute over the pros and cons of retaining the Old Testament in the church, cf. P.R.Ackroyd, 'The Old Testament in the Christian Church', *Theol* 66, 1963, 46-52). Now, however, a series of popular revivalist works, soon joined by contributions from biblical critics, called for a renewed recognition of the authority of Holy Scripture, including the Old Testament, for Christian faith.

Anderson, A.A., 'Old Testament Theology and its Methods', in *FS S.H.Hooke*, Edinburgh 1963, 7-19; Atkinson, B.F.C., *The Christian's Use of the Old Testament*, London 1952; Balmforth, H., 'The Appeal to the Bible', *Theol* 53, 1950, 210-18; Barr, J., 'The Problem of Old Testament Theology and the History of

Religion', *CJT* 3, 1957, 141-9; id., 'Biblical Theology', *IDB.S*, 1976, (104-11) 105f.; Blackman, E.C., 'The Authority of the Old Testament: Is it Christian Scripture?', *ConQ* 24, 1946, 13-24; Bright, J., *The Authority of the Old Testament*, Nashville and London 1967; Childs, B.S., *Biblical Theology in Crisis*, Philadelphia 1970, 13-60; Cunliffe-Jones, H., *The Authority of the Biblical Revelation*, London 1945, ²1948; Davey, F.N., 'Biblical Theology', *Theol* 38, 1939, 166-76; Dentan, R.C., 'The Old Testament and a Theology for Today', *ATR* 27, 1945, 17-27; Dodd, C.H., *The Bible Today*, Cambridge 1946 and New York 1947; id., 'The Relevance of the Bible', in *Biblical Authority for Today*, ed. A.Richardson and W.Schweitzer, London 1951, 157-62; Filson, F.V., 'A New Testament Student's Approach to Biblical Theology', *JBR* 14, 1946, 22-8; id., 'Biblische Theologie in Amerika', *TLZ* 75, 1950, 71-80; Fridrichsen, A. (ed.), *The Root of the Vine: Essays in Biblical Theology*, Westminster 1953; Gamble, C., 'The Literature of Biblical Theology. A Biblical Study', *Int* 76, 1953, 466-80; Hanson, R.P.C. and Harvey, B., *The Loom of God*, Dublin 1945 (²1955); Haroutunian, J., 'Recent Theology and the Biblical Mind', *JBR* 8, 1940, 18-23; Discussion (E.S.Brightman; C.T.Craig; J.Haroutunian; A.N.Wilder; V.Corwin; I.R.Beiler), ibid., 35-9; Hebert, A.G., *The Throne of David: A Study of the Fulfilment of the Old Testament in Jesus Christ and His Church*, London 1941; id., *The Authority of the Old Testament*, London 1947; id., *The Bible from Within*, Oxford 1950 (new edition, *The Old Testament from Within*, London etc. 1962); id., *Scripture and the Faith*, London 1947; Hendry, G.G., 'The Exposition of Holy Scripture', *SJT* 1, 1948, 29-47; Higgins, A.J.B., *The Christian Significance of the Old Testament*, London 1949; Johnson, D., *The Christian and His Bible*, London 1953; Lankard, F.G., *The Bible Speaks to Our Generation*, New York 1941; Lowe, J., 'The Recovery of the Theological Interpretation of the Bible', in *The Interpretation of the Bible*, ed.C.W.Dugmore, London 1944, 108-22; Lyman, M.E., 'The Unity of the Bible', *JBR* 14, 1946, 5-12; Minear, P.S., 'Wanted: A Biblical Theology', *ThTo* 1, 1944, 47-58; id., *Eyes of Faith: A Study in the Biblical Point of View*, Philadelphia 1949; Phythian-Adams, W.J.T., *The Call of Israel*, London 1934, id., 'The Foundations of Biblical Theology', *CQR* 135, 1942, 1-42; id., *The Fulness of Israel. A Study of the Meaning of Sacred History*, London, New York and

Toronto 1938; id., *The People and the Presence*, Oxford 1942; id., 'Shadow and Substance. The Meaning of Sacred History', *Int* 1, 1947, 419-35; id., *The Way of At-one-ment. Studies in Biblical Theology*, London 1944; Porteous, N.W., 'Towards a Theology of the Old Testament', *SJT* 1, 1948, 136-49 = id., *Living the Mystery*, Oxford 1967, 7-19; id., 'Semantics and Old Testament Theology', *OS* 8, 1950, 1-14 = *Living the Mystery*, 21-30; id., 'The Old Testament and Some Theological Thought-Forms', *SJT* 7, 1954, 153-69 = *Living the Mystery*, 31-46; Richardson, A., *Preface to Bible Study*, London 1941, [8]1972; id., 'Historical Theology and Biblical Theology', *CJT* 1, 1955, 157-67; Robinson, H.W., *Inspiration and Revelation in the Old Testament*, Oxford 1946; Roehrs, W.R., 'The Unity of Scripture', *CTM* 31, 1960, 277-302; Rowley, H.H., *The Relevance of the Bible*, London 1942 and New York 1944; id., *The Rediscovery of the Old Testament*, London and Philadelphia 1946; id., *The Authority of the Bible*, Birmingham 1949 = id., *From Moses to Qumran*, London 1963, 3-34; id., *The Unity of the Bible*, London 1953; cf. id., *The Biblical Doctrine of Election*, London 1950; Rylaarsdam, J.C., 'Preface to Hermeneutics', *JR* 30, 1950, 79-89; Schoder, R.V., 'The Rebirth of Scriptural Theology', *AEcR* 117, 1947, 81-101; Smart, J.D., 'The Death and Rebirth of Old Testament Theology', *JR* 23, 1943, 1-11, 125-36 = id., *The Interpretation of Scripture*, Philadelphia and London 1961, 232-304; id., 'The Need for a Biblical Theology', *RelLife* 26, 1956/57, 22-30; id., *The Old Testament in Dialogue with Modern Man*, Philadelphia 1964 and London 1965; id., *The Past, Present and Future of Biblical Theology*, Philadelphia 1979; Smart, W.A., *Still the Bible Speaks*, New York 1948; Sparks, H.F.D., *The Old Testament in the Christian Church*, London 1944; Stokes, M.B., *The Epic of Revelation: An Essay in Biblical Theology*, New York 1961; Terrien, S.L., 'The Old Testament and the Christian Preacher Today', *RelLife* 15, 1946, 262-71; Vicary, D.R., 'Liberalism, Biblical Criticism, and Biblical Theology', *ATR* 32, 1950, 114-21; Vos, G., *Biblical Theology: Old and New Testaments*, Grand Rapids 1948 (cf. id., *The Idea of Biblical Theology as a Science and as a Theological Discipline*, New York 1894); Wand, J.W.C., *The Authority of the Scriptures*, London 1949; Watson, P.S., 'The Nature and Function of Biblical Theology', *ExpT* 73, 1962, 195-200; Wilder, A.N., 'An Editorial Note', *JBR* 14, 1946, 3f.; Wolfe, R.E., 'The Terminology of

Biblical Theology', *JBR* 15, 1947, 143-7; Wood, J.W., 'The Interpretation of the Old Testament', *ExpT* 57, 1946, 165-7; Wright, G.E., *The Challenge of Israel's Faith*, Chicago 1944.

The effects of dialectical theology made themselves felt above all in America, whereas Great Britain (apart from Scotland) went its own way more markedly. The significance of Holy Scripture for the church was also discussed at an ecumenical level (see the collection edited by Richardson and Schweitzer). Theologians of different confessions, all moved by the same concerns, took part in the discussion. A series of journals came into being specifically for the purpose of providing a forum for the new movement (like *ThTo* in 1944, *Int* in 1947 and *SJT* in 1948). Often congresses and symposia were held on the problem, and the lectures given at them were published in special numbers of the leading journals (cf. *JBR* 1940; *JBR* 1946; *SJT* 1948; *Int* 1951; *RelLife* 1956). However, despite the basic agreement that the Bible must again take on a theological significance, i.e. one which was directly concerned with faith, the individual positions were very different. In this phase much that could be seen in earlier developments in Germany now recurred in the Anglo-Saxon countries (for an account of the development cf. especially Childs, *Biblical Theology*, Ch.1, 14ff.; Filson, *TLZ* 1950; also Smart, J.D., *Interpretation*, 285ff.; id., *Past, Present and Future*, 9ff.; Wood, op.cit.). Sometimes we find a christological interpretation of the Old Testament reminiscent of W.Vischer, as in A.G.Hebert, *The Throne of David* (who seeks to interpret the Old Testament in the light of its fulfilment in Christ; he calls this 'mystical interpretation', 256ff.), or in the works of W.J.Phythian-Adams, for whom the 'presence' of God in the Old Testament is the central concept, the relationship of which to the fulfilment in Christ is the basis of the unity of salvation history. Whereas marked fundamentalist features appear above all in the latter (thus in *The Call of Israel* he argues for the 'truth' of the events reported in the Old Testament including the miracles), H.H.Rowley is an outstanding professional Old Testament scholar. He emphatically stresses the need for the historical-critical method in the understanding of the Old Testament and argues that its application is no obstacle to the spiritual use of the Bible (*Relevance*, passim). The Bible is not the revelation itself but the account of the revelation; it is not infallible, and therefore is also subject to critical investigation by reason (*Authority*, 3ff.). While reason is not everything, 'Yet within its own sphere reason is supreme, and... the judgment of reason must be free and final' (ibid., 6). 'This means that a truly historical outlook is essential for the understanding of the Old Testament, and the mere reading back of the New into the Old is misleading' (*Rediscovery*, 11). Nevertheless he is convinced of the significance of the Old Testament for Christian faith and sees the two Testaments belonging together as in a relationship of promise and fulfilment (*Unity*, 90ff.). Alongside this, however, he stresses the multiplicity in unity (*Unity*, 1-29), and emphasizes that the principle of scholarly work is that, 'Each Testament is to be read first and foremost in terms of itself and its own *Sitz im Leben...* before they are related to one another' (*Unity*, 20). In his book *Eyes of Faith*, the New Testament scholar P.Minear stresses the faith-relationship to the Bible: 'The Bible calls for witnesses, not for teachers. It is written from faith to faith; not from objective knowledge to faith, or from faith to objective knowledge. It demands subjective appropriation' (3). It is not concerned with a theological system: 'Our task... lies in the direction of so seeing ourselves in relation to their [the biblical witnesses] God that a kind of inner life may ensue that will be productive of their perspective.' 'The message of the Bible seems more easily grasped in the chapel than in the classroom' (12). 'Sympathetic imagination' is called for (3f.).

Although there is no direct connection, much here recalls the programme of 'pneumatic exegesis'. It is illuminating that above all in America in the years immediately after the Second World War there was a vigorous discussion about the approach to a biblical theology. In it we find exactly the same opposition as the one which governed the argument between O.Eissfeldt and W.Eichrodt in the 1920s (see my *Problems of Old Testament Theology*). On the one hand are those who think that a purely historical approach to the Bible must be transcended in favour of a direct commitment in faith (G.F.Hasel, *Old Testament Theology. Basic Issues in the Current Debate*, Grand Rapids 1972, ²1975, 39ff., calls this the 'Confessional Method'), and on the other side the members above all of the old liberal school who, if they do not want to maintain a purely history-of-religions approach to the Old Testament, also call for an objective and descriptive approach in any presentation of the theology of the Old Testament (Hasel, 35ff., 'Descriptive Method'). They often also criticize the theological position of what they call (cf. F.Hahn,

The Old Testament in Modern Research, Philadelphia 1954 and London 1956, Philadelphia [3]1970, 237-42) 'neo-orthodoxy' (there is especially vigorous criticism in Morton Smith, 'The Present State of Old Testament Studies', *JBL* 88, 1969, 19-35). K.Stendahl has emerged as the most prominent spokesman for the historical-descriptive task of biblical theology.

Stendahl, K., 'Biblical Theology, Contemporary', *IDB* I, 418-32; id., 'Implications of Form-Criticism and Tradition-Criticism for Biblical Interpretation', *JBL* 77, 1958, 33-8; id., 'Method in the Study of Biblical Theology', in *The Bible in Modern Scholarship*, ed. J.P.Hyatt, Nashville 1965, 196-209. Cf. also Allen, E.L., 'The Limits of Biblical Theology', *JBR* 25, 1957, 13-18; Branton, J.R., 'Our Present Situation in Biblical Theology', *RelLife* 26, 1956/7, 5-18; M.Burrows, 'The Task of Biblical Theology', *JBR* 14, 1946, 13-15; Cwiekowski, F.J., 'Biblical Theology as Historical Theology', *CBQ* 24, 1962, 404-10; Dentan, R.C., 'The Nature and Function of Old Testament Theology', *JBR* 14, 1946, 16-21 (but cf. *ATR* 1945, above, 2); id., *Preface to Old Testament Theology*, New York 1950, [2]1963, 89ff.; Enslin, M.S., 'The Future of Biblical Studies', *JBL* 65, 1946, 1-12; Irwin, W.A., 'The Reviving Theology of the Old Testament', *JR* 25, 1945, 235-46; id., 'Trends in Old Testament Theology', *JBR* 19, 1951, 183-90; cf. also id., 'A Still Small Voice... Said, What Are You Doing Here?', *JBL* 78, 1959, 1-12; King, W.L., 'Some Ambiguities in Biblical Theology', *RelLife* 27, 1958, 95-104; Lacheman, E.R., 'The Renaissance of Biblical Theology' (review of Dentan, *Preface*), *JBR* 19, 1951, 71-5; Martin, I.J., 'Higher Criticism and Biblical Problems', *JBR* 3, 1947, 148-52; Moore, J.M., 'Recent Theological Tendencies and the Teaching of Religion to Under-graduates', *JBR* 8, 1940, 24-6; Pfeiffer, R.H., 'Facts and Faith in Biblical History', *JBL* 70, 1951, 1-14; Pittenger, W.N., 'Biblical Religion and Biblical Theology', *JBR* 13, 1945, 179-83; Pritchard, J.B., 'Some Strange Fruit of Old Testament Criticism', *RelLife* 18, 1948, 34-47; Rylaarsdam, J.C., *JR* 1950 (see above, 3); Teeple, H.M., 'Notes on a Theologian's Approach to the Bible', *JBL* 79, 1960, 164-6 (for Ferré, see below, 8). For the general intellectual situation in the USA as a background to this attitude cf. also Wilder, A.N., 'Biblical Hermeneutics and American

Scholarship', *Neutestamentliche Studien R.Bultmann...*, Berlin 1954, 24-32; Smart, *Past, Present and Future* (above, 3), 43-8.

The arguments of this group are predominantly the same: all of them regard biblical theology (by which sometimes they mean mainly the theology of the New Testament) as a historical task which must be carried out in a descriptive way (that even applies to a group in the conservative camp, as e.g. in Vos's book written in his old age [1948]). Among his followers are J.Murray, 'Systematic Theology', *WTJ* 25, 1963, 133-42, and O.Robertson, 'The Outlook for Biblical Theology', in *Towards a Theology for the Future*, ed. D.F.Wells and C.H.Pinnock, Carol Stream, Ill., 1971, (65-91) 66, 70. J.Bright, *Authority* (see above, 2), 115, also holds the same position on quite different presuppositions. So they maintain the development introduced by Gabler. Their fear is that the 'biblical theology movement' will lead to enthusiasm, arbitrariness and the loss of scientific objectivity. It is often conceded that the greatest possible sympathy by the exegete for the content of the Bible is helpful and perhaps necessary. So in terms of method they keep to the standpoint of historicism.

A smaller group defends the concern for a biblical theology related to faith and focussed on preaching against these attacks. An important representative of it is B.S.Childs (see 'Interpretation in Faith, The Theological Responsibility of an Old Testament Commentary', *Int* 18, 1964, 432-9). He argues against a merely 'objective' description of the religious content of the Bible that the task of a biblical theology is to achieve the Reformation relationship to the Bible: the Reformers read the Old Testament in order to hear the Word of God (437). The theological task of biblical interpretation can only be fulfilled in the framework and on the presuppositions of faith. Similarly, as early as 1946 G.E.Wright already called for a view which departed from the misleading quest for 'objectivity' and adopted the confessional standpoint of the biblical narrator ('Neo-orthodoxy and the Bible', *JBR* 14, 1946, 87-93; later ['Biblical Archaeology Today', in *New Directions in Biblical Archaeology*, ed. D.N.Freedman and J.C.Greenfield, New York 1969, 159] Wright again saw biblical theology as a 'descriptive discipline'). Here the biblical scholars had to take the lead, as the danger of dogmatism among the systematic theologians of 'neo-orthodoxy' (like Barth, Brunner and Niebuhr) could not in fact be disregarded (87). To the same effect see N.F.Ferré, 'Living Light and Dedicated Decision: Comments on the Relation between Biblical and Systematic Theology', *Int* 6, 1952, 1-16; id., 'Notes by a Theologian on Biblical Hermeneutics', *JBL* 78, 1959, 105-44; F.V.Filson, *JBR* 1946 (see above, 2). We can find the arguments for and against in a short form as early as the discussion carried on in *JBR* in 1940 (see above, 2); the positions remained essentially the same for a long time. However, the representatives of the 'confessional method' defended themselves against the charge that they were arguing for an unscholarly interpretation of the Bible. In 1964, B.S.Childs stressed that the descriptive task was included in the theological task; all critical methods were to be used, as the Old Testament is the testimony of a historical people. Classical Reformation exegesis had not paid enough attention to this. However, 'The final task of exegesis is to seek to hear the Word of God'; to this degree a commentary on the Bible has a normative task (443). However, there is no absolute norm but only what is found in the testimony of the witnesses. (J.Smart, *Old Testament* [above, 3], uses the dialogue between God and Israel which already takes place in the Old Testament as a basis for hearing the word of God in the present.) A.Dulles ('Response to Krister Stendahl's "Method in the Study of Biblical Theology"', in *The Bible in Modern Scholarship*, ed. J.P.Hyatt [above, 6], 210-16) regards descriptive (historical or history-of-religions) and biblical-theological (normative confessional) work as equally justified. 'Normative theology, then, is theology in direct discourse. It is the theologian's own effort to set forth the contents and implications of God's revelation, as he himself understands it within the tradition of the church to which he belongs' (213). However, in his view (cf. R.de Vaux, 'Method in the Study of Early Hebrew History', ibid., [15-29] 15f.) this kind of confessional biblical theology, which after some hesitation he feels able to regard as legitimate, is to be regarded as a separate field of study from historical description and the history of religions. 'On the level of objective scientific history, therefore, there are enormous possibilities of fruitful collaboration between Protestant and Catholic, Christian and Jew, believer and agnostic' (211). However, a position of this kind, in which the hermeneutical approaches are completely disjoined, can hardly be satisfactory.

In fact at the beginning of the 1960s the American 'Biblical Theology Movement' found itself in a state of crisis (cf. Childs,

Biblical Theology, 51ff.). The criticism by L.Gilkey ('Cosmology, Ontology and the Travail of Biblical Language', *JR* 41, 1961, 194-205) and J.Barr ('Trends and Prospects in Biblical Theology', *JTS* 25, 1974, 265-82) of the historical hermeneutical approach of Wright and Anderson – the American representatives of the movement which had started from Europe – provided a decisive stimulus here. Changes came in the general intellectual and theological climate which at this time made themselves felt throughout the Western world. (Cf. J.Barr, 'The Old Testament and the New Crisis of Biblical Theology', *Int* 25, 1971, 24-40; id., *The Bible in the Modern World*, London 1973, paperback 1977, 5ff.; id., *JTS* 1974; for the effects in America cf. Childs, *Biblical Theology*, 77ff.; cf. also B.W.Anderson, 'The Crisis of Biblical Theology', *ThTo* 28, 1971, 321-32; G.M.Landes, 'Biblical Exegesis in Crisis: What is the Exegetical Task in a Theological Context?', *USQR* 26, 1971, 273-98; also M.Barth, 'Whither Biblical Theology?', *Int* 25, 1971, 350-4; J.C.Becker, 'Reflections on Biblical Theology', *Int* 24, 1970, 303-20; D.E.Nineham, 'The Use of the Bible in Modern Theology', *BJRL* 52, 1969, 178-99; also the review of Childs by J.A.Sanders, *USQR* 26, 1971, 299-304). The attention of the church public was to a large degree directed towards questions arising out of sociology and other humane disciplines which 'neo-orthodoxy' had either failed to integrate or which had so far remained outside its perspective. (The most recent sharp criticism of 'biblical theology', that of N.K.Gottwald, *The Tribes of Yahweh*, Maryknoll NY and London 1979, also comes from this direction; he criticizes previous attempts at a 'biblical theology' for having an idealistic basis and puts forward 'Biblical Theology or Biblical Sociology?' [665] as an alternative.) Thus the Bible largely came to be silent in the church, a fact which J.D.Smart lamented at the height of this crisis (Smart, *The Strange Silence of the Bible in the Church. A Study in Hermeneutics*, Philadelphia and London 1970, Philadelphia ⁵1976, cf. also Landes, op.cit., and the review by M.C.Howard, *USQR* 26, 1971, 305-10). However, the publication of the laments of Smart and Childs already introduced a new phase, which will be dealt with later (see below, 135ff.).

II

The Relationship between the Old Testament and the New

Surveys:

'De Verhouding van Oud en Nieuw Testament' (Berkhof, H., Baarda, T., and others – Report for Faith and Order), *KeTh* 25, 1974, 318-27; Baker, D.L., *Two Testaments, One Bible*, Leicester 1976; Barr, J., *Old and New in Biblical Interpretation*, London 1966; Eichrodt, W., 'Les Rapports du Nouveau et de l'Ancien Testament', in *Le Problème Biblique*, ed. J.Boisset, Paris 1955, 105-31; Filson, F.V., 'The Unity of the Old and the New Testaments: A Bibliographical Survey', *Int* 5, 1951, 134-52; Goppelt, L., *Theologie des Neuen Testaments*, Göttingen ³1980 = ET *Theology of the New Testament* (two vols), Grand Rapids 1981, 1982, passim; Jasper, F.N., 'The Relation of the Old Testament to the New', *ExpT* 78, 1967, 228-32; Kapelrud, A.S., 'Det Gamle Testamente og den hermeneutiske nøkkel', *NTT* 74, 1973, 207-15; Mayo, S.M., *The Relevance of the Old Testament for the Christian Faith*, Washington, DC 1982; Murphy, R.E., 'The Relationship between the Testaments', *CBQ* 26, 1964, 349-59; Oeming, M., *Gesamtbiblische Theologien der Gegenwart. Das Verhältnis von Altem Testament und Neuem Testament in der hermeneutischen Diskussion seit Gerhard von Rad*, Stuttgart 1985; Preuss, H.D., *Das Alte Testament in christlicher Predigt*, Stuttgart 1984; Ridderbos, N.H., 'De verhouding van het Oude en het Nieuwe Testament', *GTT* 68, 1968, 97-110; Roloff, J., *Neues Testament* (Neukirchner Arbeitsbücher), Neukirchen-Vluyn 1977, 259-77; Roscam Abbing, P.J., *Inleiding in de bijbelse theologie*, Amsterdam 1983; Schwarzwäller, K., 'Das Verhältnis Altes Testament – Neues Testament im Lichte der gegenwärtigen Bestimmungen', *EvTh* 29, 1969, 281-307; Smart, J.D., *Interpret-*

ation, 65-133; Tengström, S., 'Kristen tolkning av Gamla testamentet', *SEÅ* 48, 1983, 77-101; Verhoef, P.A., 'The Relationship between the Old and the New Testament', in *New Perspectives on the Old Testament*, ed. J.B.Payne, Waco, Tx. 1970, 280-303.

As we have seen (*Problems of Old Testament Theology*, 13ff.), a desire to recover the theological relevance of the Old Testament as well as of the New proved to be an important element within the development of theology as a whole, above all in Germany and the neighbouring countries of Holland and Switzerland, both predominantly bound up with the Reformed tradition, in the first twenty years after the Second World War. The christological approach adopted by Barth, and also by others, had an important influence. Many agreed that the relationship between the Testaments had a decisive role here. (N.H.Ridderbos, 97, even thinks: 'The relationship between Old and New Testaments: that is just about the whole story; the whole of theology is involved in that.') Most writers took it for granted that the Old Testament could only take on theological significance within Christian theology if a positive solution could be found for its relationship to the New Testament. Only a few found satisfaction in the more or less negative proposals put forward by Hirsch, Bultmann or Baumgärtel and Hesse. However, sometimes the authors stopped at a demand for an interpretation related to Christ, which then could not be implemented adequately in the actual construction of a theology of the Old Testament. This is the case not only with Procksch (see *Problems of Old Testament Theology*, 49f.), but also with Vriezen (ibid., 52; see Baker, *Two Testaments* [above, 10], 335-8, and the literature given there – in addition, above all A.J.Bjørndalen, 'Det Gamle Testamentets Teologie. Metodiske hovedproblemer', *TTK* 30, 1959, 22-38, 92-116; V.Hamp, 'Neuere Theologien des Alten Testamentes', *BZ* NF 2, 1958, 303-13) and for G.A.F.Knight, *A Christian Theology of the Old Testament*, London 1959; for him see *Problems of Old Testament Theology*, 53, and especially Baker, 232f., and the literature mentioned there).

The relationship between the Testaments inevitably became a central problem above all in the context of the salvation-historical approach which was characteristic of this period. It was discussed at length especially in Germany. Here it is no coincidence that the

various explanations of this relationship put forward reflect closely
the theological approaches of the partners in the discussion.

1. The model of an ongoing salvation history

The most prominent representative of a salvation-historical
approach covering both Testaments is G.von Rad. Part Three of
the second volume of his *Old Testament Theology* is devoted to an
extended account of the problem (*Theologie des Alten Testaments*,
II: *Die Theologie der prophetischen Überlieferungen Israels*, Munich
1960, 329-424, ⁴1965 [⁶1969], 380-436 = ET of first edition only, *Old
Testament Theology* II, Edinburgh and New York 1965, reissued
London 1975, 319-429). The traditio-historical approach through
the 'historical traditions of Israel' (cf. *Problems of Old Testament
Theology*, 59ff.) logically leads von Rad beyond his initial consideration of the Old Testament itself. The tradition history of the
historical traditions as reflected in the texts of the Old Testament is
at the same time the history of constantly new interpretations which
regularly relate the old traditions to the present (*Theologie* II⁴,
381ff., cf. ET, 320ff.); in this process it is usually possible to see
increasingly large complexes. In principle there is no limit to
these interpretations; they became necessary through the constantly
changing situations in which Israel found itself, but were also already
given in the nature of the historical traditions themselves. (For this
cf. M.Noth, 'Die Vergegenwärtigung des Alten Testaments in der
Verkündigung', *EvTh* 12, 1952/53, 6-17 = *Probleme alttestamentlicher Hermeneutik*, ed.C.Westermann, TB 11, Munich 1960 [1968],
54-68 = ET 'The "Re-presentation" of the Old Testament in
Proclamation', in *Essays on Old Testament Hermeneutics*,
ed.C.Westermann, Richmond, Va 1963[= *Essays on Old Testament
Interpretation*, London 1963], 76-88, who refers to the great feasts
of Israel as the place where the events of salvation history are represented.) 'Every Old Testament account of history is already
intrinsically open in one way or another to a future... The constantly
new interpretation to which... the old stories of Yahweh were
exposed did not do anything new to them. Rather, they already
pointed in this direction of their own accord' (384f.; this passage is
not in the ET). Nor does this ongoing new interpretation stop with
the end of the Old Testament canon; it is also taken up again in the
New Testament, 'starting from a completely new event' (384). Thus

no violence is done within the context of the 'radical openness for the future' (ibid.), which is characteristic of the Old Testament account of history; rather, the New Testament fulfilment already has its place within the inner movement of the dialectic of the Old Testament salvation history (for the regular progress from promise to fulfilment within the Old Testament see *Problems of Old Testament Theology*, 75ff.). However, this ongoing line is only one side of the picture; the impact of the 'discontinuity of the revelations of God experienced by Israel' (385) is almost as strong. This impact prevents von Rad simply from following von Hoffmann's view of a divine plan of salvation which embraces both Testaments (*Problems of Old Testament Theology*, 91ff.) and leads him to resort to the expedient of typology (see below), which makes it possible to put the relationship between the Testaments on an even broader basis.

Since I have already devoted a lengthy chapter to the problem of salvation history (*Problems of Old Testament Theology*, 87ff.), we need not take up the question again here. A concern to arrive at a view which embraces both Testaments is inherent in the salvation-historical approach. A large number of other exegetes in addition to von Rad have argued for a salvation-historical view of the relationship between the Testaments in one form or another. A prominent representative of this view is B.S.Amsler (*L'Ancien Testament dans l'Église*, Neuchâtel 1960; cf. also id., 'Lecture juive et lecture chrétienne de l'Écriture Sainte', *Jud* 17, 1961, 24-39. – For Amsler cf. Baker, *Two Testaments*, [above, 10], 315-26 [and bibliography]). According to Amsler, a historical event stands at the centre of the witness of the New Testament (whose use of the Old Testament he has first thoroughly investigated, 15-99): the person and work of Jesus Christ. Now according to the New Testament understanding God himself has acted in the Christ event. Following Cullmann (cf. *Problems of Old Testament Theology*, 101f.), Amsler sees this event as the central event of a history which extends from creation to the end of time, in which all God's historical acts and acts of revelation belong (106). Therefore the witnesses of the New Testament understand the Christ-event in direct connection with the action of God in creation and in the history of Israel. In it there takes place the goal of this history which God had in mind from creation onwards (107). However, Amsler already finds testimony to this salvation history expressed in a great variety of ways throughout the Old Testament (107ff.); its perspective orientated on a future which is still open but structured by the events in past salvation history is particularly significant (114ff.). So while the Old Testament perspective on salvation history is still open in a forward direction, the New Testament perspective indicates that the end-time of salvation history has now come and has already dawned in Jesus Christ (119). Because of this all the events of the Old Testament are interpreted by the New in the light of fulfilment, since the New Testament begins from the direct connection of all past, present and future events of salvation history in this light. The various individual perspectives of the New Testament exegesis of the Old must be understood in terms of this basic understanding: the pattern of promise and fulfilment (125ff.); the interpretation of individual writings (136ff.); the typological approach (see below). G.E.Wright (*God Who Acts. Biblical Theology as Recital*, SBT 8, London 1952 [⁹1969], 56) is similar to Amsler in also seeing Christ as the goal of the Old Testament salvation history; this likewise produces perspectives in terms of promise and fulfilment (56f.) and typology (61-6). In conservative circles, especially in older Roman Catholic publications, we still often find the model of a salvation history unfolding in accordance with God's plan of salvation, coming to a climax in Christ and including the church. Cf. e.g. E. O'Doherty, 'The Unity of the Bible', *BiTod* 1, 1962, 53-7; F.E.Elmo, 'Christ – The Fulfillment of the Old Testament', *DunR* 3,1, 1963, 5-38, and also in the Protestant evangelical O.P.Robertson ('Outlook' [above, 7]), who thinks in terms of an organic process of development in Old Testament salvation history leading up to the fulfilment in Christ. It is easy to multiply approaches of this kind. In contrast to them we should recall, with P.Pokorny ('Probleme biblischer Theologie', *TLZ* 106, 1981, [1-8] 3f.), that of itself 'the Christ event attested in the New Testament is not a direct continuation or development of the Old Testament event'. It was only faith, in the light of the experience of Christ, that discovered the historical dimension of God's address in the Old Testament witnesses, which is necessarily extended in time.

2. The typological approach

Alfrink, B.J., *Over 'typologische' exegese van het Oude Testament. Rede...*, Nijmegen and Utrecht 1945; id., 'Rondom de "spiri-tueele" verklaring van de H.Schrift', *NKS* 43, 1947, 289-95, 329-

37; Amsler, S., *Où en est la typologie de l'Ancien Testament?'*, *ETR* 27, 1952, 75-81; id., 'Prophétie et typologie', *RTP* 3, 1953, 139-48; Baker, D.L., 'Typology and the Christian Use of the Old Testament', *SJT* 29, 1976, 137-57; id, *Two Testaments* (above, 10), 239-70; Barr, J., *Old and New* (above, 10), 103-48; Barosse, T., C.S.C, 'The Senses of Scripture and the Liturgical Pericopes', *CBQ* 21, 1959, 1-23; Baumgärtel, F., *Verheissung. Zur Frage des evangelischen Verständnisses des Alten Testaments*, Gütersloh 1952, 124ff., 138ff.; cf. also id., 'Das hermeneutische Problem des Alten Testaments', *TLZ* 79, 1954, (199-212) = *Probleme*, ed. C.Westermann, (114-39) = ET 'The Hermeneutical Problem of the Old Testament', in *Essays*, ed. Westermann (above, 12), (134-59) 208/131 = ET, 154, esp. 204f./ 123f. = ET, 143f.; Breytenbach, A.P.B., 'Die tipologie as 'n metode van uitleg van die Ou Testament', *HTS* 28, 1971, 17-21; Bultmann, R., 'Ursprung und Sinn der Typologie als hermeneutischer Methode', *FS G. van der Leeuw*, Nijkerk 1950, 89-100 = *TLZ* 75, 1950, 205-12 = id., *Exegetica*, Tübingen 1967, 369-80; P.J. Cahill, 'Hermeneutical Implications of Typology', *CBQ* 44, 1982, 266–81; Conzelmann, H., 'Fragen an Gerhard von Rad', *EvTh* 24, 1964, 113-25; Coppens, J., *Les Harmonies des Deux Testaments*, Tournai and Paris 1949, 78-94 (cf. also the expanded bibliography, *Vom christlichen Verständnis des Alten Testaments*, FolLov.3-4, Brussels, Paris and Freiburg im Breisgau 1952; id., 'Subsidia Bibliographica', in *Exégèse et Théologie. Les Saintes Écritures et leur interprétation théologique [Donum Natalicium J.Coppens]*, ed. G.Thils and R.E.Brown, Gembloux and Paris 1968, 282-315 [review by J.Daniélou, *DViv* 16, 1949/50, 149-53]; Daniélou, J., *Sacramentum Futuri. Études sur les origines de la typologie biblique*, Paris 1950; id., 'Traversée de la Mer rouge et baptême aux premiers siècles', *RSR* 33, 1946, 402-30; id., 'Les divers sens de l'Écriture dans la Tradition chrétienne primitive', *ETL* 24, 1948, 119-26; id., 'Exégèse et dogme', *DViv* 14, 1949, 90-4; id., 'La typologie de la femme dans l'Ancien Testament', *VS* 34, 1949, 491-510; id., 'Qu'est-ce que la typologie?' in *L'Ancien Testament et les Chrétiens*, ed. P.Auvray et al., Paris 1951, 199-205; Davis, L., 'Typology in Barth's Doctrine of Scripture', *ATR* 47, 1965, 33-49; Dentan, R.C., 'Typology. Its Use and Abuse', *ATR* 34, 1952, 211-17; Edsman, C.M., 'Gammal och ny typologisk tolkning av Gamla Testamentet', *SEÅ* 12, 1947, 85-109; Eichrodt, W., 'Ist die typologische Exegese sachgemässe Exegese?', *TLZ* 81, 1956, 641-54 = *SVT* 4, 1957, 161-80 = *Probleme*, ed. Westermann (above, 12), 205-26 = ET 'Is Typological Exegesis an Appropriate Method', in Westermann, 224-45; id., 'Vom Symbol zum Typos. Ein Beitrag zur Sacharja-Exegese', *TZ* 13, 1957, 509-22; Ellison, H.L., 'Typology', *EvQ* 25, 1953, 158-66; Fairbairn, P., *The Typology of Scripture*, Edinburgh 1857 (^{5}1870, reprinted Grand Rapids, Mich. nd [1950]); Fascher, E., 'Typologie auslegungsgeschichtlich', *RGG*[3] VI, 1095-8; Foulkes, F., *The Acts of God: A Study on the Basis of Typology in the Old Testament*, London 1958; Fritsch, C.T. 'Typological Interpretation in the New Testament (Biblical Typology II)', *BS* 104, 1947, 87-100; id., 'Principles of Biblical Typology (Biblical Typology, IV)', *BS* 104, 1947, 214-22; id., TO'ANTITYΠON, *Studia Biblica et Semitica, FS T.C. Vriezen*, Wageningen 1966, 100-7; Fuchs, E., *Hermeneutik*, Bad Canstatt 1954 (^{4}1970), 192-201; Gerleman, G., 'Gamla testamentet i förkunnelsen', *SvTK* 32, 1956, 81-94; Goppelt, L., *Typos. Die typologische Deutung des Alten Testaments im Neuen*, Gütersloh 1939 (reprinted Darmstadt 1966) = ET *Typos. The Typological Interpretation of the Old Testament in the New*, Grand Rapids 1982; Gundry, S.N., 'Typology as a Means of Interpretation: Past and Present', *JETS* 12, 1969, 233-40; Gunneweg, A.H.J., *Vom Verstehen des Alten Testaments. Eine Hermeneutik* (ATD Erg.R.5), Göttingen 1977, 97f., 157-9, 164-75, 175-80 = ET *Understanding the Old Testament*, OTL, London and Philadelphia 1978, 112-3, 186-9, 209-17, 218-23; Haag, H., 'Typologisches Verständnis des Pentateuch?', in *Studien zum Pentateuch, FS W.Kornfeld*, Vienna 1977, 243-55 = id., *Das Buch des Bundes*, Düsseldorf 1980, 234-49; Hanson, R., 'Moses in the Typology of St Paul', *Theol* 48, 1945, 175-7; Hummel, H., 'The Old Testament Basis of Typological Interpretation', *BR* 9, 1964, 38-50; id., 'Christological Interpretation', *Dialog* 2, 1963, 108-17; Irwin, W.A., *JBL* 1959 (above, 6); Jacob, E., 'L'Ancien Testament et la prédication chrétienne', *VC* 16, 1950, 151-64; Jewett, P.K., 'Concerning the Allegorical Interpretation of Scripture', *WTJ* 17, 1954/5, 1-20; *Essays on Typology*, ed. G.W.H.Lampe and K.J. Woollcombe, SBT 22, London 1957 (containing Lampe, 'The Reasonableness of Typology', 9-38; Woollcombe, 'The Biblical Origins and Patristic Development of Typology', 39-75); Lampe, G.W.H., 'Typological Exegesis', *Theol* 56, 1953, 201-8; id.,

'Hermeneutics and Typology', *LQHR* 6, 1965, 17-25; Lys, D., 'A la recherche d'une méthode pour l'exégèse de l'Ancien Testament', *ETR* 30, 1955, 1-73 (cf. id., *Nephesh*, Paris 1959, 9f., 11-22); id., *The Meaning of the Old Testament*, Nashville 1967; Marcus, R.A., 'Presuppositions of the Typological Approach to Scripture', *CQR* 158, 1957, 442-51; Martínez, E., 'El sentido tipico en la Sagrada Escritura', *MCom* 2, 1943, 1-34; Michaeli, F., 'La "typologie" biblique', *FV* 50, 1952, 11-18; Miller, A., 'Zur Typologie des Alten Testaments', *Anton* 25, 1950, 425-34 = *BenM* 27, 1951, 12-19; Minear, P., *Horizons of Christian Community*, St Louis 1959, 63-70; Miskotte, K.H., *Letter en geest. Om het verstaan van het Oude Testament in de rooms-katholieke theologie*, Nijkerk 1966, 62-76, 123-38; Preuss, H.D., 'Das Alte Testament in der Verkündigung der Kirche', *DtPfrBl* 68, 1968, 73-9; id., *Predigt* (above, 10), 112ff.; von Rad, G., 'Typologische Auslegung des Alten Testaments', *EvTh* 12, 1952/53, 17-33 = *Vergegenwärtigung*, ed. H.Urner, Berlin 1955, 47-65 = ET 'Typological Interpretation of the Old Testament', *Int* 15, 1961, 147-92 = (extract) 'Das Alte Testament ist ein Geschichtsbuch', in *Probleme*, ed. Westermann (above, 12), 11-17 = ET, 17-39; cf. id., 'Predigt über Ruth 1', *EvTh* 12, 1952/3, 1-5 = *Predigten*, ed. U.von Rad, Munich 1972, 45-51; Ridderbos, N.H., 'Het Oude Testament in de prediking', *GTT* 56, 1956, 142-53, esp. 149-51; id., 'Typologie', *VoxTh* 31, 1960/61, 149-59; Roscam Abbing, *Inleiding* (above, 10), 159ff.; Schilling, O., 'Hat das AT ein ΤΥΠΟΣ-Verständnis seiner selbst?', in *Universitas. FS A.Stohr*, Mainz 1960, 28-35; Smart, *Interpretation* (above, 3), 93-133; Stek, J.H., 'Biblical Typology Yesterday and Today', *CTJ* 5, 1970, 133-62; Takamori, A., 'Das Vorkommen der Termini Typus und Typologie seit der Aufklärung', *STU* 37, 1967, 30-41 (= *Typologische Auslegung des Alten Testaments? Eine wortgeschichtliche Untersuchung*, theol.diss. [typescript] Zurich 1966, 90-105); Uhlig, S., 'Die typologische Bedeutung des Begriffes Babylon', *AUSS* 12, 1974, 112-25; Verhoef, P.A., 'Some Notes on Typological Exegesis: New Light on Some Old Testament Problems', *OTWSA.P* 5, 1962, 58-63; Wildberger, H., 'Auf dem Wege zu einer biblischen Theologie. Erwägungen zur Hermeneutik des Alten Testaments', *EvTh* 19, 1959, 70-90; Wolff, H.W., 'Der grosse Jesreeltag (Hos 2.1-3)', *EvTh* 12, 1952/3, 78-104 = id., *Gesammelte Studien zum Alten Testament*, TB 22, Munich 1964,

²1973, 151-81; id., 'Erwägungen zur typologischen Auslegung des Alten Testaments', *ZdZ* 10, 1956, 446-8 = *MPT* 45, 1956, 471-3; id., 'Zur Hermeneutik des Alten Testaments', *EvTh* 16, 1956, 337-70 = *Probleme*, ed.c.Westermann, 140-80 = *Gesammelte Studien*, 251-288 = 'The Hermeneutics of the Old Testament', *Int* 15, 1961, 439-72 = *Essays*, ed. Westermann (above, 12), 160-99; id., 'Alttestamentliche Predigten mit hermeneutischen Erwägungen', Neukirchen-Vluyn 1956, 7-28 = id., 'The Old Testament in Controversy. Interpretative Principles and Illustration', *Int* 12, 1958, 281-91; Woollcombe, K.J., 'Le sens de type chez les pères', *VS*, Suppl.5, 1951, 84-100; Zimmerli, W., 'Verheissung und Erfüllung', *EvTh* 12, 1952/3, 34-59 = *Vergegenwärtigung*, ed. H.Urner, 7-34 = *Probleme*, ed. Westermann, 69-101 = ET 'The Interpretation of the Old Testament III. Promise and Fulfilment', *Int* 15, 1961, 310-38 = *Essays*, ed. Westermann, 89-122.

With renewed reflection on the relationship between the Testaments at the beginning of the 1950s, attention was directed towards a method which the historical-critical approach had seemed long since to have made obsolete, but which now came back into the discussion in different ways, namely typology.

(a) Typology as the correspondence of facts, persons and events

The classical definition of typology can be found in C.T.Fritsch (*BS* 1947, 214): 'A type is an institution, historical event or person, ordained by God, which effectively prefigures some truth connected with Christianity.' In the nineteenth century P.Fairbairn wrote a significant work about typology (cf. especially Stek). In accordance with the positivistic thinking of his time, he sees types as historical realities (facts, persons or events reported by the biblical narratives) which are used by God within the framework of his economy of salvation as pedagogical instruments to prefigure to the pre-Christian church (Israel) the 'spiritual and divine truths' which would be embodied in the person and work of Jesus Christ so that it would be able to recognize these when they happened. This model is still by no means dead even in the present, but continues to find supporters. Thus E.Jacob (*VC* 1950, 160), who otherwise puts typology in the framework of salvation history, the goal of which is Christ, distinguishes three ways in which the Old Testament types are related to the antitype (Christ): 1. a relation of similarity, 2. a relation of opposition (e.g. Adam-Christ), 3. a relation of progress (from the imperfect to the perfect). S.Amsler cites the same characteristics (*ETR* 1952, 79f.) and adds that the types have to have been appointed by God and may not first be discovered by interpreters in the present (this point is stressed by a large number of exegetes, cf. Verhoef, *OTWSA* 1962, 59; Baker, *Two Testaments*, 260). So types have an ontological quality. The demand is also often made that typology should be limited to the examples explicitly mentioned in the New Testament (thus e.g. Marcus, 446f.).

As von Rad stresses ('Typologische Auslegung', 17/272 = ET, 17), typological thought is an elementary function of all human thought, a concern to understand the world by way of analogy. So it is not surprising that such thinking in terms of analogy should also relate to the Bible. Bultmann ('Ursprung und Sinn der Typologie') thinks that he can recognize in typological thought the effect of the cyclical conception of time and history current in antiquity and for this reason rejects it as being untenable in the light of the insight into the linear course of history gained in the context of the Old Testament. Von Rad rejects this view: 'One must see the basic ideas of typology less in the notion of repetition than in that of correspondence' ('Typologische Auslegung', 19/274 = ET, 20).

The attention of modern hermeneutics was drawn to typology as an exegetical method not least by the exegesis in the New Testament itself and – above all as a result of the work of Catholic theologians – by an evaluation of the methods used by the early church in biblical exegesis. Here the work of L.Goppelt (*Typos*) was pioneering in connection with the New Testament. In a broad sweep through the whole of the New Testament Goppelt demonstrated that the typological approach of the Old Testament in the New, which he regards as 'the method of interpreting Scripture that is predominant in the NT and characteristic of it' (239, = ET, 198), is not just an outdated exegetical method (which was earlier often identified with allegorical exegesis) but embodies one of the basic concerns of the New Testament: 'It is an excellent witness to the NT's consciousness of its own place in redemptive history. The NT knows itself to be in some way the fulfilment of the types found in the redemptive history of the OT and to be a prophecy in type concerning the future consummation' (248 = ET, 205). 'The results of typological exegesis are primarily statements about NT salvation' (242 = ET, 200); by connecting it with the previous Old Testament saving event, the writer stresses the messianic consummation of salvation in the present (for this whole question cf. also id., 'Apokalyptik und Typologie bei Paulus', *TLZ* 89, 1964, 321-44). Stimulated by Goppelt, in the post-war period a large number of further New Testament works concerned themselves with the use of scripture in the New Testament and its individual authors. Here the basic insight of Goppelt into the theological function of its exegetical methods was confirmed, even if they were now seen in a more sophisticated way (Qumran and other contemporary Jewish interpretations have made the context of the New Testament method clearer: typology is just one, rather rare, way in which the Old Testament is used in the New).

Cf. esp. Aalen, S., 'Jesu kristologiske selvbevissthet', *TTK* 40, 1969, 1-18; Albertz, R., 'Die "Antrittspredigt" Jesu im Lukas-evangelium auf ihrem alttestamentlichen Hintergrund', *ZNW* 74, 1983, 182-206; Anderson, H., 'The Old Testament in Mark's Gospel', in *The Use of the Old Testament in the New and Other Essays. Studies in Honor of W.F.Stinespring*, ed. J.M.Efird, Durham NC 1972, 280-306; Balentine, S.E., 'The Interpretation of the Old Testament in the New Testament', *SWJT* 23, 1981, 41-57; Barth, M., 'The Old Testament in Hebrews. An Essay in Biblical Hermeneutics', in *Essays in Honor of O.A.Piper*, ed. W.Klassen and G.F.Snyder, New York 1972, 53-78; Berg, W., *Die Rezeption alttestamentlicher Motive im Neuen Testament – dargestellt an den Seewandelerzählungen*, Freiburg 1979; Black, M., 'The Christological Use of the Old Testament in the New Testament', *NTS* 18, 1971/72, 1-4; Braun, H., 'Das Alte Testament im Neuen Testament', *ZTK* 59, 1962, 16-31; Bruce, F.F., *Biblical Exegesis in the Qumran Texts*, Ex.3,1, The Hague 1959; Cerfaux, L., 'Simples réflexions à propos de l'exégèse aposto-lique', *ETL* 25, 1949, 565-76 = *Recueil L.Cerfaux*, II, Gembloux 1954, 189-203; id., 'L'exégèse de l'Ancien Testament par le Nouveau Testament', in *L'Ancien Testament et les Chrétiens*, ed. P.Auvray et al. (above, 15), 132-48 = *Recueil Lucien Cerfaux*, II, 205-17; Clavier, H., *Les variétés de la pensée biblique et le problème de son unité*, *NT.S* 43, Leiden 1976, 348-56; Decock, P.B., 'The Understanding of Isaiah 53:7-8 in Acts 8:32-33', *Neotestamentica* 14. *The Relationship Between the Old and New Testament. Proceedings of the Sixteenth Meeting of the NTSSA/NTWSA*,

Potchefstroom 1980, 1981, 111-33; Dodd, C.H. *According to the Scriptures: The Substructure of New Testament Theology*, London 1952 (1965); Ellis, E.E., *Paul's Use of the Old Testament*, Edinburgh and London 1957 (reprinted 1981); id., 'Midrash, Targum and New Testament Quotations', in *Neotestamentica et Semitica. Studies... M.Black*, Edinburgh 1969, 61-9; Fitzmyer, J.A., 'The Use of Explicit Old Testament Quotations in Qumran Literature and in the New Testament', *NT.S* 7, 1960/1, 297-333 = id., *Essays on the Semitic Background of the New Testament*, London 1971, 3-58; Farrer, A., 'Important Hypotheses Reconsidered: Typology', *ExpT* 67, 1955/56, 228-31; Flesseman-van Leer, E., 'Die Interpretation der Passiongeschichte vom AT aus', in *Die Bedeutung des Todes Jesu*, ed. F.Viering, STAEKU, 1967, 81-96; France, R.T., 'In all the Scriptures – A Study of Jesus' Typology', *TSF Bulletin* 56, 1970, 13-16; id., *Jesus and the Old Testament: His Application of the Old Testament Passages to Himself and His Mission*, London 1971; Freed, E.D., *Old Testament Quotations in the Gospel of John*, *NT.S* 11, Leiden 1965; Goulder, M.D., *Type and History in Acts*, London 1964; Grant, R.M., 'The Place of the Old Testament in Early Christianity', *Int* 5, 1951, 186-202; Grogan, C.W., 'The Experience of Salvation in the Old and New Testaments', *VoxEv* 5, 1967, 4-26; Gundry, R.H., *The Use of the Old Testament in St Matthew's Gospel*, *NT.S* 18, Leiden 1967; Hänel, J., *Der Schriftbegriff Jesu*, BFCT 24, 5/6, 1919; Hanson, A.T., *Jesus Christ in the Old Testament*, London 1965 (cf. also the review by A.R.C.Leaney, *JTS* 18, 1967, 207f.); id., *Studies in Paul's Technique and Theology*, London 1974; Holtz, T., *Untersuchungen über die alttestamentlichen Zitate bei Lukas*, TU 104, Berlin 1968; id., 'Zur Interpretation des Alten Testaments im Neuen Testament', *TLZ* 99, 1974, 19-32; Hooker, M.D., 'Beyond the Things That are Written? St Paul's Use of Scripture', *NTS* 27, 1981, 295-309; Hübner, H., 'Biblische Theologie und Theologie des Neuen Testaments', *KuD* 27, 1981, 2-19; Jeremias, J., 'Paulus als Hillelit', in *FS M.Black*, 88-94; Kleinknecht, K.T., *Der leidende Gerechte*, WUNT II, 13, Tübingen 1984; Koole, J.L., *De overname van het Oude Testament door de christlijke kerk*, Hilversum 1938; Larcher, C.L., *L'actualité chrétienne de l'Ancien Testament d'après le Nouveau Testament*, Paris 1962; Lindars, B., *New Testament Apologetic: The Doctrinal Significance of the Old Testament Quotations*, London and Philadelphia

1961 (reprinted London 1973; cf. the review by C.F.D.Moule, *TLZ* 87, 1962, 680f.); Lindblom, J., 'Gamla testamentet i urkristendom. Tillika ett bidrag till bibeltolkningens historia', *SEÅ* 6, 1941, 23-42; Lohfink, N., 'De Moysis epicinio', *VD* 41, 1963, 227-89 = id., 'Das Siegeslied am Schilfmeer', in id., *Das Siegeslied am Schilfmeer*, Frankfurt 1965 (²1966), 102-28; Lohse, E., 'Die alttestamentlichen Bezüge im neutestamentlichen Zeugnis vom Tode Jesu Christi', in *Bedeutung...*, ed. F.Viering, 99-112; Longenecker, R., *Biblical Exegesis in the Apostolic Period*, Grand Rapids 1975; Malan, F.S., 'The Use of the Old Testament in I Corinthians', *Neotestamentica* 14, 1981, 134-70; Manson, T.W., 'The Argument from Prophecy', *JTS* 46, 1945, 129-36; id., 'The Old Testament in the Teaching of Jesus', *BJRL* 34, 1951/55, 312-32; Mayo, S.M., *Relevance* (above, 10), 21-7; McCaffrey, U.P., 'Psalm Quotations in the Passion Narratives of the Gospels', *Neotestamentica* 14, 1981, 73-89; Michel, O., *Paulus und seine Bibel*, BFCT 2, 18, Gütersloh 1929, reprinted Darmstadt 1972 (with supplement 213-21); Miller, M.P., 'Targum, Midrash and the Use of the Old Testament in the New Testament' (bibliography), *JSJ* 2, 1971, 29-82; Nicole, R., 'The Attitude of Jesus Toward Scripture', in *Evangelicals and Jews in Conversation on Scripture, Theology, and History*, ed. M.H.Tanenbaum, M.R.Wilson and A.J.Rudin, Grand Rapids, Mich. 1978, 197-205; Rothfuchs, W., *Die Erfüllungszitate des Matthäusevangeliums*, BWANT V, 8, Stuttgart 1969; Ruppert, L., 'Die alttestamentlich-jüdischen Messiaserwartungen in ihrer Bedeutung für Jesus und seine Zeit', *MTZ* 35, 1964, 1-16; Saebø, M., 'Das Alte Testament – christlich interpretiert', in *Der Herr ist einer, unser gemeinsames Erbe*, ed. K.-J.Illman and J.Thuren, Åbo 1979, 81-97; Schaefer, P., 'Das Alte Testament im Neuen Testament', in *Israel und Kirche Christi*, ed. F.Heiler, Sonderheft *EHK* 16, 1934, 98-102; Schmitz, O., 'Das Alte Testament im Neuen Testament', in *Wort und Geist, FS K.Heim*, Berlin 1935, 49-74; Seeligman, I.L., 'Voraussetzungen der Midraschexegese', in *Congress Volume Copenhagen 1953*, SVT 1, 1953, 150-81; Shires, H.M., *Finding the Old Testament in the New*, Philadelphia 1974; Smith, D.M., Jr, 'The Use of the Old Testament in the New', in *Studies...* *Stinespring*, 3-65; Schröger, F., 'Das hermeneutische Instrumentarium des Hebräerbriefverfassers', in *Schriftauslegung*, ed.J.Ernst, Munich and Paderborn 1972, 313-29; Smits, C., *Oud*

Testamentische Citaten in het Nieuwe Testament, 's Hertogenbosch 1952-1953 (four vols); Sowers, S.G., *The Hermeneutics of Philo and Hebrews,* BSt 1, Zurich 1965; Stendahl, K., *The School of St Matthew and its Use of the Old Testament,* ASNU 20, Uppsala 1954; Suhl, A., *Die Funktion der alttestamentlichen Zitate und Anspielungen im Markusevangelium,* Gütersloh 1965 (cf. the review by E.Grässer, *TLZ* 91, 1966, 667f., and M.Rese, 'Die Rolle des Alten Testaments im Neuen Testament', *VF* 12, 1967, 87-97 [also on Ulonska, see below]); Tasker, R.G.V., *The Old Testament in the New,* London 1946 (Grand Rapids, Mich. ²1964); Thyen, H., *Studien zur Sündenvergebung im Neuen Testament und seinen alttestamentlichen und jüdischen Voraussetzungen,* FRLANT 96, Göttingen 1970; Ulonska, H., *Paulus und das Alte Testament,* Munich 1964; Vielhauer, P., 'Paulus und das Alte Testament', in *Studien zur Geschichte und Theologie der Reformation. FS E.Bizer,* ed. L.Abramowski and J.F.G.Goeters, Neukirchen 1969, 33-62 = id., *Oikodome, Aufsätze zum Neuen Testament,* II, ed. G.Klein, TB 65, Munich 1979, 196-228; Vorster, W.S., 'The Function of the Use of the Old Testament in Mark', *Neotestamentica* 14, 62-72; Wilckens, U., 'Die Rechtfertigung Abrahams nach Römer 4', in *Studien zur Theologie der alttestamentlichen Überlieferungen, FS G.von Rad,* ed. R.Rendtorff and K.Koch, Neukirchen 1961, 111-27 = id., *Rechtfertigung als Freiheit, Paulusstudien,* Neukirchen 1974, 33-49. Cf. also Sailer, J., 'Über Typen im Neuen Testament', *ZKT* 69, 1947, 490-6 (New Testament themes also have a typological function).

The results of this great variety of investigations have made it clear that the Old Testament quite naturally became Holy Scripture for earliest Christianity, as it also was for the synagogue. Therefore Christians could also take over without further ado the contemporary exegetical methods as practised in Judaism. It emerges from an investigation like that of Vielhauer that Paul could even use Old Testament quotations to express the radically new element in the Christian message: final salvation has come with Jesus Christ. However, that does not invalidate the past action of God attested by the Old Testament – and this excludes the erroneous conclusions that have often been drawn from this finding, especially by the Bultmann school. The New arose out of the Old and can only be understood by reference back to the Old as the will of God. That is why Paul and the authors of the other New Testament works quote abundantly from the Old Testament.

However, views of modern exegetes continue to differ widely over precisely how the relationship between the two parts of the Bible is to be understood.

(b) Typology as a method of salvation-historical hermeneutics

At the beginning of the 1950s, a group of German Old Testament scholars formed around a plan to produce a 'Biblical Commentary' (Biblischer Kommentar) combining historical criticism with the task of kerygma (cf. also Baker, *Two Testaments* [above, 10], 307-10). In a programmatic volume of *EvTh* 1952/53 the group developed its ideas of an exegesis of the Old Testament which would lead up to proclamation of the kind that this commentary series was to offer (the series has been continued down to the present). Here they accorded a central place to typology. At the centre of the issue stood G.von Rad's article 'Typological Interpretation of the Old Testament' (above, 17 – cf. also Ridderbos), which was specifically concerned with this approach; however, the contributions by Noth, Zimmerli and Wolff were closely associated with it. In the course of his remarks (in which the organizing principle of his later *Theology* appears) von Rad acknowledges that he is impelled by one question above all, namely the degree of faith that the church and he personally can have in the salvation-historical action of the God of Israel as attested in the Old Testament. Can the salvation that once held for Israel continue to hold in the same way today for the church and the individual Christian? 'But I belong to none of the twelve tribes, I do not offer sacrifice in Jerusalem... I am not even a proselyte, and so able to appropriate for myself the greathearted consolation of TritoIsaiah... God's gracious provisions, so lavishly bestowed on Israel, seem to pass me by, because I do not belong to the historical people Israel...'(31/286 = ET, 35). Typology, long forgotten, presents itself as a solution: 'Rather we see everywhere in this history brought to pass by God's Word, in acts of judgment and acts of redemption alike, the prefiguration of the Christ-event of the New Testament' (ibid.). According to von Rad, typology is based on the faith that the same God who has revealed himself in Christ was already at work in the Old Testament history, was already speaking with the fathers through the prophets as he now speaks to us through Christ. Within the rules for the application of typological exegesis which he goes on to sketch out, it is particularly important that this refers exclusively to the kerygma of the divine event and may not concern itself with every possible historical or archaeological detail which is common to both Testaments, that it does not do away with the difference in the substance of salvation in the Old and New Testament, and that it cannot 'serve as a heuristic principle for the elucidation of particular philological and historical problems' (32/287 = ET, 37).

Thus within a system orientated on salvation history and an exegesis concerned with kerygma, typology is a means of discovering structural analogies between the saving events attested by both Testaments which bridge the gap produced by our loss of a direct relationship in faith to the events of the Old Testament and disclose to faith in the context of an overall view ('Typological interpretation has to do with the entire Old Testament', 31/286 = ET, 36) the testimony of the Bible to revelation which according to von Rad is a testimony to Christ only when the Old Testament is included (33/288/39). In the years after his article appeared von Rad found support for his adherence to the method in the ensuing discussion in which the significance and utility of typology was partly disputed sharply, and partly defended by new arguments; his account in the *Old Testament Theology* (II⁴, 387ff., cf. ET, 364ff.) makes even more clear what he had only hinted at in the 1952 article, namely that he understands typology strictly in terms of salvation history, in the context of a divine, linear saving action which spans both Testaments in an event (cf.395 = ET, 371) characterized at the same time by the 'area of tension constituted by promise and fulfilment' (ibid.). In this context typology not only presents itself as an analogy between the two Testaments; it is also a structure to be observed within the Old Testament itself, for analogies of salvation, or promises already being fulfilled, were found here in a constant ongoing movement (II⁴, 396f. = ET, 372f.). Here von Rad seems to be taking up ideas which Zimmerli had developed in his contribution on 'Promise and Fulfilment' which appeared at the same time as von Rad's article on typology, about the progress in the divine action from promise to fulfilment already within the Old Testament (cf. further below, 50ff.), and also Noth's ideas, also expressed then, about the 'representation' of the central saving acts of God within the kerygmatic narrative of the Old Testament (see my *Problems of Old Testament Theology*, 75f.), which von Rad similarly understands in terms of the relationship between the Testaments (II[4], 339ff., cf. ET, 319ff.).

Von Rad's remarks represent a quite specific view of typology which is certainly not understood in the same way by all who use the term. He himself also used the term for his traditio-historical approach, in the context of which it helps him to bridge the gap between the two Testaments. However, it could not serve as more than an auxiliary approach, so it is no wonder that vigorous criticism was also made of its use.

Criticism was expressed above all by F.Baumgärtel, first of all in his book *Verheissung* (above, 15) and then in reply to von Rad's review of this book in *EvTh* 1953 ('Verheissung. Zum gleichnamigen Buch Friedrich Baumgärtels', *EvTh* 13, 1953, 406-13), in his contribution in *EvTh* 1954 ('Der Dissensus im Verständnis des Alten Testaments', *EvTh* 14, 1954, 298-313), at the same time in *TLZ* 1954, and finally in the review of von Rad's *Old Testament Theology* in *TLZ* 86, 1961, 905-7 (for the sometimes passionate discussion cf. R.Hermann, 'Offenbarung, Wort und Texte', *EvTh* 19, 1959, 99-116 = id., *Bibel und Hermeneutik. Gesammelte und nachgelassene Werke* III, Göttingen 1971, 201-15; Ludwig Schmidt, 'Die Einheit zwischen Altem und Neuem Testament im Streit zwischen Friedrich Baumgärtel und Gerhard von Rad', *EvTh* 35, 1975, 119-39). Baumgärtel's main objection to von Rad's typological model is that it is a purely theoretical construction which cannot have any effect on the faith of the simple Christian towards the Old Testament: 'If today we are referred to the type as the foreshadowing of the New Testament event in the Old, we are being confronted with a thought process, an abstraction' (*EvTh* 1954, 305; cf. *Verheissung*, 138f.). Eichrodt, in particular, defended the typological method against these objections by Baumgärtel. In his view (and here he also differs from the view of H.W.Wolff, see below), typology is 'not a rational demonstration, as Baumgärtel thinks, but the believing understanding of the divine moulding of history on the basis of an experience, founded upon Christ, of the God who is mighty in history' ('Is Typological Exegesis an Appropriate Method?', 176/221 = ET, 241); Eichrodt understands this view as an understanding which relates 'to the realization of salvation through a history', and thus in this respect, despite differences elsewhere, comes very close to von Rad. By contrast the criticism of E.Haenchen ('Das alte "Neue Testament" und das neue "Alte Testament"', in id., *Die Bibel und wir, Gesammelte Aufsätze* II, Tübingen 1968, 13-27) belongs among the group of those who object to von Rad's historical starting point: according to Haenchen only events which are confirmed by historical-critical scholarship could be evaluated in typological terms, and not legends like those in Josh.7; 8.

Foremost in explaining the typological approach along the lines of von Rad has been H.W.Wolff: at the time, in 1956, in a series of theses ('Erwägungen...') and in an extended article ('Zur Hermeneutik'). Wolff understands typology as a working hypothesis (he is well aware of the possibility of misunderstanding the term [cf. 'Zur Hermeneutik', 356/162 n.74 = ET 181f. n.74]. A. Jepsen, *Wissenschaft vom Alten Testament*, AVTRW 1, 1958 = id., *Der Herr ist Gott*, Berlin 1978, 13-38 n.17, also thinks that the words correspondence and analogy better describe what Wolff really means. However, he himself rejects this hermeneutical approach [cf. below, 60]) which can say something about the relationship between the Testaments, but strictly as a method which is 'of help in *approaching* and *carrying out* historical understanding and should not merely serve for concluding considerations of a meditative nature' ('Zur Hermeneutik', 359/275 = ET, 185). Fundamental to typology is the pre-existing correspondence between the Testaments, since the New Testament witness to the Christ of God can only be heard in constant reference to the Old Testament. Conversely, we have no unbroken relationship to the Old Testament, but can only read it rightly in the context of our knowledge of the historical and kerygmatic connection between the Testaments and of the historical and kerygmatic difference between them. According to Wolff, typology should not do away with the historical significance of the Old Testament text; the latter is rather to be investigated 'with all the means of linguistic and historical scholarship' ('Erwägungen', 447/472). However, what is at issue here proves to be the connection of the event discovered in this way in a forward direction, in the direction of the future which it indicates (cf. above, 13f.), which, seen in the context of the whole of the Bible, is ultimately directed towards the New Testament eschaton (cf. 'Zur Hermeneutik', 358/274 = ET, 184; 'Erwägungen', 447/472). As early as 1952 Wolff already produced a case study to show how he imagined such exegesis ('Der grosse Jesreeltag'); the division of the exegetical stages recommended there ('Text, form, historical situation, word, kerygma') at the same time served as a model for the later planning of the structure within BK. Similarly, Wilckens ('Rechtfertigung Abrahams') also stresses that Paul's Abraham typology in Rom.4 is to be seen before the salvation-historical reference of the line of election which leads from the Israel of the Old Testament to us.

The view of typology in Lampe and Woollcombe also resembles that in the German exegesis mentioned above. Both agree that typology is to be limited to a search for models in the historical context of revelation, that it is an exegetical process which is meant to demonstrate the aim of God in Jesus Christ through the interpretation of the Old Testament by demonstrating the correspondence of historical events. According to Foulkes, too, it is the mighty acts of God through history (and not any random events) which form the basis of typology even in the Old Testament. Cf. also Lys.

Common to all the representatives of this view is that they understand typology as a hermeneutical procedure (Stek, 153, aptly comments: 'Typology belongs, therefore, not to the *historia revelationis...* but to the *historia theologiae* which arose in Israel and the church in response to the series of events experienced...'), which is to be put to the service of the historical understanding of the Old Testament. The relationship of this process to the exact methods developed by historical-critical scholarship remains somewhat unclear. Above all in von Rad and Eichrodt we tend to get the impression that typological understanding has an intuitive character: it happens by faith and to this degree is comparable to the 'pneumatic' approach to scripture. Nevertheless, the defenders of this method are agreed that real correspondences become evident through typology which are based on demonstrable structures of divine action in the Old and New Testaments. The saving event *runs its course* in analogies; it is structured in a particular way, and the demonstration of such structures can contribute to the understanding of salvation history and its goal. By contrast, Marcus explicitly stresses that typology is an area of historical-critical exegesis, is concerned with the literal meaning, and is to be distinguished from 'spiritual' exegesis.

The advocates of the typological approach also point out that typological thought is to be found not only in the New Testament in connection with Old Testament models but also within the Old Testament itself (cf. Baker, *Two Testaments* [above, 10], 243-5, individual examples; cf.also Lohfink, *Siegeslied*; Schilling). H.Hummel (*BR* 1964, 40) even puts forward the view that thinking in types (in the broad sense of the word) is a dominant concern of the Old Testament (in historiography, in the cult and in prophecy). He also understands the representation of a group by the individual ('corporate personality'), like the righteous sufferer in the psalms, as typology (43). W.H.Gispen (*De Christus in het Oude Testament*, Oud en Nieuwtestamentische Studien I, Delft 1952) finds 'foreshadowings' of Christ not only in the suffering servant of Isa.52.13ff. (20-32), but also in the various sacrifices (9-20), in the 'righteous' man of Proverbs and Psalms (34-42), and in many individual episodes of the historical books of the Old Testament (which as a whole depict the salvation history). The best known example of typological thought in the Old Testament is certainly the exodus theme in Deutero-Isaiah (cf.B.W.Anderson, 'Exodus Typology in Second Isaiah', in *Israel's Prophetic Heritage, FS J.Muilenburg*, New York and London 1962, 177-95).

As Fritsch (*FS Vriezen*) in particular has made clear, there are, moreover, two forms of typology in the Old Testament: a horizontal one and a vertical one. The vertical one (which is also taken up in Heb.8-10) is originally of Babylonian origin; it appears above all in the Priestly writing (Ex.25.9; Gen.2.1-4a; cf. 1.27) but also in I Chron. 28.11-19; Ezek.40-48 and is concerned with the heavenly model of earthly cultic institutions: the horizontal one compares recurring basic models in history. Minear (*Horizons*, 63) derives both forms from the common basis of archetypal thought which sees the Jerusalem that is above and the Jerusalem to come as one. Minear sees typological thought as being closely connected with mythical thought, and would accord it a permanent place: 'Typology is a form of mythological thinking in which there may be a seriously ontological thrust; that is, by typology, men attempt to communicate their conviction about ultimate reality'(64). In that typology discovers invisible but real connections between persons and communities, it calls attention to a reality which also applies to us: we are members of the heavenly Jerusalem and thus also of the Old Testament city of David (68).

Criticism of typology orientated on salvation history has not been silenced since Baumgärtel. Barr's objections (*Old and New* [above, 10], Ch.1V) are connected with his suspicion of the salvation-historical approach generally (see *Problems of Old Testament*

Theology, 111f.); in particular he doubts whether the New Testament writers would have had such a perspective in their use of typologies (which in principle cannot be distinguished from allegory). Gunneweg (*Vom Verstehen*, 176-8 = ET, 209-12) follows Baumgärtel's argument, the background to which is similarly a criticism of salvation history (above, 26f.) There is also recent criticism from H.Haag, cf. *Das Buch des Bundes*, 247ff.; also id., 'Das Plus des Alten Testaments', in id., *Buch des Bundes*, 289-305 (there is also a shorter form, 'Vom Eigenwert des Alten Testaments', *TQ* 160, 1980, [2-16], 290ff. [3ff.]). Irwin (*JBL* 1959, 6) dismisses typology even more radically as unscientific: 'In reality it is a homiletic, not a hermeneutic, study of the Bible.' There is also a sharp criticism in van Ruler (below, 54), 58ff., which in many respects is indebted to Baumgärtel.

E.Fuchs puts forward a special form of existential typology (the expression occurs explicitly in Preuss, 78, though it is not clear there what gives it its distinctive character). Following his hermeneutical approach he understands the significance of typology in Paul, in contrast to salvation-historical thinking of a linear kind, in terms of the eschatological contemporaneity of the witnesses of the Word of God (like Adam, Abraham, Moses and Elijah). Gunneweg (180 = ET, 213) also seems to give typology a chance in this form. However, as in any form of existential theology, we must ask whether typological thought is not the element which stresses the continuity in the community of faith and puts the *kairos* in the context of history.

The method of inner-biblical correlation put forward by M.Hohmann (*Die Korrelation von Altem und Neuem Bund*, TA 37, Berlin 1978) is a distinctive form of typology on a salvation-historical basis. In his systematic approach, starting from P.Tillich, Hohmann incorporates into the perspective of salvation history an existential world horizon for which the Old Testament provides the model: 'The Old Testament is to be read in the light of the New Testament prototypically as a claim on *all* aspects of the world and of life by Jesus Christ to the goal of salvation history' (117). For the application of the principle of the correlation of Old and New Testaments in the specific praxis of preaching Hohmann proposes that in each case an Old Testament and a New Testament text should be put side by side ('series of pericopes of double texts', 118; for examples cf. 119ff.).

At all events, typology as a means of determining the relationship between the Testaments remains a topic for discussion. Baker (*Two Testaments* [above, 10], 268-70, 368f.) again understands it as an analysis of content: it is 'not a method of exegesis or interpretation but the study of historical and theological correspondences between different parts of God's activity among his people': its task is 'to point to the consistent working of God in the experience of his people'. Typology is not the task of exegesis proper, but of biblical theology; the former examines the literary testimony to an event; the latter connects it with other events which are reported in the Bible.

(c) The typological method in Roman Catholic theology

In addition to the development within Protestantism which I have just sketched out, typology as a method also had an important role in Catholic theology of the same period. Here the situation was different in that the historical-critical method had only made slow progress within Catholic exegesis (following the encyclical *Divino afflante spiritu* of 1943), while traditional exegesis still remained largely within the system of neo-scholasticism (for the development see more recently L.Ruppert, 'Der Weg der neueren katholischen Exegese vornehmlich im Bereich des Alten Testaments', in *Tendenzen der katholischen Theologie nach dem Zweiten Vatikanischen Konzil*, ed. G.Kaufmann, Munich 1979, 43-63). In this period thinking schooled by Thomas Aquinas dominated all areas, including that of biblical exegesis, as we can see from books of method like the official *Institutiones Biblicae* (Vol.I, *De sacra Scriptura in universum*, Rome 1925, [6]1956), from A.Robert and A.Tricot, *Initiation Biblique*, Paris and Tournai [3]1954, or J.Coppens, *Les harmonies des deux Testaments* (above, 15) (cf. the review by R.de Vaux, *RB* 57, 1950, 280f.; also *Problèmes et méthode d'exégèse théologique*, ed. L.Cerfaux, J.Coppens and J.Gribomont, Louvain and Paris 1950) (cf. the review by J.P.Weisengoft, *CBQ* 14, 1952, 83-5) – but also in a popular work like J.Schildenberger, *Vom Geheimnis des Gotteswortes*, Heidelberg 1950 (see the review by J.Ziegler, *MTZ* 1, 1950, 83-90; J.Coppens, 'Pour une meilleure intelligence des Saintes Ecritures', *ETL* 27, 1951, 500-7). Certain dogmatic preconditions, like the doctrine of verbal inspiration (cf. especially A.Bea, *De Scripturae Sacrae Inspiratione Quaestiones Historicae et Dogmaticae*, Rome 1935; P.Benoit, *La Prophétie. Somme théologique*, Appendix II, 'L'inspiration scripturaire', 293-

376, Paris 1947; K.Smyth, 'The Inspiration of Scripture', *Scripture* 6, 1954, 67-75 [shorter version, 'The Inspired Writer as God's Instrument', *ThD* 8, 1960, 15-19] and the associated doctrine of the inerrancy of scripture (both go back to Augustine [cf. H.Sasse, 'Sacra Scriptura – Bemerkungen zur Inspirationslehre Augustins', *FS F.Dornseiff*, Leipzig 1953, 262-73], but were never made a formal dogma), which were further accentuated in the Modernist crisis under Leo XIII (Encyclical *Providentissimus Deus*, 1893, *Acta Leonis XIII* 13, 1893, 326-64 = *EnchB*[4], 34-62) and Pius X, also shaped the picture (cf. J.T.Burtchaell, *Catholic Theories of Biblical Inspiration since 1810*, Cambridge 1969). On the other hand, after the war and in the first post-war years a newly revived interest in the Bible, including the Old Testament, could be seen everywhere (cf.J.Coppens, 'Vom christlichen Verständnis des Alten Testaments [above, 15], 9-27; A.Ibañez Arana, 'La moderna exégesis espiritual', *Lum* 1, 1952, 193-212), for which a few great individuals were also the driving force. Catholic France in particular played a prominent part here; through the work of poets and writers like P.Claudel and H.Daniel-Rops the Bible, and in particular the Old Testament, became popular again, and two Jesuits, H. de Lubac and J.Daniélou (who ended up being a cardinal), advanced the biblical movement theologically, each in his characteristic way.

It is worth noticing that neither of these were professional exegetes, but patristic scholars, for whom patristic exegesis (which was never completely forgotten in Catholic exegesis, although it was displaced by Scholasticism) was the great model. In particular, a concern with the most significant exegete of the early church, Origen, from whom they acknowledged that they had learned (albeit not uncritically), and the multiple sense of scripture for which he had argued (this also remained in force even in the mediaeval church, cf. E. von Dobschütz, 'Vom vierfachen Schriftsinn', in *Harnack-Ehrung*, Leipzig 1921, 1-13; C.Spicq, *Esquisse d'une histoire de l'exégèse latine au Moyen Age*, BiblThom 26, Paris 1944; B.Smalley, *The Study of the Bible in the Middle Ages*, Oxford 1952; H. de Lubac, *Exégèse médiévale. Les quatre senses de l'Écriture*, Paris I, 1959; II.1, 1961; II.2, 1964) had decisively influenced both. However, their positions differed. As the sub-title indicates, in his main work *Histoire et Esprit: Intelligence de l'Écriture d'après Origine*, Paris 1950 (cf. the reviews by J.L.McKenzie, *TS* 12, 1951, 365-81; J.Coppens, *ETL* 27, 1951, 145-50 – partial survey also in H.

de Lubac, *Der geistige Sinn der Schrift*, Einsiedeln 1952, cf. also id.,
'Sens spirituel', *RSR* 36, 1949, 542-76), H. de Lubac (cf. K.Neufeld
and M.Sales, *Bibliographie Henri de Lubac 1925-1974*, Einsiedeln
[1971] ²1974) presents, with reference to Origen, a 'spiritual exegesis'
which in its somewhat obscure character can be compared with the
'pneumatic exegesis' of Girgensohn (cf. *Problems of Old Testament
Theology*, 17f.). Through historical criticism of the literal sense (the
need for which de Lubac does not deny) and beyond it he is
concerned with a direct encounter beween people of today and the
revelation of God in Jesus Christ. 'Spiritual exegesis' means reading
scripture under the guidance of the Holy Spirit. C.Charlier ('La
lecture sapientielle de la Bible', *MD* 12, 1947, 14-52) similarly sees
turning to the text of the Bible in prayer as the highest stage of Bible
reading (see further his main work, *La lecture chrétienne de la Bible*,
Charleroi 1950 [⁶1957]; id., 'Méthode historique et lecture spirituelle
des Écritures', *BVC* 18, 1957, 7-26).

J.Daniélou has a specific purpose in his various writings, above
all in his main work *Sacramentum futuri*, which is also based on
Origen (cf. also id., *Origène*, Paris 1948, 83-9 = ET *Origen*, London
1955); he calls for a return to typology (in principle the Protestant
F.Michaeli also agrees with Daniélou). There is profound
justification for the typological exegesis practised by the Fathers,
even in the present. Not only is it extremely biblical, as Daniélou
shows in detail, because it is practised both in the New Testament
towards the Old and in the Old Testament itself (in the exodus
typology, 131ff.), but it is also the only approach which makes it
possible for Christians to read the Old Testament in an edifying
way, since its literal sense can hardly be affirmed in a Christian
pulpit. Moreover, for Daniélou the boundary between the Bible
itself and the church fathers is very fluid, as we can see in the
structure of his book; here, in connection with each theme (Adam-
Christ; flood and baptism; the sacrifice of Isaac; the exodus; Joshua-
Jesus) first Holy Scripture and then patristic exegesis is discussed.

As we can see from Daniélou, typology is taken over as a method
in the Catholic sphere above all as a means of spiritual reading of
scripture (Daniélou actually calls it 'spiritual exegesis'). Not only
was it possible to refer to Thomas Aquinas in this respect (cf. e.g.
J.Gribomont, 'Le lien des deux Testaments selon la Théologie de
S.Thomas', *ETL* 22, 1946, 70-89), but in addition, even if one leaves
room for a historical-critical approach – which had in fact been

encouraged officially by the *magisterium* (cf. already the letter from
the papal Biblical Commission to the Italian episcopate, *AAS* 33,
1941, 465-72 = *EnchB*⁴, 192-202) in connection with the literal
meaning of scripture since it had explicitly been allowed by the
encyclical *Divino afflante spiritu* of Pius XII (*AAS* 35, 1943, 297-
325 = *EnchB*⁴, 205-32; cf. also A.Bea, *Bib* 24, 1943, 313-23), it
made it possible to affirm a spiritual level alongside the literal
meaning (T.G.Chifflot, 'Comment lire la Bible', *VS* 1949, 232-61,
even wants explicitly to arrive at the 'spiritual' = typological meaning
by way of the literal meaning [cf. also P.Samain, 'Note sur le sens
spirituel de l'Ecriture', *RDT* 3, 1948, 429-33; H.Renard, 'L'objet
de la Bible', *MSR* 11, 1954, 121-32 = id., 'Problemi scelti di teologia
contemporanea', *AnGr* 68, Rome 1954, 281-92], like the Protestant
R.A.Marcus) and thus solve by reference to the church's tradition
of exegesis the problem of 'theological exegesis' which proved so
difficult in Protestantism (e.g. C.H.Giblin, 'As it is Written. A Basic
Problem in Noematics and Its Relevance to Biblical Theology',
CBQ 20, 1958, 327-54, 477-98, speaks explicitly of a 'theological
insight' [344, etc.] gained at this higher level, supported by the
authority of the *magisterium*, in an 'analogous fulfilment' [494 n.87]
in the context of an overall divine plan of salvation history which
becomes rational to the biblical theologian. Therefore 'metahistor-
ical analogy' seems to him to be a more appropriate designation
than typology, which he thinks to be more technical [494f.]. Note
the terminology, which still has a marked scholastic stamp.) (There
was also a similar interest among the Anglicans and other high-
church groups. Cf.D.Stone, 'The Mystical Interpretation of the Old
Testament', in *A New Commentary on Holy Scripture*, ed.C.Gore
et al., London 1928 and New York 1929, 688-96, who speaks of
a 'mystical' interpretation of scripture. Cf. also the works by
W.J.Phythian-Adams [above, 2] and Hebert, *The Throne of David*
[above, 2]; cf. also Edsman [above, 15], 96f.). In this connection
B.Alfrink (later to become a cardinal but at that time an Old
Testament scholar in Utrecht), in a speech in 1945 which specifically
referred to the encyclicals and the open letter, stressed that every
sensus typicus rests on the *sensus literalis* and that the latter must
first be studied carefully before the reader moves on to the typology
which is relevant for salvation history. This typology is in no way an
arbitrary, allegorical explanation of scripture in the style of Philo.
Later (*NKS* 1947) he made more critical remarks about patristic

exegesis: the typological meaning of the Old Testament has indeed been assured by the pre-understanding of Christ and the New Testament writers, but the Fathers often extended typology to any object in the Old Testament at random; the limits of the method must be defined by the standards of the New Testament (330). By contrast A.Miller 1950 ('Typologie' [above, 17], 425/12) thinks that a 'happy, peaceful relationship' can be arrived at between patristic exegesis and modern scholarship, between reason and faith. Typology allows the literal meaning to be related to the christological-pneumatic meaning if it is assumed that over the course of the slow progress of a development, the literal meaning, once bound up with a particular event as a starting point, changes in content until it arrives at the Christ event.

'Any interpretation of an Old Testament fact, event or person which displays an inner similarity with a New Testament truth of salvation could be... accepted as having a spiritual meaning' (431/17). Here we recognize a certain affinity to the significance of typology in von Rad's traditio-historical view, though the terminology is different. These ideas are taken further in Barosse's article in *CBQ* 1959 (above, 15) which brings out 1. the ongoing reinterpretation of the written tradition, which is regarded as definitive, already within the Old Testament and then further in the New, and 2. the continuity of divine interventions in history as the two basic presuppositions of the typological view, and above all puts the liturgical use of scripture (cf. here also L.Bouyer, 'Liturgie et exégèse spirituelle', *MD* 7, 1946, 27-50) on the same level – an important idea, which hardly appears in Protestant literature (but cf.R.E.Clements, below 143). The issue here is similarly the way in which there is often a reinterpretation of the word of scripture, which is treated definitively in the context of the continuity of a divine action that extends up to the present.

While in Alfrink we can already see the beginnings of a move towards historical-critical exegesis focussed on the literal meaning, and Daniélou even stands out in having to defend himself against a strong repudiation of typology and any kind of spiritual interpretation of scripture whatsoever, made by J.Steinmann in the form of a fictitious conversation between Pascal and the famous father of Catholic biblical criticism, Richard Simon ('Entretien de Pascal et du Père Richard Simon', *VieI* 17, 1949, 239-53 = id., *R.Simon et les origines de l'exégèse biblique*, Paris 1959, 423-31; against this see

P.Claudel, 'Lettres au Révérend Père Maydieu, directeur de *La Vie Intellectuelle*', *DViv* 14, 1949, 76-81; J.Daniélou, *DViv* 1949 (above, 15); cf. further J.Steinmann, 'Apologie du littéralisme', *VieI* 16, 1948, 15-22; id., *La Critique devant la Bible*, Paris 1956 – C.Charlier, 'La lecture chrétienne de la Bible' [above, 33], already argued resolutely for the literal meaning which alone [in the light of the whole of scripture] also contained the spiritual meaning; cf. id., 'Typologie ou évolution. Problèmes d'exégèse spirituelle', *EeV* 8, 1949, 578-97; id., *BVC* 1957 [above, 33]; C.Courtade, 'Le sens de l'histoire dans l'Écriture et la classification usuelle des sens scripturaires', *RSR* 36, 1949, 136-41; T.G.Chifflot, 'Exégèse littérale, exégèse religieuse', in Auvray, P., et al, *L'Ancien Testament* [above, 15], 187-98; A.Ibañez Arana, 'La verdadera exégesis espiritual', *Lum* 1, 1952, 288-306) similarly carry on an extended debate on the spiritual interpretation of scripture in a group strongly indebted to Thomistic thought. Here typology as a method also plays a role. E.Martínez (*MCom* 1943 [above, 17]) distinguishes between literal meaning (direct meaning) and real meaning (indirect meaning). The real meaning is divided into (*a*) symbolic and (*b*) typical meaning. The difference between the two is that the symbol can be used many times, the type only once. The type exists for itself; it is earlier than the antitype and is similar to it. Fernández (*Institutiones biblicae* [above, 31], 377) also distinguishes between literal meaning and real meaning: *Sensus typicus...non sequitur ex ipsis verbis in se consideratis, sed cum rebus per illa verba expressis connectitur ex positiva ordinatione Dei* ('The typical meaning... does not follow from the words considered in themselves, but is connected with the things expressed by those words through a positive ordering on the part of God'). The type is a fact which also has an intrinsic ground for existence; it takes on additional typological meaning in that this is explicitly revealed by God (and only in that way). In that case, however, the meaning is so certain that dogmatic statements can also be built on it. Cf. also the table in P.Grelot (*Sens chrétien de l'Ancien Testament*, BT.D 3, Tournai ³1962, 457) with the same distinction between real meaning and textual meaning. Of course, according to Martínez the Old Testament as a whole is a type of the New. But typological exegesis may not be extended to just any texts (see above); it is important to guard against excesses of this kind. However, Martínez thinks that the tradition can also confirm new types – though this is also disputed in the Catholic discussion. In the end all types go back to the purpose of the Holy Spirit as the first author of scripture (here the doctrine of inspiration has a role). Cf. also the literature on the next section, and for the whole question, S.Siedl, 'Das Alte und das Neue Testament.Ihre Verschiedenheit und Einheit', *TPQ* 119, 1971, 314-24.

3. The *sensus plenior* debate

Ambroggi, M.de, 'Il senso litterale pieno nelle divine Scritture', *SsC* 60, 1932, 296-312; id., 'Il senso "pieno" del Protevangelo (Gen.3.15)', ibid, 193-205, 277-88; Bellet, P., '¿Utilizaron los santos padres, especialmente los antioquenos, el "sensus plenior" en sus comentarios?', *SBEsp* 12, 1952, 381-402; Benoit, P., 'La plénitude de sens des livres saints', *RB* 67, 1960, 161-96 = id., *Exégèse et Théologie* III, Paris 1968, 31-68 (short version *TD* 9, 1961, 3-8 - cf. also Bourke, M.M., 'Letter to the Editor of Benoit's Article', ibid., 66); Bierberg, R., 'Does Sacred Scripture have a Sensus Plenior?', *CBQ* 10, 1948, 182-95; Bover, J.M., 'El problema del sentido biblico ampliado a la luz de la filosofia del lenguaje', *SBEsp* 12, 1951, 261-82; Braun, F.-M., 'Le sens plénier et les Encycliques', *RThom* 49, 1951, 294-304; Brown, R.E., *The Sensus Plenior in Sacred Scripture*, Diss.Baltimore, Md 1955, reprinted 1960 (cf. the review by P.Benoit, *RB* 63, 1956, 285-7 = *Exégèse et Théologie* I, Paris 1961, 19-21 and S.de Ausejo, 'El "sensus plenior" de la Sagrada Escritura', *EstB* 15, 1956, 95-104); id., 'The History and Development of the Theory of a Sensus Plenior', *CBQ* 15, 1953, 141-62; id., 'The Sensus Plenior in the Last Ten Years', *CBQ* 25, 1963, 262-85; id., 'The Problems of the Sensus Plenior', *FS Coppens* (above, 15), 72-81; Bullough, S., 'The Spiritual Senses of Scripture', *LoS* 8, 1954, 343-53; Buzy, D., 'Un Problème d'herméneutique sacrée: sens plural, plénier et mystique', *ATh* 5, 1944, 385-408; Colunga, A., 'Dós palabras aun sobre los sentidos de la S.Escritura', *CTom* 64, 1943, 327-46; id., '¿Existe pluralidad de sentidos literales en la Sagrada Escritura?', *EstB* 2, 1943, 423-47; id., 'Habitaré en medio de ellos y seré su Dios (Ex 29,45). Un ejemplo de sentido pleno', *SBEsp* 12, 1951, 463-81; Coppens, J., *Harmonies* (above, 15), 31-68; id., 'Le problème d'un sens biblique plénier', in *Problèmes et méthode d'exégèse theologique*, ed. Cerfaux, Coppens and Gribomont (above, 31), 11-19; id., 'Le protévangile', ibid., 45-77; id.,

'Nouvelles réflexions sur le divers sens des Saintes Ecritures', *NRT* 74, 1952, 3-20; id., 'Le problème du sens plénier', *ETL* 34, 1958, 1-20; Courtade, G., 'Le sens de l'histoire dans l'Ecriture et la classification usuelle des sens scripturaires', *RSR* 36, 1949, 136-41; id., 'Les Ecritures ont-elles un sens "plénier"?', *RSR* 37, 1950, 481-99 (cf. also the review by J.Coppens, *ETL* 27, 1951, 145-50); Encisco, J., 'Observationes acerca del sentido pleno', *EstB* 13, 1954, 325-31; Fernández, A., *Institutiones Biblicae* (above, 31), *Liber IV, Pars I, Cap.II, De sensu typico*, 303-6 (377-81[6]). *Cap.III. De sensu pleniori, consequenti, accommodato, spirituali, supraliterali, historico et dogmatico*, 306-11 (381-393[6]); id., *'Sensus typicus, sensus plenior'*, *Bib* 33, 1952, 526-8; id., 'Sentido plenior, literal, tipico, espiritual', *Bib* 34, 1953, 299-326; id., 'Nota referente a los sentidos de la S.Escritura', *Bib* 35, 1954, 72-9; Franquesa, P., 'Inspiración, causalidad instrumental y sentido pleno', *SBEsp* 14, 1954, 187-208; Grelot, P., *Sens chrétien* (above, 36), 449-55, 458-99; id., *La Bible parole de Dieu* (BT.D 5), Tournai [2]1965, 314-89; id., 'La lecture chrétienne de l'Ancien Testament', in *Où en sont les études bibliques*, ed. J.J.Weber and J.Schmitt, Paris 1968, 29-50; Gribomont, J., 'Sens plénier, sens typique et sens littéral', in L.Cerfaux et al., *Problèmes*, 21-31; Harrington, W., *The Path of Biblical Theology*, Dublin 1973, 293-304; Hessler, B., 'Zur Frage nach dem "Vollsinn" der heiligen Schrift', *WiWei* 21, 1958, 134-41; Ibañez Arana, A., 'El concepto de inspiración y el provenir del "sensu plenior"', *Lum* 2, 1953, 193-219; id., 'Inspiration and the Fuller Sense', *TD* 4, 1956, 59-64; Kehoe, R., 'The Spiritual Sense of Scripture', *Bl* 27, 1946, 246-51; Krumholtz, R.H., 'Instrumentality and the "Sensus Plenior"', *CBQ* 20, 1958, 200-5; Leal, J., 'El sentido "plenior" de la Sagrada Escritura', *RF* 144, 1951, 474-82; Mayo, *Relevance* (above, 10), 81-7; Michl, J., 'Dogmatischer Schriftbeweis und Exegese', *BZ* NF 2, 1958, 1-13; Miskotte, K.H., *Letter* (above, 17), 76-95, 138-52; Muñoz Iglesias, S., 'Problemática del "sensus plenior"', *SBEsp* 12, 1951, 223-59; id., 'El llamado sentido tipico no es estrictamente sentido biblico viejo-testamentario', *EstB* 12, 1953, 159-83; Murnion, P.J., 'Sensus plenior and the Progress of Revelation', *DunR* 2, 1962, 117-42; Nacar, E., 'Sobre la unidad o multiplicidad del sentido literal en las Escrituras', *CTom* 64, 1943, 193-210; Nicolau, M., 'Sentido "plenior" de la Sagrada Escritura', in *Miscellanea Biblica Andrés Fernández*, ed. J.Sagiis, S.Bartina and M.Quera,

45-55 = *EE* 34, 1960, 349-59; O'Flynn, J., 'The Senses of Scripture', *ITQ* 21, 1954, 181-4; 22, 1955, 57-66; Onate, J.A., 'El llamado sentido tipico ¿es estrictamente sentido biblico viejo-testamentario?', *EstB* 13, 1954, 185-97 = *Problemi Scelti di Teologia Contemporanea*, Rome 1954, 307-17; del Paramo, S., 'El "mysterio" paulino y el sentido literal pleno', *SBEsp* 15, 1955, 247-66; Peinador, M., 'Justificatión del sentido "plenior" dentro de las necesidades a que responde', *SBEsp* 14, 1954, 421-38; Prado, J., 'Criterios de fijacion de un "sensus plenior" y de su uso en la argumentacion teologica', *SBEsp* 12, 1951, 403-61; Robinson, J.M., 'Scripture and Theological Method: A Protestant Study in Sensus Plenior', *CBQ* 27, 1965, 6-27; O'Rourke, J., 'Marginal Notes on the Sensus plenior', *CBQ* 21, 1959, 64-71; id., 'Theology and the Sensus Plenior', *AEcR* 143, 1960, 301-6; id., 'Notes on the Sensus Plenior', *AEcR* 145, 1961, 319-25; Schildenberger, J., 'Altes Testament', in *Fragen der Theologie heute*, ed. J.Feiner, J. Trütsch and F.Böckle, Einsiedeln, etc. 1958, 123-48; Schilling, O., 'Der geistige Sinn der Heiligen Schrift', *ThGl* 44, 1954, 241-54; Schmid, J., 'Die alttestamentlichen Zitate bei Paulus und die Theorie vom sensus plenior', *BZ* NF 3, 1959, 161-73; Schückler, G., 'Der theologische Aufbruch in der protestantischen Bibelwissenschaft des AT', *Cath (M)* 11, 1958, 108-24; Stuhlmueller, C., 'The Influence of Oral Tradition upon Exegesis and the Senses of Scripture', *CBQ* 20, 1958, 299-326; Suarez, P.L., 'El sensus plenior y la XII semana Biblica Española', *IluCle* 45, 1952, 21-8; Sutcliffe, E., 'The Plenary Sense as a Principle of Interpretation', *Bib* 34, 1953, 333-43; id., 'The Plenary Sense, Original or Superimposed?', *HeyJ* 1, 1960, 68-70; Tamisier, R., 'The Total Sense of Scripture', *Scripture* 4, 1950, 141-3; Temino Sáiz, A., 'En torno al problema del "sensus plenior"', *EstB* 14, 1955, 5-47; Turrado, L., '¿Se demuestra la existencia del sensus plenior por las citas que el Nuevo Testamento hace del Antiguo?', *SBEsp* 12, 1951, 333-78; Tuya, M.de, '¿El sentido tipico, es sentido biblico?', *CTom* 78, 1951, 571-4; id., 'Si es posible y en qué medida un "sensus plenior" a la luz del concepto teológico de inspiración', *SBEsp* 12, 1952, 283-329; id., 'El sentido tipico del Antiguo Testamento es "verdadera y estrictamente" sentido de la Biblia', *CTom* 80, 1953, 625-61; id., 'Anotaciones a un articulo sobre el sensus plenior', *CTom* 81, 1954, 627-44; id., 'Respondiendo a un articulo de D.Angel

Temino Sáiz', *CTom* 82, 1955, 625-43; Vawter, B., 'The Fuller Sense: Some Considerations', *CBQ* 26, 1964, 85-96; de Vine, C., 'The Consequent Sense', *CBQ* 2, 1940, 145-55.

In the same two post-war decades the discussion over the so-called *sensus plenior* occupied a central place in the debate within Catholicism over the 'spiritual' sense of the Old Testament – to put it in terms of content, over its relationship to the New Testament and its christological references. It had a particular centre in Spain, where neo-scholastic thought had flourished longest, but also found lively spokesmen elsewhere (like J.Coppens in Louvain, P.Benoit in Jerusalem and R.E.Brown in Baltimore). The Twelfth Spanish Bible Week was completely devoted to this theme (cf. the reports in *RET* 11, 1951, 536-55; *EstB*, 1951, 358f., 454-73; Suarez, op.cit.).

The theory of the *sensus plenior* is to be seen in close association with the traditional doctrine of inspiration which derives from mediaeval scholasticism and was also supported officially by the Council of Trent, Vatican I and other statements of the *magisterium* (for this see J.Beumer, *Die katholische Inspirationslehre zwischen Vatikanum I und II*, SBS 20, Stuttgart 1966). Nevertheless, recognition of the way in which the Bible had come into being in a historical context had also extended more and more through Catholic exegesis; the *sensus plenior* debate can be incorporated into the history of attempts to bring historical perspectives and the scholastic doctrine of inspiration into accord (for theories of inspiration, cf. further J.T.Burtchaell, *Catholic Theories* [above, 32]; D.M.Stanley, 'The Concept of Biblical Inspiration', in *Proceedings of the Catholic Theological Society of America* 13, 1958, 65-95 [especially on P.Benoit, J.Coppens, K.Rahner and B.Brinkmann]; O.Loretz, *Das Ende der Inspirations-Theologie* I,II, Stuttgart 1974-1976).

The encyclical *Divino afflante spiritu* (for this see also J.Levie, *L'encyclice sur les études bibliques*, Paris 1947; id., 'A la lumière de l'encyclice *Divino afflante spiritu*', in *L'Ancien Testament* [above, 15], 89-111) had provided a decisive stimulus to historical-critical scholarship by an express demand that the literal sense of the Bible should be investigated by all available methods (including form criticism). Nevertheless Pius XII had also wanted to give 'spiritual' exegesis its due: *Non omnis sane spiritualis sensus a Sacra Scriptura excluditur. Quae enim in Vetere Testamento dicta vel facta sunt, ita a Deo sapientissime sunt ordinata atque disposita, ut praeterita spirituali modo ea praesignificarent, quae in novo gratiae foedere essent futura* ('By no means is all spiritual meaning excluded from Holy Scripture. For what is said or done in the Old Testament is most wisely ordained and disposed by God in such a way that past things prefigure in a spiritual way what is to come in the new covenant of grace', *EnchB*, 552).

Catholic hermeneutics had developed a complicated system on the basis of the old doctrine of the threefold or fourfold sense of scripture in which the relationship of the different 'senses' to one another was defined (albeit still in different ways). There was a main distinction between the literal sense and the 'spiritual' ('secondary') sense; the latter could then be sub-divided into various lesser kinds – cf. e.g. the system in F.X.Patrizi, *Institutio de Interpretatione Bibliorum*, Rome (1844), ²1876; in Coppens, *Harmonies* (above, 15); in R.Cornely and A.Merk, *Introductionis in S.Scripturae Libros Compendium*, CSS.V.Editio Nova, Paris 1934, *Introductio Generalis. III. De Interpretatione SScr.I. Systema hermeneuticum*, 233-50 (¹1885, 513-49), the tables in Grelot, *Sens chrétien* (above, 36) 457; Schildenberger, *Vom Geheimnis* (above, 31f.), Ch.7, 392ff., esp. 452ff., etc.

The so-called *sensus plenior* or 'fuller meaning' fits into this scheme. The person who introduced the phrase as a technical term (for its prehistory in the nineteenth century cf. e.g. Brown, *Sensus plenior*, 89-92; Coppens, *Harmonies*, 33-36 [with bibliography]) is the Spanish Jesuit A.Fernández, who used it for the first time in his contribution to the handbook *Institutiones Biblicae* in 1925. There is a definition in Brown (*Sensus plenior in Sacred Scripture*, 92): 'The sensus plenior is that additional, deeper meaning, intended by God but not clearly intended by the human author, which is seen to exist in the words of the biblical text... when they are studied in the light of further revelation or development in the understanding of revelation' (similarly also O'Flynn, *ITQ* 1954, 181 n.1). This relates to the Old Testament as follows: in particular passages of the Old Testament it is thought possible to see a deeper significance (or 'fuller meaning', related to the Christ-event) hidden in the wording; this is only disclosed to the Christian interpreter in the New Testament or in the light of the New Testament. It is important that this is meant to be a form of the literal sense which according to those who support this theory is therefore to be distinguished from the various 'secondary' senses. The difference from the typical sense is seen to lie in the fact that it relates to the wording of the Old Testament texts themselves, whereas types named in the text are realities which have their correspondence in the Christ event (see above).

The theory of the *sensus plenior* is the attempt to resolve the problem of the theological relevance of the Old Testament for the Christian, whose faith is directed towards the Christ-event attested in the New Testament as a focal point, on the presupposition of the doctrine of inspiration and by means of scholastic thought. So the basic question shares common ground with the attempts from the sphere of Protestant theology described above: J.M.Robinson has rightly pointed out that in the *sensus plenior* debate the basic problem of the 'new hermeneutics' is discussed along the lines of H.G.Gadamer. This is the question of the existential claim of a matter which, although at first it appears in the form of a thoroughly time-conditioned expression set down in writing, and therefore needs 'translation', nevertheless directly concerns the hearer or reader, because he himself stands in the tradition which goes out from this text.

> Behind this there is indeed often an explicit assertion that the historical-critical method is an indispensable presupposition for Catholic exegesis as well (cf. e.g. B.O'Flynn, *ITQ* 1955, 59f.). However, the *sensus plenior* has also been criticized specifically from this perspective: it is said already to presuppose part of the way from the text to the interpreter, the dogmatic tradition, whereas exegesis must begin with the original literal sense, and no insuperable discontinuity should arise between it and dogmatic theology (L.Scheffczyk, 'Die Auslegung der Heiligen Schrift als dogmatische Aufgabe', *MTZ* 15, 1964, 190-204 = W.Joest et al., *Was heisst Auslegung der Heiligen Schrift?*, Regensburg 1966, [135-71] 161f.).

However, the philosophical tools used in this debate are taken from a period in intellectual history that is now long past and therefore lead to what to contemporary eyes are often strange distinctions and concepts. A basic presupposition of all the participants in the debate is the so-called doctrine of instrumentality, which is closely connected with inspiration. This doctrine distinguishes between God as the *auctor primarius* (or the *causa principalis*) and the biblical author as the *auctor secundarius* (the *causa instrumen-*

talis) of the text. One point of dispute which is discussed with great vigour centres on the question of the involvement of the author/instrument in the origin of the text, including any 'fuller sense' that may possibly be contained in it. Some of those who reject the *sensus plenior* do so because of a deliberately narrow definition of the literal sense: the literal sense can only be the intentional content as meant and understood by the author himself, which relates to the circumstances of the composition of the text. Any hidden sense which goes beyond this is no longer intrinsic to the text itself but is rather added by later insights or revelation and is therefore a secondary sense (examples in Brown, *Sensus Plenior in Sacred Scripture*, 123ff.). A further disputed question connected with this was whether the author of the biblical text did or did not have a clear or only a vague knowledge of such a 'fuller sense'. The doctrine of instrumentality (from the time of Franzelin who, all things considered, was the most significant of the fathers at Vatican I) attached great importance to the human 'co-author' of the word of the Bible being no will-less instrument but playing a part in its origin with all his human capacities (for the debate cf. also e.g. Beumer [above, 40], 22ff.; Loretz, *Ende*, I [above, 40], 71ff.). But the opponents of the *sensus plenior* (Bellet, Bierberg, Courtade, Ibañez, Muñoz, and so on) ask whether he could have composed a text the meaning of which he did not understand. That is irreconcilable with his role as one who is consciously involved and responsible. Therefore the theory is to be rejected. Its defenders (Benoit, Brown, Coppens, Krumholtz, Nacar, O'Rourke, de Tuya, etc.) either think that the author could indeed have had some inkling, albeit obscure, that what he had said had a deeper meaning which one day would become significant in a later fulfilment in salvation history; or they think it enough if the *auctor primarius*, God, had already envisaged the fullness of the testimony of the Bible as a whole when causing each individual text to be written.

Cf. the definition by A.Bea, *De Inspiratione et Inerrantia Sacrae Scripturae*, Rome 1947, 32: *Inspiratio biblica est donum transiens, gratis datum, quo Deus hagiographo utitur tamquam instrumento ad communicanda scripto, sine errore, ea quae hagiographus aut ex divina revelatione novit aut propria ratione vel experientia percepit aut ab aliis didicit et de quibus, supernaturali lumine adiutus, cum certitudine divinae veritatis iudicavit* ('Biblical inspiration is a passing gift, freely given, by which God uses the sacred writer as an instrument for communicating in writing, without error, what the sacred writer either knows by divine revelation or perceives by his own reason or experience or has learned from others and about which, with the aid of supernatural light, he has judged with the certainty of divine truth').

It is not necessary to go further into the finer points of this controversy, which went on for years (for the various forms of *sensus plenior* cf. also Miskotte, *Letter* [above, 17], 80ff.). The problem largely settled itself over the course of the further development of Catholic hermeneutics. Thus as early as 1963 R.E.Brown stresses that the demand that the human author must himself have known the *sensus plenior* is a pseudo-problem, since modern literary criticism is increasingly turning from the intention of the author to the present meaning of the text (*CBQ* 1963, 264). In fact the theory of instrumentality in the form it took in the nineteenth century is also based on a type of hermeneutics following the model of Schleiermacher and Dilthey, whereas modern theories of the text treat it as an independent entity. Specifically in connection with the Old Testament, the traditio-historical view has demonstrated that the development of what is now the final text, which went through many hands, is to be far removed beyond the possible intentions of a first author (cf. J.Scharbert, 'Probleme der biblischen Hermeneutik', in *Neue Erkenntnisprobleme in Philosophie und Theologie*, ed. J.B.Lotz, Freiburg im Breisgau 1968, 180-211; P.Asveld, *Exégèse critique et exégèse dogmatique*, BETL 26, Vol.III, *FS J.Coppens* [above, 15], [17-31] 25f.). The question was indeed touched on in the discussions during Vatican II, but not decided (cf. A.Grillmeier, 'Die Wahrheit der Heiligen Schrift und ihre Erschliessung', *TP* 41, 1966 [161-87] 183; Beumer, op.cit., 96); in 1968 (in his last statement on the complex of problems, *FS Coppens*, 73f.) Brown comments that the earlier problems are no longer really relevant. The theory of instrumentality is disappearing, and the *sensus plenior* theory is of little use. Probably, in the next century, at most it will appear as a footnote in textbooks on hermeneutics. In particular, the apologetic feature inherent in some of these investigations is out of date. In part they also represented an attempt to salvage traditional dogmatic interpretations of particular Old Testament passages (like the so-called Protevangelium in Gen.3.15

– cf. e.g. F.Ceuppens, *Quaestiones selectae ex historia primaeva*, Rome and Turin [2]1948; J.F.Bonnefoy, *Le mystère de Marie selon le Protévangile et l'Apocalypse*, Paris 1949; P.de Ambroggi, 'I sensi biblici. Direttive e studi recenti', *ScC* 78, 1950, 444-56 and bibliography; cf. Benoit, review of Brown, 286/19: 'Pour justifier *a posteriori* ces façons traditionelles d'interpréter l'Ecriture').

However, the question raised in the *sensus plenior* debate should not be regarded as settled. If the significance of scripture did not extend beyond the time-conditioned intention of its authors, the labours of biblical theology over it would get nowhere. The 'modern' element in the *sensus plenior* theory is that it refers to the text itself for the Christian significance of the Old Testament and thus argues in a more direct way than any typology. However, its entanglement with the scholastic theory of instrumentality means that the details of arguments used in connection with it would seem to be no longer viable.

Since the heyday of the *sensus plenior* debate, Catholic hermeneutics has undergone a radical revolution (there is an instructive survey of developments by R.E.Brown, 'Rome and the Freedom of Catholic Biblical Studies', in *Search the Scriptures, FS R.T.Stamm*, Leiden 1969, 129-50). The scholastic way of thinking has largely disappeared. Granted, even Vatican II has repeated the doctrine of inspiration in the 'Dogmatic Constitution on Divine Revelation', ch.III, no.11 (*Dei verbum*: the official German text is in O.Semmelroth and M.Zerwick, *Vaticanum II über das Wort Gottes*, SBS 16, Stuttgart 1966; ibid., in *LTK*.E 2, 504-83 [Introduction by J.Ratzinger, 498-503, on chs.I-II; commentary by A.Grillmeier, 528-44, on ch.III]; cf. also K.Rahner and H.Vorgrimler, *Kleines Konzilskompendium*, Freiburg im Breisgau [1966] [3]1967, 361-82; for the English text see Abbott, *The Documents of Vatican II*, New York and London 1966, 111-28; *Vatican Council II, The Conciliar and Post Conciliar Documents*, ed. A.Flannery OP, New York 1975, [5]1980, [760-5] 765f. Cf. also D.Arenhovel, *Was sagt das Konzil über die Offenbarung?*, Mainz 1967; Beumer [above, 40], 83ff.; G.G.Blum, *Offenbarung und Überlieferung*, Göttingen 1971, 16ff.; Grillmeier, op.cit.; N.Lohfink, *Bibelauslegung im Wandel*, Frankfurt am Main 1967, 13ff.; E.Stakemeier, *Die Konzilskonstitution über die göttliche Offenbarung. Werden, Inhalt und theologische Bedeutung*, KKTS XVIII, Paderborn 1966), but in the adjoining passage on the inerrancy of scripture (the wording was hotly disputed and changed several times; for its prehistory cf. e.g. Grillmeier, *TP* 1966; id., *LTK*.E 2, 528-37; Semmelroth and Zerwick, op.cit., 28ff.; Stakemeier, op.cit., 151ff.; for the subject matter cf. N.Lohfink, 'Über die Irrtumslosigkeit und die Einheit der Schrift', *StZ* 174, 1964, 161-81 = 'Die Irrtumslosigkeit', in *Siegeslied* [above, 22], 44-80; Italian translation also in *La verità della Bibbia nel dibattito attuale*, ed. I.de la Potterie, Brescia 1968, 19-63) there was a breakthrough to the recognition of the historical character of revelation, above all in the version of the concept of truth which was conceived of in terms of salvation history (cf.Grillmeier, *TP* 1966, 178ff.; Stakemeier, op.cit., 155ff.; I. de la Potterie, 'La vérité de la Sainte Écriture et l'Histoire d'après la Constitution dogmatique *Dei Verbum*', in *Die hermeneutische Frage in der Theologie*, ed.W. Stolz, Freiburg 1968, 469-500; Loretz, *Ende* I [above, 40], 184; he has also written a monograph on the question: id., *Die Wahrheit der Bibel*, Freiburg im Breisgau 1964; cf. also N.H.Cassem, 'Inerrancy after 70 Years: The Transition to Saving Truth', *ScEs* 22, 1970, 189-202). This put the whole of Catholic exegesis on a new basis. Though not everyone goes as far as O.Loretz, who proclaims the 'end' of the theory of inspiration (*Ende*, esp.I, 170ff.), in subsequent years praxis developed just as rapidly as within Protestantism in the direction of historical-critical exegesis and away from dogmatic preconditions.

Cf. the plea for the historical-critical method in H.Petri, *Exegese und Dogmatik in der Sicht der katholischen Theologie*, APPR NF 11/12, Paderborn 1966, 12-67; N.Lohfink, *Bibelauslegung* (above, 45). For the critical function of the Bible studied by historical criticism, even over against the church, see J.Blank, 'Das politische Element in der historisch-kritischen Methode', in *Die Funktion der Theologie in Kirche und Gesellschaft*, ed. P.Neuenzeit, Munich 1969, 39-60.

Conversely, we might ask whether this development towards a 'presuppositionless discipline' (cf. R.Schnackenburg, 'Der Weg der katholischen Exegese', *BZ* NF 2, 1958, 161-76 = id., *Schriften zum Neuen Testament*, Munich 1971, 15-33; he is more cautious in 'Haben wir die Bibel bisher falsch ausgelegt?', in *Alte Fragen – Neue Antworten? Neue Fragen – Alte Antworten?*, ed. W.Kasper, L. Scheffczyk and R.Schnackenburg, Würzburg 1967, 105-25) has not obscured the legitimate hermeneutical approaches of the Bible movement shortly after the end of the war (there is a recent plea for mediaeval exegesis in D.G.Steinmetz, 'The Superiority of Precritical Exegesis', *ThTo* 37, 1980, 27-38). That is particularly true of Old Testament theology. Recently there have even been open complaints about the small part which the Old Testament plays in the praxis of the church (M.Limbeck, 'Bedarf der Christ des Alten Testaments?', *HerKorr* 29, 1975, 77-84; but cf. J.Ratzinger, 'Bedarf der Christ des Alten Testaments?', ibid., 253f.; J.Marböck, 'Zur Verkündigung des Alten Testaments', *BiLe* 52, 1979, 22-6; A.Deissler, 'Wozu brauchen wir das Alte Testament?', *HerKorr* 35, 1981, 618-24). On the other hand we have the observation that the role of the Bible is growing within Catholic theology (cf. R.E.Murphy and C.J.Peter, 'The Role of the Bible in Roman Catholic Theology', *Int* 25, 1971, 78-94). Because the old (Thomistic) system no longer holds, but a new basis for thought has yet to be discovered (cf. ibid., 86), a transitional situation has come about in which, as on the Protestant side, no clear contours of a new way are yet discernible – cf. esp. the valuable comments by K.Lehmann, 'Der hermeneutische Horizont der historisch-kritischen Exegese', in *Einführung in die Methoden der biblischen Exegese*, Würzburg 1971, 40-80; also (in brief) N.Lohfink, *Katholische Bibelwissenschaft und historisch-kritische Methode*, Kevelaer 1966; H.Halbfas, 'Die Schriftauslegung in der katholischen Kirche', in K.Frör, *Wege zur Schriftauslegung* (new edition of *Biblische Hermeneutik*, Munich 1961), Düsseldorf ³1967, 384-91, and the prospect in J.Ernst, 'Das hermeneutische Problem im Wandel der Auslegungsgeschichte', in *Schriftauslegung*, ed.J.Ernst (above, 22), (17-53) 47ff.

4. Promise and Fulfilment

The scheme of promise and fulfilment, like typology, goes back as far as the use of scripture in the New Testament itself.

As is well known, the proof from scripture has an important role, especially in Matthew ('All this took place to fulfil what the Lord had spoken by the prophet': Matt.1.22; 2.15, etc.; cf. e.g. G.Delling, πλήρης, κτλ, *TWNT* 6, [283-309] 293-5 = *TDNT* 6, [283-311], 294-6; G.Strecker, *Der Weg der Gerechtigkeit*, Göttingen [1962] ³1971, 49-85; W.Grundmann, *Das Evangelium*

nach Matthäus, THK, Berlin [1968] ⁴1975, 71-3). For Matthew
(which stands in the tradition of Jewish-Christian scribal groups,
for which there is a significant model in the understanding of
scripture in the Qumran sect) the word of scripture is to be
referred to the story of Jesus, which is decisive for the Christian
community; the actual occurrence of this story is understood as
the fulfilment of the will of God as set down in the words of the
prophets. This takes into consideration a far larger area than the
'messianic prophecies' in the traditional sense.

More recent research has brought considerable changes to
exegetical knowledge both with respect to the so-called 'messianic'
sections in the Old Testament and to the use of messianic
conceptions in the New Testament. Both the time of origin and
the character of the classical 'messianic prophecies' like Isa.9.1-
6; 11.1-5; Micah 5.1-5 are still disputed (bibliography in e.g.
Gressmann, H., *Der Messias*, Göttingen 1929; Bentzen, A.,
Messias-Moses redivivus-Menschensohn, ATANT 17, Zurich
1948 = *King and Messiah*, ed.G.W.Anderson, Oxford 1955
[²1970]; de Fraine, J., *L'aspect religieux de la royauté israélite*,
AnBib 3, Rome 1954; Mowinckel, S. *He That Cometh*, Oxford
1956 = *Han som kommer*, Copenhagen 1951; Coppens, J.,
Le messianisme royal, LeDiv 54, Paris 1968; Rehm, M., *Der
königliche Messias im Licht der Immanuel-Weissagungen des
Buches Jesaja*, ESt NF 1, Kevelaer 1968; Kellermann, U., *Messias
und Gesetz*, BSt 61, Neukirchen 1971; Seybold, K., *Das davidi-
sche Königtum im Zeugnis der Propheten*, FRLANT 107,
Göttingen 1972; Dexinger, F., 'Die Entwicklung des jüdisch-
christlichen Messianismus', *BiLi* 47, 1974, 5-31, 239-66; Schmidt,
W.H., 'Die Ohnmacht des Messias', *KuD* 15, 1969, 18-34; id.,
Alttestamentlicher Glaube in seiner Geschichte, Neukirchen ⁴1982,
207-15 = ET *The Faith of the Old Testament*, Oxford 1983,
182-206; id., *Zukunft und Hoffnung* [with J.Becker], Biblische
Konfrontationen, Stuttgart 1981, 45-65; Becker, J., *Messiaserwartung im Alten Testament*, SBS 83, Stuttgart 1977, 32ff. = ET
Messianic Expectation in the Old Testament, Nashville and Edinburgh 1980, 37ff.; Gese, H., 'Der Messias', in id., *Zur biblischen
Theologie*, BEvTh 78, Munich 1977 [²1983], 128-51 = ET *Essays
on Biblical Theology*, Minneapolis 1981, 141-66; Lang, B.,
'Messias und Messiaserwartung im alten Israel', *BiKi* 33, 1978,
110-5 = id., *Wie wird man Prophet in Israel?*, Düsseldorf 1980,

69-79; Cazelles, H., *Le Messie de la Bible*, Paris 1978;Werner, W., *Eschatologische Texte in Jesaja 1-39. Messias, Heiliger Rest, Völker*, FzB 46, Würzburg 1982; Strauss, H., *Messianisch ohne Messias*, EHS.T 232, Frankfurt am Main, Berne and New York 1984). At all events, no matter whether it envisages, in the pre-exilic period, a son of David on the throne who, within the framework of the idea of law and order in the ancient Near East, was responsible for the preservation of righteousness and peace and the embodiment of order, or – as evidently happened in the post-exilic period – turns its expectation to a ruler figure who would bring salvation in the future, the conception of a royal messiah represents only a narrow area within the Old Testament traditions and is certainly not its centre (thus above all G.Fohrer, *Messiasfrage und Bibelverständnis*, Tübingen 1957; id., 'Das Alte Testament und das Thema Christologie', *EvTh* 30, 1970, 281-98; id., 'Theologische Grundstrukturen des Alten Testamentes, Berlin 1972, 17-22; however, for criticism see the review by S.Herrmann, *TLZ* 85, 1960, 662-6). On the other hand, however, it has become clear that the significance of the word 'messianic' (cf. E.Kutsch, *Salbung als Rechtsakt im Alten Testament und im Alten Orient*, BZAW 87, Berlin 1963) covers a far wider range of charismatic offices which come into question as 'mediators of salvation' (cf. J.Scharbert, *Heilsmittler im Alten Testament und im Alten Orient*, QD 23/4, Freiburg im Breisgau 1964; id., 'Der Messias im Alten Testament und im Judentum', in *Die religiöse und theologische Bedeutung des Alten Testaments*, ed. H.Gross et al., SBKAB 33, Würzburg nd [1965], 47-78), so that recently scholars have also felt able to speak of a 'prophetic' and an 'apocalyptic' messianism (cf. J.Coppens, *Le messianisme et sa relève prophétique*, BETL 38, Gembloux 1974; id., *La relève apocalyptique du messianisme royal* I, BETL 50, Louvain 1979) – one might also follow Scharbert and others in adding a 'priestly' messianism. For the relationship between the Old and New Testaments it must be said that the absolute use of the designation '*the* messiah' as a royal figure of the end-time first appears in Jewish writings of the Christian era (Syrian Baruch and IV Ezra; cf. A.S.van der Woude, Χρίω, κτλ, *TWNT* IX, 500 = *TDNT* IX, 509; M.de Jonge, ibid., 502-8 = 511-18; Becker, 82ff. = ET 87ff. [with bibliography]) and then in the New Testament itself. On the other hand it may be taken to be the result of critical research into

Jesus that 'The Gospel witness does not offer incontestable proof of the Messianic consciousness of Jesus' (W.Grundmann, Χρίω, κτλ', op.cit., [518-70] 530 = [527-80] 537). That is also very improbable against the background of the nationalistic political understanding of the messiah-figure in contemporary Judaism. It was the cross and resurrection which first caused the earliest community to transfer the honorific title Christ (which then soon became a proper name) to the risen Lord (for the problem cf. recently also E.Zenger, 'Jesus von Nazareth und die messianischen Hoffnungen des alttestamentlichen Israel', in *Christologische Schwerpunkte*, ed.W.Kasper, Düsseldorf 1980, 37-78; L.Ruppert, 'Die alttestamentlich-jüdischen Messiaserwartungen in ihrer Bedeutung für Jesus und seine Zeit', *MTZ* 35, 1984, 1-16). In addition, however, there are the traditions of the other charismatic offices of the Old Testament (cf. F.Hahn, *Christologische Hoheitstitel*, FRLANT 83, Göttingen 1963 [⁴1974] = partial ET, *The Titles of Jesus in Christology*, London 1969) so that the whole range of the Old Testament expectation of salvation comes together in the New Testament Christ-event. H.J.Kraus, 'Perspektiven eines messianischen Christusglaubens', in *Offenbarung im jüdischen und christlichen Glaubensverständnis*, ed.J.J.Petuchowski and W.Strolz, QD 92, Freiburg im Breisgau 1981, 237-61, has recently undertaken an attempt at a messianic christology.

The scheme of promise and fulfilment has also continued to play something of a role in the sphere of the theology of the Old Testament as a specialist discipline, even in recent times (cf. also Preuss, *Predigt* [above, 10], 62ff.). However, the traditional model of the 'messianic promises' which find their fulfilment in the New Testament in Jesus Christ has long since come to an end in serious scholarly discussion as a result of the exegetical developments described above (here, too, one of the last advocates was E.König, *Die messianischen Weissagungen des Alten Testaments*, Stuttgart [1923] ²,³1925; cf. also A.H.Edelkoort, *De Christusverwachting in het Oude Testament*, Wageningen 1941). Eichrodt (*Theologie des Alten Testaments* I-III, Leipzig 1933-1939 [later editions were published as two volumes, I, Stuttgart and Göttingen, ⁵1957, ⁸1968, Vol.II/III, Göttingen ⁴1961, ⁷1974] = ET *Theology of the Old Testament*, London and Philadelphia I, 1961; II, 1967; *Theologie* I,

11, IV, 'Weissagung und Erfüllung' [⁵342ff.] = ET I, XI, 4, 'Prediction and fulfilment', 501ff; cf. also id., *Israel in der Weissagung des Alten Testaments*, Zurich 1951) therefore already concentrated the relationship between the Testaments by means of these concepts on the 'real communion between God and man' (⁵345 = ET, 506) as the nucleus of the order of salvation, hoped for in the Old Testament, which finds its fulfilment in Jesus, but similarly still thinks in terms of the prophetic proclamation of salvation. In the context of the revival of typology in the salvation-historical kerygmatic school in Germany after the Second World War (cf. above, 24f.), the bridge between the two Testaments was also sought, especially by von Rad and Zimmerli ('Promise and Fulfilment' [above, 17f.]), in the correspondence of promise and fulfilment (cf. also C.Westermann, 'Zur Auslegung des Alten Testaments', in *Vergegenwärtigung*, ed. Urner [see above, 18], [88-120] 99ff. [in Westermann, ed., *Probleme*, 18-27 = ET *Essays* deleted except for the beginning] – but similarly e.g. also J.Scharbert, 'Was ist Heilsgeschichte?, *SBEsp* 26, 1970, 21-34, esp.29f.). In von Rad and Zimmerli this is essentially an aspect within the Old Testament saving event itself, which runs in 'an area of tension constituted by promise and fulfilment' (von Rad [above, 25]) in a 'movement from promise towards fulfilment' (Zimmerli, 51/25f./91 = ET, 111f.). Here Zimmerli also includes prophecy, where the terms 'promise' and 'fulfilment' are used indiscriminately (even resulting in the paradoxical phrase a 'dark language of promise' (= proclamation of disaster), 46/19/84 = ET, 104 – cf. also the criticism by F.Mildenberger, *Gottes Tat im Wort*, Gütersloh 1964, 76f., who wants to see the still unfulfilled divine action rather than the unfulfilled word as the element which holds the Testaments together). According to von Rad the Old Testament can 'only be read as a book in which expectation keeps mounting up to vast proportions' (*Theologie* II⁴, 341 = ET, 321); here we find the influence of an idea which becomes visible in the overall structure of his work, that classical prophecy introduced an 'eschatologizing of historical thought' (II⁴, 121ff. = ET, 112ff.). However, in its character as promise the Old Testament history points beyond itself; all its fulfilments have only provisional character, and some fulfilments are still completely lacking (von Rad, *Theologie* II⁴, 397 = ET, 372): the promise continues to lie unfulfilled (Zimmerli, 'Promise', 52/26/92 = ET, 113). The final fulfilment in Christ is first attested by the message of the New Testament: the 'nucleus of the good news of the New Testament' is 'the preaching that the fulfilment is today' (Zimmerli, ibid., 52f./27/93 = ET, 113f.). However, as Christians, too, still walk in faith and not already in sight, and the final disclosure of what is already fulfilled is still to come, it can be said that the existence of the believer also again 'comes to stand in a new way under an arc of tension between promise and fulfilment' (Zimmerli, ibid., 53/28/94 = ET, 114). The Christian community, too, finds itself (according to Heb.4.1ff.) again on the way from a promise to a fulfilment (von Rad, *Theologie* II⁴, 408 = ET, 383f.). According to Kraus, 'Perspektiven', 260, 'The promise is fulfilled' does not mean that the promise has come in Jesus Christ, 'but the promise is endorsed, is sealed, is brought near and effectively spoken in Jesus as the Christ with the "Yes and Amen" of God'. The redemption and consummation of the world as the object of the promise are still to come. The terms 'hope-fulfilment', 'expectation-fulfilment' or 'question-answer' are variations of the same scheme (cf. J.Barr, 'Tradition und Expectation in Ancient Israel', *SJT* 10, 1957, 24-34 [an early article of Barr's] and L.E.Toombs, *The Old Testament in Christian Preaching*, Philadelphia 1971, 27ff. Cf. also G.G.Oxtoby, *Prediction and Fulfilment in the Bible*, Philadelphia 1966; F.F.Bruce, *The Time is Fulfilled. Five Aspects of the Fulfilment of the Old Testament in the New*, Exeter 1978). E.Achtemeier (*The Old Testament and the Proclamation of the Gospel*, Philadelphia 1973 [cf. already P. and E.Achtemeier, *The Old Testament Roots of Our Faith*, New York and Nashville 1962; E.Achtemeier, 'The Relevance of the Old Testament for Christian Preaching', in *A Light unto My Path. Old Testament Studies in Honor of Jacob M.Myers*, Philadelphia 1974, 3-24]) even wants to elevate the correspondence of promise and fulfilment (77-115) to a binding homiletic practice: every sermon on an Old Testament text calls for the searching out of a corresponding New Testament section as a help in interpretation (142ff., 146ff.). Jesus Christ is the fulfilment of the Old Testament word of God, and the life of the church is analogous to that of the Old Testament people of God (163). Therefore analogy and 'promise and fulfilment' become valid methods for preparing a sermon (165ff., 172ff.). The ecumenical study conference in Wadham College, Oxford (1949), in whose guidelines for the interpretation of Holy Scripture (A.Richardson and W.Schweitzer, *Biblical Authority for Today* [above, 2], 240-44) the then ecumenical consensus in biblical hermeneutics had been formulated, had already in principle called for a similar procedure.

F.Baumgärtel criticized this approach vigorously (*Verheissung*, 95-101, 106-127; cf. also his other works mentioned above, 26), as he had typology, in connection with his own understanding of promise (see *Problems of Old Testament Theology*, 40ff.). For him the distinction between 'promise' as a divine promise and 'foretelling' as a purely human forecasting of future events is decisive. He attacks the vagueness in the use of the two terms by Eichrodt, Zimmerli and von Rad. There is certainly some justification in his objection (cf. also Smart, *Interpretation* [above, 11] 82 – but cf. Verhoef, 'Relationship' [above, 3], 290). However, Baumgärtel orientated his conceptuality exclusively on the New Testament (cf. Westermann, in Urner [above, 18], 103); his own use of the term 'promise' in the sense of a timelessly valid basic promise of God has, however, proved just as untenable as the distinction between word of God and prophetic word. In the context of his general scepticism about the whole view of history in contemporary exegesis (cf. *Problems of Old Testament Theology*, 115f.), Barr's criticism is specifically also directed against the use of the term 'promise'; he does not think that it can be derived from the New Testament conceptuality, and in any case that is no longer applicable (*Old and New* [above, 10], 113ff.). However, in a way the semantic components in his approach do not seem compatible with that of Zimmerli, whom he is criticizing (cf. 123f.). Both approaches have to be relativized, each in its own way.

The model of promise and fulfilment also found supporters outside this debate. Thus H.H.Rowley (*The Unity of the Bible* [above, 3], 90-121, [for Rowley cf. also Baker, *Two Testaments*, above, 10, esp.343-8]) sees a decisive connecting link between the two Testaments in the fact that the same God is attested as acting in both of them, not only in the messianic expectation and suffering servant (Isa.53), but also in a large number of unfulfilled hopes of the Old Testament which are fulfilled in Christ (and in part still wait for their final fulfilment). R.E.Murphy (*CBQ* 1964 [above, 10]) understands the scheme in terms of the preparatory development of religious concepts and notions and of realities in the life of Israel (monotheism, the doctrine of immortality, the suffering servant, the Son of Man), which lead up to the New Testament, i.e. markedly in terms of the history of ideas. B.Childs ('Prophecy and Fulfillment', *Int* 12, 1958,

259-71) begins from the literal sense of 'fulfil': in Jesus Christ there appeared the 'fullness' of a reality which had already taken shape in embryo in the Israel of the Old Testament in the prophets, in the servant of God, and the 'I' of the psalms. In the context of this speculation the author himself recalls W.Vischer, whose attempt has in his view provided a more solid biblical basis than most (270). The example shows that the terms allow some exploitation (also in the typological sense).

The scheme has continued to play a significant role in Roman Catholic publications down to most recent times: cf. e.g. H.Gross, 'Zum Problem Verheissung und Erfüllung', *BZ* NF 3, 1959, 3-17; J.Daniélou, 'Die Gottmenschheit als Formalprinzip der Heilsgeschichte', in *Der historische Jesus und der kerygmatische Christus*, ed.H.Ristow and K.Matthiae, Berlin 1961, (495-509) 496-500; P.Grelot, 'L'accomplicement des Ecritures en Jésus-Christ', *BCES* 35, 1961, 365-86; id., *Sens chrétien* (above, 36), 327ff.; J.Kahmann, 'De eenheid van Oud en Nieuw Testament', *NKS* 53, 1963, 353-67; L.Krinetzki, 'Das Verhältnis des Alten Testaments zum Neuen Testament. Seine Bedeutung für den Christen', in *Wort und Botschaft*, ed.J.Schreiner, Würzburg 1967 (³1975), 343-58; W.Harrington, *Path* (above, 38), 334-6; H.Gross and F.Mussner, 'Die Einheit von Altem und Neuem Testament', *IKaZ* 3, 1974, 544-55. Cf. also C.van Leeuwen, 'Hoe moeten wij het Oude Testament uitlegen?', in *Op het spoor van Israel*, The Hague 1961, 84-118; K.Schwarzwäller, *Das Alte Testament in Christus*, TS 84, Zurich 1966 (the Christ-event is *the result* [cf. Rom.10.4, 39f.] of the saving action of God to Israel attested by the Old Testament).

5. The superiority of the Old Testament

Great excitement was caused in 1955 by the appearance of a slim volume by the Utrecht Reformed theologian A.A.van Ruler, *Die christliche Kirche und das Alte Testament*, BEvTh 23, Munich 1955 (= ET *The Christian Church and the Old Testament*, Grand Rapids, Mich 1966, reprinted 1971), in which he intervened in an original way in the hermeneutical debate about the Old Testament sparked off by the group centred on BK.

For discussion cf. esp. J.J.Stamm, 'Jesus Christus und das Alte

Testament', *KBRS* 112, 1956, 27f. = *EvTh* 16, 1956, 387-95 = *Probleme*, ed. Westermann (above, 00), 181-91 = ET 'Jesus Christ and the Old Testament', in *Essays*, ed. Westermann (above, 12), 200-10; T.C.Vriezen, 'Theokratie und Soteriologie', *EvTh* 16, 1956, 395-404 = *Probleme*, ed.Westermann, 192-204 = ET 'Theocracy and Eschatology', in *Essays*, ed. Westermann, 211-23; N.H.Ridderbos, *GTT* 1956 (above, 17); I.J.Hesselink, 'Recent Developments in Dutch Theology', *RTR* 28, 1969, (41-54) 46-50; Baker, *Two Testaments*, 97-136; F.Hesse, 'Die Israelfrage in neueren Entwürfen Biblischer Theologie', *KuD* 27, 1981, (180-97) 181-9; for van Ruler's general approach cf. also W.H.Velema, *Confrontatie met van Ruler*, Kampen 1962; there are further works of van Ruler in Baker, *Two Testaments*, 99.

Van Ruler's starting point, which takes the form of a question, is the assumption (the positive answer is only to be inferred) that Yahweh, the God of Israel, and the Father of Jesus Christ are one and the same God (13-16 = ET, 15-18). Van Ruler is certainly not alone here, nor is he in what he goes on to say about the question of revelation in the Old Testament, and in particular about the relationship between exegesis and revelation; in the last resort faith is a decision of the conscience (17 = ET, 18) which has to 'cut through the knot' (21= ET, 22) if it assumes that it finds revelation in the Old Testament, because its authority is supported by the authority of Jesus himself (17= ET, 19). Starting from this basis, despite all the difficulties of its task, scholarly exegesis is in principle also capable of getting through to this content (21, = ET, 21). Van Ruler's view that, according to the Old Testament, revelation is the action of God in history, is wholly in keeping with the salvation-historical perspective (with Vriezen, van Ruler expresses his hesitations about the application of the theology of the Word to the Old Testament, 22 = ET, 24).

Van Ruler's own line appears at the point where he asks '*to what end* God is present in Israel and has dealings with Israel'. He argues that the usual one-sided soteriological view is wrong; rather, what is at issue is the establishment of the kingdom of God, i.e. theocracy (26f.= ET, 28). While this still corresponds to the usual Reformed approach, van Ruler goes on to press his consequences deliberately to an extreme point; the interest in the earthly, the concrete, the 'clinging to the material' (Baumgärtel's term, which is now

deliberately assessed in quite the opposite way, 27 n.42= ET, 30
n.42), which emerges in the Old Testament view of revelation is to
be seen as an advantage of the Old Testament, and the stronger
spiritualism of the New Testament is seen 'not as a plus but as a
minus, albeit as a minus which is perhaps necessary' (32, cf.46= ET,
34, cf.54). If, as van Ruler thinks, it is the task of Christian preaching
to be 'not only a preaching of Christ but also a preaching of the
kingdom' (ibid.), the New Testament is not enough. The Old
Testament is indispensable. A whole series of further conclusions
follows from this: not only does the people 'Israel' regain a permanent place in the saving plan of God (the Jews, the synagogue, the
state of Israel, 33= ET, 35. 'To the very depths of Old Testament
expectation the people of Israel as a people, the land, posterity, and
theocracy play a role that cannot possibly be eliminated', 42f.= ET,
45). The significance of Jesus Christ is also relativized (in deliberate
antithesis to the Christomonism of K.Barth and his disciples – cf.
also Velema, *Confrontatie* [above, 55], 104ff.): 'Certainly... he is at
least one act among others in this history of God with his people'
(37 = ET, 40); 'the incarnation is exclusively motivated by sin' (64 =
ET, 68), 'Jesus Christ is an emergency measure that God postponed
as long as possible' (65= ET, 69). On the other hand, in the last
resort the issue is not that of Israel as such (any more than it is a
matter of Jesus Christ as such) but God's action both with Israel and
with the church (the Christian peoples are 'incidental repetitions of
Israel', 33, cf. 31ff. = ET 35, cf.34ff.; the church is, in an analogous
way to Israel, a foreshadowing of the future, 39 n.25 = ET, 42 n.25)
relates to the world and its eschatological consummation which is
still to come (for the overall eschatological orientation of van
Ruler's theology cf. Velema, *Confrontatie*, passim). In Israel God is
concerned with the nations of the world (64, 73 = ET, 67, 79); it is
a means to the kingdom, just as Jesus Christ is a means to the
kingdom (73 = ET, 79); if one respects the Old Testament in its
independence, 'we shall see that God is always concerned only
about the earth' (33 = ET, 35). Thus, 'the quintessence is to be
found in politics in the broadest sense of the term: the state, social
and economic life, culture – in a word, the santification of the earth'
(85 = ET, 91). However, this is not an end in itself (van Ruler is in
no way a materialist!), but if God is concerned with created reality,
it is in order 'that it may stand before his presence' (64 = ET, 68).
'Sanctification is greater than reconciliation' (65 = ET, 69), 'The

doxological is more than the soteriological' (46 n.47 = ET, 55 n.47); van Ruler's thought has its real centre in God's honour, in the coming of his kingdom – here he is a true follower of Calvin (for his overall theocratic approach, cf. also B.Engelbrecht, 'A.A.van Ruler, Moderne Teokraat', *NGTT* 12, 1971, 188-211).

An important final conclusion for the canon also follows from this; 'The Old Testament is and remains the true Bible' (68 = ET, 72). Not only can van Ruler find six ways of arguing that the Old Testament is indispensable for the Christian church (69ff. = ET, 73ff.); he even asks whether there is 'only one canon... the Old Testament alone is the canon, and the New has just been added at the end as an explanatory glossary?' (88 = ET, 94), but leaves the question open (in contrast to his own early statement [in *Religie en Politiek*, Nijkerk 1945, 123-49; cf. 68 n.125 = ET, 70 n.125] a plurality of authorities has to be recognized, 89 = ET, 95). At all events, the emphasis lies on the Old Testament, even when van Ruler concedes 'that as a Christian church we have to accept our position as such in the New Testament' (52f. = ET, 56). Here, though, there is a plus over and above the Old: the New contains the kingdom of God in the form of suffering, which represents a greater depth and also the unique testimony to the divinity of Jesus Christ (47 = ET, 54). Yet, 'This plus is thus a minus too': 'The definitive revelation of created reality and the beauty of the world and hence the full glory of God are all absent from the Gospel of Jesus Christ' (52 = ET, 54).

However, the Reformed atmosphere of Holland was particularly favourable to such developments (cf. also Hesselink [above, 55]). It is certainly no coincidence that the second significant theologian in whom we can see a similarly high estimation of the Old Testament was also from the Netherlands: K.H.Miskotte. His main work is *Als de goden zwijgen*, Amsterdam 1956 = German (revised) *Wenn die Götter schweigen. Vom Sinn des Alten Testaments*, Munich 1963 = ET, *When the Gods are Silent*, London 1967. For further important works by Miskotte cf. Baker, *Two Testaments* (above,10), 482f.; K.A.Tangberg, 'Det gamle testamentes plass i Kornelis Heiko Miskottes teologi', *TTK* 49, 1978, 197-208. For Miskotte's influence in Holland (especially on F.H.Breukelman) and later developments see 'Een geschil over de uitleg van het Oude Testament (Studie des Raad voor de zaken van Kerk en Theologie [Komissionsbericht])', *KeTh* 27, 1976, 89-101. Specifically on Miskotte, cf. K.K.Deurloo et al., *De weg der verwachting*, Amsterdam 1975; de Kruijf, G.G., *Heiden, Jood en Christen*, Diss. Utrecht 1981. Cf. also especially Baker, *Two Testaments*, 139-46 (which is limited to the aspect of the relationship between the Testaments). For Miskotte's relationship to F.Rosenzweig see Liebster, W., 'Franz Rosenzweig und Kornelis Heiko Miskotte', in *'Wenn nicht jetzt, wann dann?'* FS *H.J.Kraus*, Neukirchen-Vluyn 1983, 209-21.

Because of its meditative, essayistic character, Miskotte's main work is not easy to describe; many thoughts are associated in an almost aphoristic way. One can also recognize the influences of a variety of contemporary theological ideas, both general and specific: the argument over the 'fourth man' (Alfred Weber), with modern nihilism of an existentialist stamp as a late flowering of Christian religion, 'when the gods are silent', but also over Bonhoeffer's thesis of man come of age serves to provide a comprehensive description of the situation (11-105 = ET, 14-101) as a background to the task of proclaiming the 'word' from scripture, which is a proclamation of the 'name', as Miskotte writes, taking up Jewish terminology (73ff., 127ff. = ET, 73ff.,119ff.). Two great lines of thought which have shaped Miskotte's thought world are particularly striking: first, dialectical theology of a Barthian stamp (from which derives not only the emphasis on the 'Word' and its proclamation as a central task, but also the characterization of religion as purely human and therefore misplaced action, a mere ingredient of culture [cf. e.g. 46ff., 73ff. = ET 49ff.,73ff.], while only faith, which depends on the free spontaneous approach of God, is worth living); secondly, his thorough attention to statements from Jewish piety, as is attested not only by the numerous mentions of Buber, Rosenzweig, Ben Chorin and Hasidism but also the deliberate adoption of central terms like 'the Name', which he uses throughout (the tetragrammaton cannot be spoken or translated, 127ff. = ET, 119ff.) and the rabbinic formula, the abbreviation, 'Tenach' for Holy Scripture (Old Testament). (There were even protests against this from the Jewish side; for the problem cf. also R.Zuurmond, 'Twee voetnoten bij K.H.Miskotte's theologie van het Oude Testament', in Deurloo et al, *De weg der verwachting*, [24-33] 26ff.) In fact Miskotte's dissertation (*Het wezen der joodse religie*, nd [1932, Haarlem ²1962]) was already concerned with the phenomenology of Jewish religion (cf. also id., *Edda en Thora*, Nijkerk 1939), and the juxtaposition of church and synagogue as a problem (we are confronted with the unfathomable schism in God's community which is alien to its nature) dogged him all his life (cf. still *Das Judentum als Frage an die Kirche*, Wuppertal 1970). He sees 'no overshadowing, but a help towards clarifying the message' in the question which Judaism puts to the church (311ff. = ET, 309ff.). The Old Testament in particular is common to them both; this, the Tenach, is also Holy Scripture for Christians in the real sense. 'Everything is there'. 'When we say that "everything" is there we certainly also mean to include, as Christians, the New Testament... But where it is a matter of God and his name, where the consecutive evaluations of history, the law, man, the priest, the prophet, the king are compared, where reconciliation and forgiveness, faith and sanctification, tribulation and the future are spoken of, we must say: all the essentials have been said in the Tenach' (166). Miskotte does not in any way want to do without the New Testament; on the contrary, he presupposes a fundamental accord in the structure of the two Testaments (167 = ET, 159; the same categorial reality, 176 = ET, 169), which he demonstrates in seven points (168-70 = ET, 161-3). He is sceptical about the usual patterns used to define this relationship, like typology, law and gospel, promise and fulfilment (115ff. = ET, 107ff.). However, it hardly seems to him to be possible to establish a 'plus' for the New Testament (a failing of the Old, the multiplicity of things, the provisionality of the doctrine of God, can be mentioned in passing, but it is not decisive, 176 = ET, 169f.). What is decisive is that 'the newness of the new *covenant* lies in the fact that the Word has been made flesh. The time of God has come. The promise is fulfilled. The shadows have fled' (171 = ET, 164). Yet the Tenach above all remains scripture in the real sense. Miskotte changes Vischer's slogan (cf. my 'Der Konflikt zwischen Exegese und Dogmatik. Wilhelm Vischers Ringen um den Christus im Alten Testament', in *Textgemäss*, FS E. *Würthwein*, Göttingen 1979, 110-22), by saying, 'To know *who* he (Christ) is, is the ground of the church. *What* he is, we must be constantly taught afresh by the Torah and the prophets' (167 = ET, 160). Miskotte sees the decisive 'profit' of the Old Testament in the way in which it speaks of God: precisely in the anthropomorphism, the apparently 'primitive' nature of this image of God, we have an expression of the concrete, a demonstration of the direct presence of the name of the one who stands in the midst (179ff. = ET, 173ff.). Here it is a matter of the world as creation, the inclusiveness of salvation; the Old Testament

preaching of salvation is a decisive hindrance to any dualistic
spiritualism (191ff. = ET, 191ff.). Areas like erotic love and politics
also belong to it (267ff., 273ff. = ET, 264ff., 271ff.). We are
reminded of similar remarks of van Ruler's (similarly, following
Miskotte, cf. recently also H.Kremers, 'Die Wiederentdeckung des
Alten Testaments in der evangelischen Kirche der Gegenwart', in
id. [ed.], *Juden und Christen lesen dieselbe Bibel*, Duisburg 1973
[²1977], 26-37; cf. also H.Haag, *Das Buch des Bundes* [above, 16],
299ff. = *TQ* 1980 [above, 60], 11ff.). Like van Ruler, Miskotte
similarly includes in the 'profit' of the Old Testament the fact that
the future is open, that the consummation of the kingdom of God
is still to come (211ff. = ET, 207ff. – on the other hand, however,
Miskotte sees that there is also mention of this in the New Testament,
298 = ET, 298), that expectation is an essential element (284ff. =
ET, 283ff.). The debate with E.Bloch's *Das Prinzip Hoffnung*
(297ff. = ET, 297ff.) in which he criticizes above all the absence of
the idea of creation, also belongs in this context.

All in all, Miskotte's attitude to the two Testaments is rather more
restrained than that of van Ruler. In drawing up his 'profit and loss
account' he himself describes it as 'more sophisticated' (176 = ET,
176). Central for him is the fact that both Testaments are testimony
to the one word of the same God (one can also apply the same
description to the attitude of A.Jepsen [*Wissenschaft vom Alten
Testament*, above, 27], for whom the Old Testament is concerned
above all with an independent testimony to the one God and his
 action which leads to its goal in Christ. As such testimony the Old
Testament must be taken seriously in its own right. Cf. also id,
'Theologie des Alten Testaments', in *Bericht von der Theologie*, ed.
G.Kulicke et al., Berlin 1971, 15-32 = id., *Der Herr ist Gott* [above,
27], [142-54] 149ff.). In addition to the 'voice' of scripture as
Word, Miskotte also attaches importance, particularly in the Old
Testament, to its 'function' as 'instruction' (64ff. = ET, 65ff.); again
and again its teaching is important, particularly its doctrine of God.
In this connection he takes up the term 'torah' in a positive way
(231ff. = ET, 228ff.; cf. also the index): it is concerned with the
benefits and obligations of the covenant, of faith as action, 'of
knowing God through his acts' (232 = ET, 229). In this way
commands and narrative (the two ingredients of the Pentateuch)
take on a positive theological significance for Christians as well.

In his concern for the theological significance of Judaism Miskotte deliberately follows Karl Barth (cf. 85 = ET, 80), who here introduced a discussion which has gone on down to the present day, sometimes with very controversial standpoints. The problem does not belong in the traditional sphere of Old Testament theology, but must nevertheless be mentioned, because the relationship between the Testaments and thus the theological evaluation of the Old Testament is directly affected by it.

Karl Barth (for the theme cf. F.W.Marquardt, 'Die Entdeckung des Judentums für die christliche Theologie', in *Israel im Denken Karl Barths*, ACJD 1, Munich 1967; W.L.Dekker, *Getuige Israel. Dogmatische en bijbels-theologische studie over de plaats van Israel in het denken van Karl Barth, met name in zij Kirchliche Dogmatik*, Wageningen 1974; B.Klappert, *Israel und die Kirche, Erwägungen zur Israellehre Karl Barths*, ThExH 207, Munich 1980; also A.T.Davies, *Antisemitism and the Christian Mind. The Crisis of Conscience after Auschwitz*, New York 1969, 113ff.; E.Borowitz, 'Anti-Semitism and the Christologies of Barth, Berkouwer and Pannenberg', *Dialog* 16, 1977, 38-41), however, had still internalized the relationship between Israel and the church, something that also happens (though not exclusively, cf. *KD* II/2, 215ff. = *CD*, 195ff.) with his concept of the church, which has an individualist framework. For him it is certain that 'the history of Israel is not continued after the crucifixion of Christ', because 'the Church has no history in the strict sense': 'Christians have their being as a whole elected race... a holy people... every one of them on the basis of his personal election' (*KD* II/2, 377 = *CD*, 342). Moreover, the messiah Jesus is 'in so far as he is also the end of the history of Israel', 'the foundation, the content and the goal of the covenant of God with humanity': 'His coming, appearance, birth and historical existence... are what follows that which came before, so that it is broken off and no longer continues as such. When that which follows comes, the history of Israel and its prophecy find in it their fulfilment and therefore *cannot have any continuations*' (*KD* IV/3, 76 = *CD*, 69). Consequently the concern of theology can only be the history of Israel *before* Christ, which in its totality in connection with Old Testament prophecy is type, i.e. prefiguration or the prehistory of Jesus Christ (cf. *KD* II/2, 52ff. = *CD*, 55ff.), which has its theological value as the time of expectation (*KD* I/2, 77ff. = *CD*, 70ff.). 'What might seem to be such are only recollections of their former occurrence which is now broken off and concluded...' (*KD* IV/3,

76 = *CD*, 69). 'The election of Israel is not for this reason denied or invalidated. But the election of Israel itself, as its election for the sake of Jesus Christ, is the election of those who believe in him, the election of the *Church*' (*KD* II/2, 473 = *CD*, 427). However, talk of 'the end of history' is not limited to Israel but relates to time and history generally (in a speculative interpretation of the *telos* concept of Rom.10.4ff. [on this cf. also Marquardt, op.cit., 321ff.]): 'Jesus Christ is the end not only of Israelite history but of all human history... of the course of time' (*KD* III/2, 708 = *CD*, 633).

Another line of thought is not integrated into this one (*KD* II/2, 215ff. = *CD*, 195ff.). Here Barth speaks of the community existing in two forms: 'It exists according to God's eternal decree as the people of Israel (in the whole range of its history in past and future, *ante* and *post Christum natum*), and at the same time as the Church of Jews and Gentiles' (*KD* II/2, 218 = *CD*, 198). Here 'Israel is the people of the Jews which resists its divine election....The Church is the gathering of Jews and Gentiles called on the ground of its election' (219 = 198f.). However, the community is chosen in both its forms, as Israel and as the church. Granted, as the people who failed to recognize and rejected the Messiah, Israel cannot recognize the mysterious unity of this community (and as such it is its special task to be the reflection of judgment – but God has taken that from it and suffered it himself in the person of Jesus [226ff. = 206ff.], so that the rejection of Israel is not his last word). Yet the church may never forget it, but must itself also witness to the obdurate people of the Jews God's permanent concern even for the sinner (219f. = 199). For the mere existence of the Jews as a group who are hard to define is, in its mysterious character (a people yet not a people), a testimony only to the faithfulness of God, who continues with the election of this people as an 'unshakeable decree' (*KD* III/3, 238ff. = *CD*, 217ff.) which cannot be altered in any way by the faithlessness of Israel. Indeed – as Barth said particularly in his radio broadcast of 1949 ('Die Judenfrage und ihre christliche Beantwortung', *KBRS* of 19.1.1950 = *Jud* 6, 1950, 67-72 = *Die Juden und wir Christen*, ed. H.Kallenbach, Kirche und Welt, Schriftenreihe der Evangelischen Akademie in Hessen und Nassau 5, Frankfurt am Main 1950, 9-16), in fact it is the most impressive sign of God's permanent concern for sinful man in his free grace. The election of apostate Judaism, unwilling to recognize the Lord Christ, an election which has not failed, is the mirror that is held up in front of us all.

In his attitude towards contemporary Judaism Barth found himself all his life in a dilemma (cf. also L.Steiger, 'Die Theologie vor der Judenfrage – Karl Barth als Beispiel', in *Auschwitz – Krise der christlichen Theologie. Eine Vortragsreihe*, ed. R.Rendtorff and E.Stegemann, ACJD 10, Munich 1980, 82-98). When he speaks in this connection, in a well-known letter (to F.-W.Marquardt of 5.9.1967, *Gesamtausgabe* V, *Briefe 1961-1968*, ed. J.Fangmeier and H.Stoevesandt, Zurich 1975, no.260, [419-23] 420f. = ET *Letters 1961-1968*, Grand Rapids and Edinburgh 1981, [261-3] 262 – also in Steiger, op.cit., 89, with the wrong date and an inaccurate page reference), of a 'totally irrational aversion' which he feels when he meets a living Jew, this is probably also an indication of the roots of a restriction of his horizon in theological discussion.

Barth feels the division between the two aspects of the history of Israel which he outlines, as being closed in respect of salvation history and as going on to the present in a way which is also theologically significant in the present, himself to be problematical, and in *KD* IV/1, 749 = *CD*, 671 he says that the existing division of church and synagogue poses the most difficult existential question to the confession of the unity of the church, if we take Rom.9-11 seriously: 'But here, in the so-called Jewish question, we face the deepest obscurity which surrounds it.' The root of this division also rests in the juxtaposition of the two basic, yet disparate, theological approaches which come together in Barth: the salvation-historical perspective along biblical lines and the christocentric 'transcendentalism' whose effects we also met elsewhere (*Problems of Old Testament Theology*, 103 = ET, 95).

Barth's last comments on the problem (which have also been called his 'ecumenical testament') appear in the account of his journey to Rome in 1966, *Ad limina Apostolorum*, Zurich 1967, which is significant in many respects. Here he criticizes above all (as did H.D.Leuner [below, 103] at the same time, independently of him) the fact that the opposition between church and synagogue, 'the greatest scandal of all, the basic schism', was not discussed in the Vatican II Decree on Ecumenism, but in the Declaration on Non-Christian Religions (see below)(33), 'although (*a*) the Old Testament is in no way concerned with a "religion" but with the original form of the one *revelation of God*, (*b*) the existence of later Judaism and Judaism today (both believing and unbelieving) is the one natural *proof of God* (from world history)' (39f.).

Even in his old age the patriarch had the ability to prompt questions which led to the heart of a discussion that is extremely topical.

6. Excursus: Israel and the Church

An extended discussion on the 'Jewish question' was only begun in the Christian churches after the end of the Second World War (for the theme as a whole see W.Schweikhart, *Zwischen Dialog und Mission*, Studien zu jüdischem Volk und christlicher Gemeinde 2, Berlin 1980; C.Thoma, *Die theologischen Beziehungen zwischen Christentum und Judentum*, Grundzüge 44, Darmstadt 1982). Certainly the horrors of the Holocaust provided a decisive stimulus towards it. A series of official declarations also arose out of this discussion, the basic tenor of which is a far-reaching opening out of ecumenical conversations in the direction of Judaism as well.

The most important documents are:
'Die 10 Seelisberger Thesen von 1947 zum christlichen Religionsunterricht', *RFF* 2, 1949/50, 5f. (revised version of Schwalbach, 1950, 'Thesen christlicher Lehrverkündigung im Hinblick auf umlaufende Irrtümer über das Gottesvolk des Alten Bundes, corr.1965', *FrRu* 16/17, 1964/65, 60f. [= *Die Juden*, ed.Kallenbach, 61-5]; the Amsterdam document of the World Council of Churches, 'The Christian Approach to the Jews', in *The First Assembly of the World Council of Churches*, ed.W.A.Visser 't Hooft, London 1949, 160-6 = *Stepping Stones to Further Jewish-Christian Relations*, ed.H.Croner, London and New York 1977, 69-72; the document of the Faith and Order Commission, 'The Church and the Jewish People', in *New Directions in Faith and Order. Bristol 1967*, Geneva 1968, 69-80 = *Stepping Stones*, 73-85: Group Report A, 'Christian-Jewish-Moslem Relations in the WCC Consultation in Chiang, May 1977', in *Faith in the Midst of Faiths*, ed.S.Samartha, Geneva 1977, 150-5; World Council of Churches, 'Committee on the Church and the Jewish People', *Newsletter* 1963-1980, continued in *Current Dialogue*, 1980ff. (see most recently, 'Guidelines for Jewish-Christian Dialogue' of the CCJP Meeting, London Colney, 22-26.6.1981', 1981/2, 5-11); the Vatican II Declaration on the Relation of the Church to Non-Christian Religions, *Nostra Aetate'*, *4, in LTK* E.2, 490-4 (ET in Abbott [above, 45],660-8; Flannery [above, 45], 738-49; also in

Stepping Stones, 1f. For its earlier history see e.g. F.E.Cartus, 'Vatican II and the Jews', *Com* 29, 1965, 19-29; also the introductory commentary by J.Oesterreicher, *LTK*.E 2, 406-78; the detailed commentary by A.Bea, *La Chiesa e il populo ebraico*, Brescia 1966 = *Die Kirche und das jüdische Volk*, Freiburg, Basle and Vienna 1966; J.C.Hampe, 'Die Judenfrage auf dem Konzil', in *Judenhass – Schuld der Christen?*, ed. W.P.Eckert and E.L.Ehrlich, Essen 1964, 406-36; id., 'Aber am Morgen ist Freude. Die Judenerklärung des Konzils – Rückblick und Ausblick', in W.P.Eckert, *Judenhass – Schuld der Christen?*, Ergänzungsheft, Essen 1966, 13-45; W.Becker, 'Die Erklärung über das Verhältnis der Kirche zu den nicht-christlichen Religionen', *Cath (M)* 20, 1966, 108-35; A.Exeler, 'Das Verhältnis der Kirche zu den Juden', in *Umkehr und Erneuerung. Kirche nach dem Konzil*, ed. T.Filthaut, Mainz 1966, 235-72; C.Hollis, 'The Vatican Council and the Jews', *DublRe* 241, 1966, 24-39; A.Gilbert, *The Vatican Council and the Jews*, Cleveland 1968; W.P.Eckert, 'Forderungen und Chancen einer christlich-jüdischen Begegnung nach dem Zweiten Vatikanischen Konzil', in *Die geistige Gestalt des heutigen Judentums*, Munich 1969, 143-65; J.Oesterreicher, *The Rediscovery of Judaism*, South Orange, NJ 1971; M.B.McGarry, *Christology after Auschwitz*, New York 1977, 13ff.; K.Richter, 'Die katholische Kirche und die Juden. Zur Entwicklung von 1945-1982', in *Die katholische Kirche und die Juden. Dokumente von 1945-1982*, ed. K.Richter, Freiburg 1982, 9-24 – also the guidelines of the Vatican Secretariat for Unity for its implementation, *Stepping Stones*, 11-16 = Flannery, 743-9 = *Auschwitz als Herausforderung für Juden und Christen*, ed.G.B.Ginzel, Heidelberg 1980, 296-308 (with an introduction by W.P.Eckert, 7-31) = *Dokumente*, ed. Richter, 80-7 = P.von der Osten-Sacken, *Katechismus und Siddur*, Berlin and Munich 1984, 292-7 (cf. also W.Becker, 'Schritte zur Versöhnung zwischen Christen und Juden', in *Versöhnung. Gestalten – Zeiten – Modelle*, ed. H.Fries and U.Valeske, Frankfurt 1975, 231-45 [236ff., 240ff.]; McGarry, *Christology*, 36ff.; also the evaluation from the Jewish side: H.Siegman, 'Jews and Christians – Beyond Brotherhood Week', *WV* 18, 1975, 31-6. For the overall development see also C.Klein, 'Catholics and Jews – Ten Years After Vatican II', *JES* 12, 1975, 471-83); the declaration of the American Committee of Bishops for Ecumenical and Inter-religious Affairs:

CMind 65, 1967, 62-5 = *Ecumenist* 5, 1967, 61-3 = *JES* 4, 1967, 568-72 = *Bridge* V, 1970, 257-62 = *Stepping Stones*, 16-20; the declaration of the French Catholic Bishops' Conference, 'L'attitude des chrétiens à l'égard du judaisme', *Documents épiscopat. Conférence épiscopale française*, no.10, Paris avril 1973 (= *CMind* 71, no.1275, Sept.1973, 51-7 = *Stepping Stones*, 60-5 = *Auschwitz*, ed.Ginzel, 294-5 = Richter, *Dokumente*, ed.Richter, 71-9 – some with discussions and commentaries). Also, the declaration of the Chief Rabbi of France, Jacob Kaplan, *Jud* 29, 1973, 54f.; the 18 theses of the Belgian 'National Catholic Commission for Relations between Christians and Jews' of 1973: L.Dequeker, 'Le dialogue judéo-chrétien un défi à la théologie?', *Bijdr* 37, 1976, 2-35 = *Stepping Stones*, 55-9; resolution of the synod 'Unsere Hoffnung': *Gemeinsame Synode der Bistümer in der Bundesrepublik Deutschland – Beschlüsse der Vollversammlung. Offizielle Gesamtausgabe*, ed. L.Bertsch, P.Boonen et al., I, Freiburg 1976, 84-111, section IV.2, 'Für ein neues Verhältnis zur Glaubensgeschichte des jüdischen Volkes', 108f. = *Auschwitz*, ed.Ginzel, 315-28 = *Stepping Stones*, 66; the working paper of the 'Jews and Christians' group of the Central Committee of German Catholics, *Theologische Schwerpunkte des jüdisch-christlichen Gesprächs*, Bonn – Bad Godesberg 8.5.1979 (privately printed) = *Auschwitz*, 315-28 = *Dokumente*, 110-21 (cf. also E.Zenger, 'Der Dialog muss weitergehen', ibid., [25-40] 25-32; cf. also id., 'Ökumene aus Juden und Christen. Zwei wichtige Anstösse aus den Jahren 1979 und 1980', *StZ* 199, 1981 [245-56], 245-50); the declaration of the German (Catholic) bishops: 'Über das Verhältnis der Kirche zum Judentum', 28.4.1980, ed.Sekretariat der Deutschen Bischofskonferenz (privately printed) = *HerKorr* 34, 1980, 292-9 = *Dokumente*, 122-50 (cf. also Zenger, ibid., 32-40; cf. also id., *StZ* 1981, 250-6); Biemer, G., (ed.), *Freiburger Leitlinien zum Lernprozess Christen-Juden*, Düsseldorf 1981, 25-133; the Declaration of the National Council of Brethren of the German Protestant Church of 8.4.1948: *RFF* 1, 1948, 5-8 = K.Kupisch, *Das Volk der Geschichte*, Berlin ²1962, 219-26 = *Der ungekündigte Bund*, ed. D.Goldschmidt and H.J.Kraus, Stuttgart 1962, 251-4 = *Die Juden*, ed.Kallenbach, 54-66; the Declaration of the Synod of the German Protestant Church in Berlin-Weissensee 1950, *Kirchenkanzlei der EKD, Berlin-Weissensee 1950*, Hanover 1950, 257f. =

KJ 77, 1950, 5f. = *Der ungekündigte Bund*, 256f. = *Auschwitz*, 339f. = *Die Juden*, 57f.; 'Juden und Christen', Declaration of the Christian participants in the leadership of the Sixth Working Party of the Tenth German Protestant Kirchentag, Berlin 1961: *Deutscher Evangelischer Kirchentag, Berlin 1961. Dokumente*, Stuttgart 1961, 487 = *LM* 1, 1962, 76f. = *Der ungekündigte Bund*, 123-5; 'Die Kirche und das jüdische Volk', Consultation of the Lutheran World Federation, Løgumkloster 1964: *LR* 14, 1964, 337-44 = *Das Zeugnis*, ed. Becker, Dobbert and Gjerding, 101-4 = *Stepping Stones*, 85f.; 'Gott ist treu zu den Juden', Declaration of the 'Jews and Christians' committee of the Lutheran World Federation: *LM* 9, 1970, 140-3 = *Stepping Stones*, 87-91; 'Das christliche Zeugnis und das jüdische Volk', Declaration of a consultation of the Lutheran World Federation, Oslo 1975: *LR* 26, 1976, 67-71 = *EvMis* 9, 1977, 94-9 = *Stepping Stones*, 127-32; *Christen und Juden. Eine Studie des Rates der EKD*, Gütersloh 1975, [3]1979 = *Stepping Stones*, 133-49 (there is also an extract in *Auschwitz*, 341-76 – cf. also e.g. W.P.Eckert, review, *FrRu* 27, 1975, 68-72; E.Flesseman-van Leer, *US* 31, 1976, 90-3; P.Lapide, 'Christians and Jews – A New Protestant Beginning', *JES* 12, 1975, 485-92; R.Rendtorff and N.P.Levinson, in *17. Deutscher Evangelischer Kirchentag, Berlin 1977. Dokumente*, 1977 = P.von der Osten-Sacken and M.Stöhr, *Wegweisung*, Berlin 1978, 72-85; *Arbeitsbuch Christen und Juden zur Studie des Rates der EKD*, ed. R.Rendtorff, Gütersloh 1979; 'Thesen zur Erneuerung des Verhältnisses von Christen und Juden', accepted by the Synod of the Protestant church in the Rhineland, 11.1.1980 (produced by the committee 'Christen und Juden') in *Handreichung für Mitglieder der Landessynode... 39* (privately printed, nd), 12-28 = *Umkehr und Erneuerung. Erläuterungen zum Synodalbeschluss der Rheinischen Landessynode 1980 'Zur Erneuerung des Verhältnisses von Christen und Juden'*, ed. B.Klappert and H.Starck, Neukirchen 1980, 267-81 = *EvTh* 40, 1980, 262-76 = epd-Dokumentation 42/80, 3-10 = *Leben und Glauben nach dem Holocaust. Einsichten und Versuche*, ed.G.Weissler, Stuttgart 1980, 112-14 = *Auschwitz*, 377-401, cf. the official resolution of the synod 'Zur Erneuerung des Verhältnisses von Christen und Juden': *Handreichung*, 9-11 = *Umkehr und Erneuerung*, 264-6 = *Auschwitz*, 402-7 = von der Osten-Sacken, *Katechismus*, 299-301 = *EvTh* 40, 1980, 260-2 = epd-Dokumentation 42/80, 1f.; the counter-declaration of the Theological Convention of Confessing Communities, 'Mission unter Israel – auch heute', *FÜI* 63, 1980, 62f. = epd-Dokumentation 42, 1980, 66f.; the statement by the professors of the Protestant Faculty of Theology of the University of Bonn, 'Erwägungen zur kirchlichen Handreichung zur Erneuerung des Verhältnisses zwischen Christen und Juden', epd-Dokumentation 42, 1980, 14-17 (cf. the response by B.Klappert, ibid., 18-43; cf. also P.von der Osten-Sacken, 'Das vergessene Skandalon', *LM* 20, 1981, 274-7; R.Rendtorff, 'Streit um die Judenmission', ibid., 716-18); the open letter by F.Hesse, 'Einige Anmerkungen zum Wort der rheinischen Landessynode über das Verhältnis von Christen und Juden', in *Umkehr und Erneuerung*, 283-6 (cf. J.Fangmeier, 'Offener Brief an Franz Hesse', ibid., 66-71); cf. also M.Honecker, 'Ein gemeinsames Glaubensbekenntnis für Christen und Juden?', *KuD* 27, 1981, 198-216; F.von Hammerstein, 'Neue Tendenzen in der christlich-jüdischen Begegnung', *Jud* 37, 1981, 2-11; U.Luz, 'Zur Erneuerung des Verhältnisses von Christen und Juden', ibid., 195-211, = *Israël en de Kerk*, The Hague 1959 = *Israel und die Kirche. Eine Studie im Auftrag der Generalsynode der Niederländischen Reformierten Kirchen, zusammengestellt von dem Rat für das Verhältnis zwischen Kirche und Israel*, Zurich 1961; *Überlegungen zum Problem Kirche-Israel*, ed. Vorstand des Schweizerischen Evangelischen Kirchenbundes, May 1977 = *FrRu* 29, 1977, 108-11; 'Kerkinformatie special, Kerk en Israël', ed. Deputaten voor Kerk en Israël, Leusden nd (1978), esp.5f.; *Kirche als 'Gemeinde von Brüdern'*. *Barmen III*, Vol.l.2, *Votum des Theologischen Ausschusses der Evangelischen Kirche der Union*, Gütersloh 1981, III.6, 'Kirche und Israel', 98-103 = von der Osten-Sacken, *Katechismus*, 301-6. – Cf. also the survey of the whole range of official and semi-official documents by C.Thoma, *Die theologischen Beziehungen zwischen Christentum und Judentum (= Beziehungen)*, Darmstadt 1982, 1-44.

The documents indicate relative agreement over the recognition of biblical Israel as the people of the old covenant and the subjects of the original election, in whose heritage the church of the new covenant has a part (here Pauline statements like Gal.3.7; Rom.11.17-24 are quoted). There is also usually a reference to the fact that in the church Jews and non-Jews ('Gentiles') are reconciled and united (Eph.2.14-16). However, different attitudes emerge when it comes to assessing the relationship of the church to Judaism today.

The Amsterdam document still exclusively envisages a mission to the Jews and the incorporation of converts into the church. However, the National Council of Brethren in 1948 already makes a more sophisticated statement about the Jewish question. On the one hand it stresses: 'The election and predestination of Israel have found their fulfilment in the fact that the Son of God was born a Jew.' 'Through and since Christ, the election of Israel has passed over to the church made up of all peoples, Jews and Gentiles.' In negative terms it is said: 'By crucifying the Messiah, Israel has rejected its election and predestination.' 'Israel under judgment is the constant confirmation of the truth and reality of the divine Word and the constant warning of God to his community. The mute preaching of the fate of the Jews is that God will not be mocked...' However, Israel's action in rejecting Jesus Christ is at the same time an example of the attitude of humanity to Christ generally: 'Here at the same time the revolt of all men and nations against the Christ of God has become an event. We all share the guilt of Christ's cross.' In that case, however, what happened on the cross also holds for the Jews: 'Christ was crucified and rose again also for the people of Israel.' Hence (one might add, in the light of the event of justification) it is also possible to speak of a 'continuation of the promise over Israel': 'God's faithfulness does not let go of Israel even in its unfaithfulness and its rejection.' However, this does not seem to envisage a *special* promise for Israel in the context of a manifestly general anthropological argument: if even Israel is not excluded from the sinfulness of all men, it is not excluded from the hope that is offered to all men either. By contrast, the Berlin-Weissensee declaration evidently already supposes that contemporary Judaism has a special theological significance. 'We believe that God's promise over the people of Israel whom he has chosen has remained in force even after the crucifixion of Jesus Christ.' In the course of ecumenical discussion considerable differences have emerged at this point; they seem above all to divide the churches of the West from those of the East, even beyond confessional boundaries (there are striking parallels between the Reformed churches and the Roman Catholic church). Here political implications are not least involved (arising out of the existence of the state of Israel and tensions between Israel and the Arab world). The Bristol document, from the Protestant side, is also illuminating. In the ecumenical commission people could agree that the existence of the Jewish people, who have been preserved down to the present day through all their persecutions, must be seen as a sign of the unchanging fidelity of God (which does not allow even that part of the Jewish people which was not prepared to recognize Jesus as Messiah to fail) and that (with Rom.11.25-32) in the end salvation is predetermined even for the Jews. But despite agreement on recognizing a degree of continuity between the biblical Israel and contemporary Judaism, opinions differed as to whether the Jews still to be regarded as God's chosen people or not. In particular the representatives of the Western churches tended to answer this question in the affirmative (this is clear from the Dutch document of 1959/61, 27ff., and the Swiss study of 1977, as examples of the Reformed position; the theses [Rhineland 1980], IV; cf. also 'Barmen III', III.6.2, p.247, are particularly forthright; on the Catholic side see the Council declaration and following that the Belgian theses, 10, cf.18, the 1979 working paper of the German Catholics, I.3, and the 1980 declaration of the German bishops, III, 1c; cf. also *Freiburger Leitlinien* 3.2; 3.5; 4.4; by contrast the 1975 German Protestant church study merely states that both Jews and Christians *understand* themselves as the people of God [13/346], while the French bishops assert that Jews and Christians find themselves 'in a state of mutual questioning'. 'Israel and the church are not two institutions which complement each other' [section 7]). The Eastern Christians see only the church as the legitimate successor in the role of people of God and inheritor of election, which is now only to be attained in Christ.

Similarly, in the preparation of the Vatican II declaration there was considerable opposition from the bishops of the Eastern church to the proposals for the formulation of the section about the Jews; indeed, they 'rose up as a phalanx against the fourth chapter' (Oesterreicher, *LTK* E.2, 430). There was even more disturbance after the release of the first outline in Arab countries (cf. Becker, *Cath [M]* 1966, 115). However, after tedious negotiations the Vatican authorities, above all through the intervention of Cardinal Bea, managed to achieve a reasonably wide assent to the final version, which was changed in many respects (cf. Oesterreicher and Becker, op.cit.). Cf. also the vigorous reactions to the declaration by the French episcopal committee (extracts in

FrRu 1973). For a similar situation in Uppsala 1968 cf. H. Berkhof, 'Israel as a Theological Problem in the Christian Church', *JES* 6, 1969, [329-47] 330; the 'Barmen III' declaration III.6.2, also failed to secure the assent of all the members of the committee, cf. 101 n.39.

The content of the dialogue to be carried on with Judaism is said above all to be the question of the significance of the Old Testament as the common biblical heritage (cf. also 'Christen und Juden', I.2; 'Barmen III', III.6.2 [which explicitly also includes the New Testament]; *Freiburger Leitlinien* 1.2, and especially Theses [Rhineland, 1980], II. A proposal is made there that the designation 'Old Testament' should be replaced with 'Hebrew Bible' [II.1 – cf. also below, 120]). It is also said that the church must rethink its understanding of election in view of the existence of Judaism. The Dutch document of 1959/61 also stresses this point (cf. I.4), but emphasizes that the election of Israel has a universal goal: Israel is elected as *pars pro toto*, by whom God seeks to show that he has intended it for the whole world. In view of the continued existence of election according to Rom.11.17ff., it would not follow that in the end Israel will be incorporated into the church; on the contrary, the nations will be 'sealed' to the church of Israel. The document sees two lines running side by side: '1. Israel is continued in the church; 2. Israel continues its existence in election, for the time being alongside the church' (31). The Swiss declaration goes even further: 'Because God has not rejected his people, there is no question that the church has taken the place of Israel as the "new people of God". There is no "new Israel"... rather, Israel and the church stand side by side' (1.4). Above all, the 1980 Rhineland theses, IV, take the same view: according to these the world of nations only has a 'share in Israel's election' through Christ. The pious observance of the Torah by modern Judaism is recognized as being completely valid: 'In the way and work of Jesus, the God of Israel demonstrates to all the world his unchangeable faithfulness and his unconditional solidarity with his elect people, which responds to him with its faithfulness to the Torah' (Thesis IV – cf. also the 1979 working paper of the German Catholics, III,1: 'Through the Jew Jesus the Torah continues to have its effect in Christianity. Through him it is given to Christians to realize, as God's promise and commandment'). According to Thesis VI, however, the Jewish people and the Christian church stand side by side; both issue their call as witnesses of the one God (the 1979 working paper of the German Catholics is similar, I,1, cf. III, 1). They also need to reckon with one another 'in consideration of the identity and witness of the other. Where they can give common witness they should do this more than hitherto' (Thesis VI). Cf. also the Belgian Theses, no.10, and the declaration by the 1961 Berlin Kirchentag, para.4.

An important idea expressed only in an abbreviated form in the Vatican II declaration (for more detailed preliminary versions cf. Oesterreicher, *LTK* E.2 and Becker, *Cath [M]* 1966), which the declaration of the French bishops develops further (section 4.a-b; cf. also the Belgian thesis 9 and the 1980 declaration of the German bishops, III,2a; V,4) is the acquittal of the Jews from the traditional charge of being 'deicides'. It already had a central place in the Seelisberger Theses (which J.Isaac played a major part in composing) 7, and from there had an influence on the preparation of the Council declaration. It had been argued with increasing urgency that this charge was untenable; even if the Jewish authorities of the time had brought about the death of Jesus, this could not be blamed on all the Jews of the time and certainly not on the Jews of today – especially as it was the Romans who put Jesus to death. The share of the guilt among the Jews of the time was to be reckoned with the general guilt of all humanity, for which Jesus had made complete atonement.

L.M.Carli ('La questione giudaica davanti al Concilio Vaticano II', *PalCl* 44, 1965, [185-203] 191ff.) criticized the Council declaration vigorously at this point; he sought to maintain the collective guilt of the Jewish people for what, in dogmatic terms, can quite properly be termed 'deicide' ('the death of Christ on the cross'), as corresponding to a biblical notion. For the controversy with Carli cf. J.M.Oesterreicher, 'Deicide as a Theological Problem', *Bridge* V, 1970, 190-206. Cf. also *inter alia* D.Crossan, 'Anti-Semitism and the Gospels', *TS* 26, 1965, 189-214 (cf. also G.O'Collins, 'Anti-Semitism in the Gospels', ibid., 663-6); E.Fischer, *Faith Without Prejudice*, New York 1977, 76-88. For the historical problems see most recently, in detail, A.Strobel, *Die Stunde der Wahrheit. Untersuchungen zum Strafverfahren gegen Jesus*, WUNT 21, 1980; cf. also J.Isaac, *L'Enseignement du Mépris*, Paris 1962 = *The Teaching of Contempt*, New York 1964, 39ff.,

109ff.; S.Zeitlin, *Who Crucified Jesus?*, New York 1964; B.Z.Bokser, *Judaism and the Christian Predicament*, New York 1967, 278ff.; H.H.Cohn, *Reflections on the Trial and Death of Jesus*, Jerusalem 1967 (also *Israel Law Review* 2, 1967, 332-79); E.M.Yamauchi, 'Concord, Conflict, and Community: Jewish and Evangelical Views of Scripture', in *Evangelicals and Jews in Conversation*, ed. M.H.Tanenbaum et al. (above, 22), (154-96) 167ff.; D.Dormeyer, 'Die Passion Jesu als Ergebnis seines Konflikts mit führenden Kreisen des Judentums', in *Gottesverächter und Menschenfeinde?*, ed. H. Goldstein, Düsseldorf 1979, 211-38; J.T.Pawlikowski, *What are They Saying About Christian-Jewish Relations?*, New York and Ramsay NJ, 1980, 1ff.; D.Flusser, *The Last Days of Jesus in Jerusalem*, Tel Aviv 1980.

The existence of the modern state of Israel and its possible theological significance pose a special problem. Is the foundation of this state and its preservation through several wars to be seen as a fulfilment of the Old Testament promise of land? Does for example the return of Israel to its land even herald the imminent dawning of the end time? The 1959/61 Dutch document goes the farthest here, supposing that in the appearance of this state 'at all events we may see a divine sign' (61), a sign above all of God's faithfulness and a new way on which God has set his people to fulfil his election (61ff.), though linked with this there is an admonition to Israel to keep peace with its Arab neighbours. This is despite the warning against a form of 'natural theology', 'in which people think that they can by-pass the revelation in Christ through the Spirit and derive from history and the events and destinies of their own time a direct knowledge of God' (61). The declaration of the French bishops is more restrained; there is certainly a recollection here of the promise of land, but it appears alongside the statement that the conscience of the world could not deny the Jewish people 'the right and the means to a political existence among the nations'; there is also thought of the victims of the return, and the declaration ends with an open question whether this will be 'one of the ways of divine justice for the Jewish people and, at the same time, for all the people of the earth' (section 5,e). Even these cautious statements caused a storm of public disturbance. The German Protestant church study on 'Christians and Jews' argues more carefully (for the phenomenological diction of the paper see Flesseman-van Leer): the state of

Israel is on the one hand explicitly termed a political entity which is organized in the form of a modern secular state; on the other hand 'it explicitly stands in the biblical tradition of Judaism and thus in the context of the history of the chosen people'. 'That is also significant for Christians' (cf. also 'Barmen III', III.6.3). However, following this there is only a plea for a just balance between Jews and Arabs, without any claim to a direct theological relevance in the founding of the state. This formulation evidently takes account of the dissent between various theological opinions which could not be resolved. The Swiss declaration speaks openly of such dissent (6.2): some (both Christians and Jews) saw the foundation of the state as the fulfilment of biblical promises, while others (Christians and Jews) saw it as a purely political act. Here too there is also a plea for the right of the Arabs to live in the land (in *Guidelines*, 5.1-6, for the rights of Jews, Christians and Moslems in respect of the land).

Finally, the theme of the mission to the Jews also plays a part in the declarations. For Amsterdam 1948 the idea of the task of mission even to the Jews was still completely taken for granted. In later declarations more than just the language has changed considerably in this respect. The American ('It is understood that proselytizing is to be carefully avoided in the dialogue...', *General Principles* [for the planned Christian-Jewish encounters], no.7), and similarly, the French bishops explicitly rule out any concern for conversion from encounters between Jews and Christians ('...without incurring the suspicion of disloyally alienating anyone from the community in order to bring him or her into one's own community', sec.6), specifically because the Jewish people is the subject of an 'eternal covenant' without which the 'new covenant' cannot exist. The 1979 working paper of the German Catholics, III, 1, takes a similar position: 'Hence in principle it is forbidden to Jews and Christians to seek to make others disloyal to the call of God which has gone out to them.'

The Report of Group A at the WCC theological consultation in Chiang Mai in 1977 (though this was only accepted in plenary session as a study document, as were all the other reports, cf. *Denkpause im Dialog*, ed. H.Mildenberger, Frankfurt 1978, 62) mentions one of the unavoidable questions in dialogues with Jews (to which different answers are said to be possible): 'What guarantees can Christians give against proselytizing among Jews?' (*Denkpause*, 65.

– *Guidelines* 1981, 3.2, however, understand proselytism more narrowly in terms of compulsory proselytism). The Dutch document of 1959/61 justifies the 1951 formulation of the church order of the Dutch Reformed Church (art. VII,2), that talk should henceforth be more of a 'conversation' than a 'mission' with Israel on the basis of the abiding 'missionary task' which (according to Rom.2.19f.) is given to Israel itself. Thus, it is said, the 'younger sister' can only enter into a conversation with the 'older brother' if she is not concerned with the conversion of individuals but with the dialogue of the whole of the church with all Israel (the Belgian theses, 18, take a similar line). The division between church and Israel is even described as 'the first schism within the one body of the community of God'. Still (according to Acts 4.12; 15.8f.,11), even for the Jews there is no exception to the fact that deliverance for humanity lies only in Christ. 'Barmen III', III.6.2, also takes a similar line: 'However, church and theology have to introduce the New Testament testimony to the saving significance of Jesus Christ into this conversation if they are to be credible conversation partners of Judaism.' Cf. also the Freiburg *Leitlinien*, 1.1.1: 'Christian recognition and appreciation of the Jewish conviction of faith, as standing firm in the revelation really given by the true God to the Jewish people, happens and can happen, regardless of the firm conviction of faith in the utterly binding character of the divine revelation of God which for Christians has taken place finally in Jesus Christ. Only in this way is true comradeship possible, which respects the existential decision of faith... as legitimate, even if the result is a mutual exclusiveness.' The 1980 Rhineland theses take christological assertion to an extreme: the church 'bears witness to the uniqueness of the Jew Jesus in the history of God with the world', and stress the abiding effect of the call of Israel for the Gentile world: 'Through this call all peoples will come to know and love God and gain a share in his salvation' (VI, 1). By contrast, the 1978 Dutch document states: 'Israel and the community from the Gentile world can only come to their full fruition in communion with Jesus Christ and with each other' (6). World Lutheranism has usually maintained the church's task of mission to the Jews very resolutely. Thus in the Løgumkloster declaration (which, however, explicitly rejects antisemitism and refers to the 'Christian responsibility to understand respectfully the Jewish people and its faith') there is a call to bear witness to the gospel and thus for organized mission even towards the Jewish people. The 1975 Oslo document juxtaposes features common to Christians and Jews (faith in the one God, the Creator) and what divides them (through the uniqueness of Christ) and recognizes a 'constant reciprocal challenge to Christians and Jews' from this dialectical relationship; however, it still issues a call to continue the preaching of Christ even to Judaism, though (as already in the declaration in *LM* 1970) it stresses the notion that as sinners together with the Jews Christians know themselves to be under the judgment of God and prove to be in solidarity with the Jews. The 1981 *Guidelines*, 3.4, note far-reaching differences of opinion among the Christians on this question. Here, too, the most balanced formulations are in the German Protestant church document 'Christen und Juden' (1975). With the common confession by Jews and Christians of the one God as a starting point (I,1 – similarly also the 1979 working paper of the German Catholics, I.1, and the 1980 declaration of the German bishops, II, 2-3; cf. also the Freiburg *Leitlinien* 1.1 and the 1981 *Guidelines*, 2.7), the task is said to be an encounter in mutual testimony to one's own faith, which is indispensable for both sides. Whereas for Jews the Torah has a central place, for Christians this place is occupied by Jesus Christ in his saving significance for all humanity. So Christians continue to be concerned (despite the many obstacles put in the way of conversation by the past) to give an account in accord with the gospel (thus, resolutely, also the Swiss declaration 5, cf. also the Belgian theses, 18). But the appropriate nomenclature for such a conversation and for the forms under which it is to be carried on must be left open, since Jews also find the term 'dialogue', as it has come to be used nowadays in ecumenical discussion, loaded (especially since Ajaltoun/Beirut, cf. *Living Faiths and the Ecumenical Movement*, ed.S.J.Samartha, Geneva 1971 = *Dialog mit anderen Religionen. Material aus der ökumenischen Bewegung*, ed. H.J.Margull and S.J.Samartha, Frankfurt 1972; cf. also below, 114. Recently, however, the limits of what is meant by the term have become clear, cf. H.J.Margull, 'Verwundbarkeit – Bemerkungen zum Dialog', *EvTh* 34, 1974, 410-20; the 1975 Nairobi Report = *Breaking Barriers, Nairobi 1975*, London and Grand Rapids 1976, 46f., but cf. also 40f.; and on it L.Vischer, *Veränderung der Welt – Bekehrung der Kirchen*, Frankfurt am Main 1976, 45ff.; M.Mildenberger, 'Nach zehn Jahren', in id. (ed.), *Denkpause* [above, 74], [9-24] 16ff. There is fundamentalist criticism in P.Beyerhaus, 'Das Programm des Dialogs mit Vertretern der Religionen und Ideologien unserer Zeit', in W.Künneth and P.Beyerhaus, *Reich Gottes oder Weltgemeinschaft?*, Bad Liebenzell 1975, 208-29).

The themes discussed in official church declarations and the differences of opinion which emerge in them are also reflected in scholarly discussion (a recent non-technical survey of them is F.Mussner, *Traktat über die Juden*, Munich 1979; for one aspect see also E.Fleischner, *Judaism in German Christian Theology Since 1945. Christianity and Israel considered in Terms of Mission*, Metuchen, NJ 1975. There is a brief general bibliographical survey of documents from the controversy between Judaism and Christianity, from the earliest church to the present, in F.E.Talmage, 'Judaism on Christianity: Christianity on Judaism', in *Disputation and Dialogue. Readings in the Jewish-Christian Encounter*, ed. F.E.Talmage, New York 1975, 361-90.) Here, too, the main concern is the possible significance of contemporary Judaism (there is also a recent general survey in J.Moltmann, *Kirche in der Kraft des Geistes*, Munich 1975, 156-71 = ET *The Church in the Power of the Spirit*, London and New York 1977, 136-49. Cf. also the dialogue between H.Gollwitzer and R.Rendtorff, *Thema: Juden-Christen-Israel. Mit einer Entgegnung von P.Levinson und einer didaktischen Skizze von H.Sorge*, Stuttgart 1978).

For the history of the conflict with Judaism since the early church cf. esp. Parkes, J., *The Conflict of the Church and the Synagogue*, London 1934 (reprinted New York 1974); cf. also id., *Judaism and Christianity*, London 1948, esp.113ff. (for Parkes cf. J.T.Pawlikowski, 'The Church and Judaism: The Thought of James Parkes', *JES* 6, 1969, 573-97); Williams, A.L., *Adversus Judaeos*, Cambridge 1935; Browe, P., *Die Judenmission im Mittelalter und die Päpste*, MHP VI, Rome 1942; Hay, M., *The Foot of Pride: The Pressure of Christendom on the People of Israel for 1900 Years*, Boston 1950 = id., *Europe and the Jews*, Boston 1960; Blumenkranz, B., *Die Judenpredigt Augustins. Ein Beitrag zur Geschichte der jüdisch-christlichen Beziehungen in den ersten Jahrhunderten*, Basle 1946 (reprinted Paris 1973); id., *Juifs et Chrétiens dans le monde occidental 430-1096*, EtJ 2, Paris 1960; id., *Les auteurs chrétiens latins du moyen age sur les juifs et le judaisme*, Paris 1963; Simon, M., *Verus Israel. Étude sur les relations entre Chrétiens et Juifs dans l'empire Romain*, Paris ²1964;

Maurer, W., *Kirche und Synagoge*, Stuttgart 1953; Kupisch, K., *Das Volk der Geschichte*. *Randbemerkungen zur Geschichte der Judenfrage*, Berlin ²1960 (*Volk ohne Geschichte*, ¹1953); Lovsky, F., *Antisémitisme et mystère d'Israël*, Paris 1955; Isaac, J., *Génèse de l'Antisémitisme*, Paris 1956; Poliakov, L., *Histoire de l'Antisémitisme*, I-IV, Paris 1955-77 = *The History of Anti-Semitism*, New York 1965 (four vols.); Strecker, G., 'Christentum und Judentum in den ersten beiden Jahrhunderten', *EvTh* 16, 1956, 458-77 = id., *Eschaton und Historie*, Göttingen 1979, 291-310; Schoeps, H.J., *Israel und Christenheit. Jüdisch-christliches Religionsgespräch in 19 Jahrhunderten*, Munich and Frankfurt ³1961 (Berlin 1937, Frankfurt am Main ²1949 = ET *The Jewish-Christian Argument. A History of Theology in Conflict*, New York 1963 and London 1965, paperback 1968); Katz, J., *Exclusiveness and Tolerance. Studies in Jewish-Gentile Relations in Mediaeval and Modern Times*, London 1961 and New York 1962 (⁴1975); *Christen und Juden. Ihr Gegenüber vom Apostelkonzil bis heute*, ed. W.-D.Marsch and K.Thieme, Mainz and Göttingen 1961; Daniélou, J., *Dialogue avec Israël*, Paris and Geneva 1963; Synan, E.A., *The Popes and the Jews in the Middle Ages*, New York 1965; Flannery, E.H., *The Anguish of the Jews: Twenty-three centuries of Anti-Semitism*, New York 1965; Veit, O., *Christlich-jüdische Koexistenz*, Frankfurt am Main (1965) ²1971; Grayzel, S., 'Evaluating the Past in Christian-Jewish Relations', in *Torah and Gospel. Jewish and Catholic Theology in Dialogue*, ed.P. Scharper, New York 1966, 5-21; Schneider, P., *Sweeter Than Honey. Christian Presence Amid Judaism [= US The Dialogue of Christians and Jews]*, London and New York 1966, paperback 1967; Lapide, P.E., *The Last Three Popes and the Jews*, New York 1967; Sheerin, J.B., 'Evaluating the Past in Catholic-Jewish Relations', in *Lessons for Today?*, 23-34; Bratton, F.G., *The Crime of Christendom: The Theological Sources of Christian Anti-Semitism*, Boston 1969; Tal, U., *Christians and Jews in Germany. Religion, Politics and Ideology in the Second Reich, 1870-1914* (Hebrew original 1969), ET Ithaca and London 1975; Hruby, K., *Juden und Judentum bei den Kirchenvätern*, SJK 2, Zurich 1971; Rivkin, E., *The Shaping of Jewish History. A Radical New Interpretation*, New York 1971; Mayer, R., *Judentum und Christentum. Ursprung, Geschichte, Aufgabe*, Aschaffenburg 1973; Conzelmann, H., *Heiden-Juden-Christen. Auseinandersetzungen in der Literatur der hellenistisch-römischen Zeit*, Tübingen 1981; Maccoby, H. (ed.), *Judaism on Trial. Jewish-Christian Disputations in the Middle Ages*, East Brunswick, NJ, London and Toronto 1982; for relations between Greek Orthodoxy and Judaism see *JES* 13, 1976.4, 517-672 (with contributions by D.J.Constantelos, Z.Ankori, S.Siegel, T.Stylianopoulos, G.S.Bebis); also the two collected volumes: Rengstorf, K.H., and Kortzfleisch, S.von, *Kirche und Synagoge*, I, II, Stuttgart 1968/70; Ruether, R., *Faith and Fratricide. The Theological Roots of Anti-Semitism*, New York 1974 (cf. also ead., 'Anti-Semitism and Christian Theology', in *Auschwitz: Beginning of a New Era? Reflections on the Holocaust*, ed. E.Fleischner, New York 1977, 79-92 – but cf. also for criticism: T.A.Idinopulos and B.Ward, 'Is Christology Inherently Antisemitic', *JAAR* 45, 1977, 193-214; J.Blank, 'Christenglaube und Judenhass', *Orien* 43, 1979, 232-5 = id., *Christliche Orientierungen*, Düsseldorf 1981, 58-72; J.Pawlikowski, 'The Historicizing of the Eschatological: The Spiritualizing of the Eschatological: Some Reflections', in *Antisemitism and the Foundations of Christianity*, ed.A.T.Davies, New York 1979, 151-66 [reply by R.Ruether, 'The Faith and Fratricide Discussion: Old Problems and New Dimensions', ibid., 30-56]; id., *Christ in the Light of the Christian-Jewish Dialogue*, New York 1982, 26ff.; H.Lindner, 'Nächstenliebe und Brudermord. Kritischer Bericht über R.Ruethers gleichnamiges Buch', *ThBeitr* 11, 1980, 177-86); Meagher, J.C., 'As the Twig Was Bent: Antisemitism in Greco-Roman and Earliest Christian Times', in *Antisemitism*, ed.A.T.Davies, 1-26; Awerbuch, M., *Christlich-jüdische Begegnung im Zeitalter der Frühscholastik*, Munich 1980; Gigon, O., 'Antiker Antisemitismus als Antijudaismus und Antichristianismus: Heiden-Juden-Christen', in *Kritik und Gegenkritik in Christentum und Judentum*, ed. S.Lauer, Judaica et Christiana 3, Berne and Frankfurt am Main 1981, 23-35; Liebeschütz, W., 'Die frühe Kirche als Verfolgerin und Verfolgte', ibid., 67-82; Schreckenberg, H., *Die christlichen Adversus-Judaeos-Texte und ihr literarisches und historisches Umfeld (1.-11.Jahrhundert)*, EHS.T 172, Berne and Frankfurt am Main 1982; Maier, J., *Jüdische Auseinandersetzung mit dem Christentum in der Antike*, EdF 177, Darmstadt 1982; Baumann, A.H., *Luthers Erben und die Juden. Das Verhältnis lutherischer Kirchen Europas zu den Juden*, Hanover 1984. It is also worth noting (for a stress on the toleration of the Jews in the Christian Middle Ages): Yerusalmi, Y.H., 'Response to Rosemary Ruether', in *Auschwitz*, ed.E. Fleischner, 97-107. This aspect has been pursued on a wider scale by A.Edelstein, *An Unacknowledged Harmony: Philosemitism and the Survival of European Jewry*, Contribution in Ethnic Studies 4, Westport, Conn. 1982. Cf. also P.von der Osten-Sacken, 'Erbe und Auftrag der christlich-jüdischen Geschichte', in id., *Anstösse aus der Schrift*, Neukirchen 1981, 124-38.

Most Christian attitudes to the problem of the church and Judaism begin from a dialectical presupposition on the basis of the New Testament evidence: on the one hand the period of Old Testament Israel as the chosen people of God and bearers of the promise has come to an end through the testimony of Christ and the time of the church, in which the promises once made to Israel have been fulfilled (cf. above, 47ff.), and a new community has come together made up of Jews and non-Jews (Gentiles). On the other hand (as is stressed with especial reference to Paul's remarks in Rom.9-11), the election of Israel, once made, is not simply done away with, since God faithfully keeps his promises, once made, despite all human disobedience (and after the rejection of the sending of Jesus).

Zimmerli, W., 'Biblische Grundlinien zur Judenfrage', *Jud* 2, 1945, 93-117; Oehmen, B.D.H., 'Le schisme dans le cadre de l'économie divine', *Irén* 21, 1948, 6-31; Weber, G., 'Das Geheimnis Israels im Zeugnis der Schrift', in *Die Juden*, ed. Kallenbach, 17-34; Ehrenberg, H., 'Acht Thesen zur Judenfrage', ibid., 35-40; Fricke, O., 'Wir Christen und die Juden', ibid., 41-9; Neill, S., Introduction to *The Church and the Jewish People*, ed. G.Hedenquist, London 1954, (11-25) 15; Torrance, T.F., 'The Israel of God: Israel and the Incarnation', *Int* 10, 1956, 305-20; Jocz, J.A., *A Theology of Election. Israel and the Church*, London 1958; Rengstorf, K.H., 'Das alte und das neue Gottes-volk', *PBL* 100, 1960, 409-19; Schooneveld, J., 'De uitverkiezing van Israel in het Oude Testament', in *Op het spoor van Israel*, The Hague 1961, 9-26; Grolle, H.J., 'Het apostolaat der kerk en het gesprek met Israel', ibid., 151-67; Vriezen, T.C., 'Die Erwählung Israels', in *Deutscher Evangelischer Kirchentag 1961* (above, 67), (414-22) 421f. (cf. 429f.) = *Der ungekündigte Bund*, ed. H.L.Goldschmidt and H.J.Kraus (above, 66), (49-56) 55f. (cf. 64f.); Lambert, B., *Le problème oecuménique*, Paris 1962 =

Das ökumenische Problem, Freiburg, Basle and Vienna 1964, II, 212ff.; Maier, R., 'Das Israel Gottes', *Christlich-jüdisches Forum* (Basle) 29, 1962, 1-8; Pfisterer, R., *Juden, Christen/getrennt, versöhnt*, Gladbeck 1964, 45ff.; Bea, A., 'Il popolo ebraico nel piano divino della salvezza', *CivCatt* 116, 1965, 209-29; Dudzus, O., 'Die bleibende Gültigkeit des Alten Testaments und Israels nicht widerrufliche Erwählung', in *Das Christentum und die Juden*, ed. W.Bienert, Cologne 1966, 9-18 (he sees the dogma of Israel's rejection as being 'something like a fall of the Christian church', 15); Quervain, A. de, *Das Judentum in der Lehre und Verkündigung der Kirche heute*, ThExH NF 130, Munich 1966, 22f.; Köberle, A., 'Israel – ein Gottesbeweis', *Jud* 22, 1966, (193-208) 199; Schelkle, K.H., 'Die Auserwählung Israels in christlicher Sicht', in *Unwiderrufliche Verheissung. Die religiöse Bedeutung des Staates Israel*, ed. W.Molinski, Recklinghausen 1968, 23-40; Harder, G., 'Die Bedeutung der Auserwähltheit Israels für die Christen', ibid., 41-66; id., 'Das christlich-jüdische Gespräch im Verhältnis zum christlichen Zeugnis an Israel', in *Der ungekündigte Bund*, ed. Goldschmidt and Kraus, (145-59) 157ff.; Vorgrimler, H., 'Ein Freundeswort', in *Die Wiederentdeckung*, ed. Oesterreicher, (21-28) 24f.; Dahl, N.A., 'Election and the People of God', *LuthQ* 21, 1969, 430-6; Wyschogrod, M., 'Israel, the Church and Election', *Bridge* V, 1970, 79-87; Oesterreicher, *The Rediscovery of Judaism* (above, 65), 47f., 49; id., *The Israel of God*, Englewood Cliffs, NJ, 1963, cf. esp.5; id., 'Unter dem Bogen des Einen Bundes – Das Volk Gottes: seine Zweigestalt und Einheit', in *Judentum und Kirche: Volk Gottes. FS J.Oesterreicher and E.Ruckstuhl*, ThBer 3, Zurich 1974, (27-69) 47ff.; Osten-Sacken, P. von der, 'Israel als Anfrage an die christliche Theologie', in *Treue zur Thora. FS G.Harder*, Berlin 1977, 72-83 = id., *Anstösse aus der Schrift*, 111-23; Mussner, F., 'Eine christliche Theologie des Judentums', in P.Lapide, F.Mussner and U.Wilckens, *Was Christen und Juden voneinander denken*, Freiburg, Basle and Vienna 1978, (40-71) 42ff.; Kremers, H., *Das Verhältnis der Kirche zu Israel*, Düsseldorf 1965, 19ff.; id., *Judenmission heute?*, Neukirchen 1979, 43ff.; Volken, L., *Jesus der Jude und das Jüdische im Christentum*, Düsseldorf 1983.

Objections have seldom (though see F.Hesse, 'Zur Profanität der Geschichte Israels', *ZTK* 71, 1974, 287ff.) been raised against the theological statement of the election of the Old Testament people of God (cf. most recently Mussner, *Traktat*, 18ff., and bibliography).

However, the real problem arises as a result of the two entities which stand over against each other as empirical communities of the faith even today: on the one hand the church (in its various confessions, which carry on an ecumenical dialogue among one another), and on the other Judaism (which is by no means an easily definable phenomenon, as Karl Barth already pointed out [above, 62; cf. also R.Pfisterer, *Im Schatten des Kreuzes*, Hamburg-Bergstedt 1966, 9f.] but is on the one hand a loosely divided confessional community and on the other a community of culture, morality and descent, even more difficult to define, spread throughout the world, and sometimes taking a strongly secularized form [Diaspora Judaism]; finally [since the foundation of the state of Israel], in the wake of the Zionist movement it is also the ruling population group in a modern multi-racial democracy). Cf. more recently also the attempt at a self-definition of Judaism in its characteristic form, over against Western Christianity, by S.Talmon, 'Kritische Anfrage der jüdischen Theologie an das europäische Christentum' ('Critical Inquiry of Jewish Theology into European Christianity'; he corrects the theme so that it is a 'Critical Inquiry of Judaism into European Christian Theology'), in *Israel hat dennoch Gott zum Trost, FS S.Ben-Chorin*, ed. G.Müller, Trier 1978, 139-57.

The most widespread view of Christian Old Testament theology against the background of ideas about the relationship between the two Testaments in a salvation-historical context is expressed e.g. by W.Zimmerli. According to him it is 'clear first of all that in Christ the Old Testament is at an end... Christ is the end of the old covenant and its promise' ('Verheissung und Erfüllung' [above, 18], 53/94f. = ET, 115; but cf. his final verdict, id., 'Biblische Theologie', *BTZ* 1, 1984, 5-26 [cf. already 'Biblical Theology', *HBT* 4, 1982, 95-130 passim, esp.26]. Here he unconsciously also agrees with the traditional verdict of Lutheran dogmatics, which we already find in P.Althaus. Althaus asserts: 'Christ is the Messiah promised to Israel, but Christ is also the end of the Messiah'; the expectations of Israel 'are broken off and finished in their earthly, national "Judaistic" nature by Christ with the *spiritual* fulfilment.' 'The church has its foundation in Israel as the elect people of God, but Israel also issues in the church' (*Die letzten Dinge*, Gütersloh [1933] [8]1961, 309f., 313). Many New Testament scholars also pass a similar judgment.

According to E.Lohse (*Israel und die Christenheit*, Göttingen 1960, 14), the original community does not understand itself as a sect, group or distinctive synagogue within Judaism but as the holy eschatological people of God. The Christian community transferred to their Lord all the honorific titles which were already present in the expectation of Judaism; even Gentiles now belong to the Israel of God apart from the law (21ff.). H.Huffmon ('The Israel of God', *Int* 23, 1969, 66-77) makes a similar statement: only the church is the real Israel of God (which is not to be understood wrongly, in political terms); cf. also L.Richard, 'Israël et le Christ', in H.de Lubac et al., *Israël et la foi chrétienne*, Fribourg 1942, ch.3, 83-119; L.Cerfaux, 'Le peuple de Dieu', in *Populus Dei: Studi in onore del Card. A.Ottaviani*, Rome 1966, 803-64; id., 'La Survivance du peuple ancien à la lumière du Nouveau Testament', ibid., 916-26; Judant, D., *Jalons pour une théologie chrétienne d'Israël*, Paris 1975, esp.43ff. – F.Mussner, 'Volk Gottes im Neuen Testament', *TTZ* 72, 1963, 169-78 = id., *Praesentia Salutis*, Düsseldorf 1967, 244-52 (earlier literature, ibid., 244 n.1), shows how in the New Testament the old honorific titles 'people' and 'Israel' are transferred to the Christian community as the eschatological people of God in the continuity of salvation history. According to H.Wiesemann (*Das Heil für Israel*, Stuttgart 1965), all the promises which originally applied to the Old Testament Israel have now passed over to the new people of God, the community (similarly also L.Richard, 'Israel', 92f., 117; A.Oepke, *Das Neue Gottesvolk*, Gütersloh 1950). Cf. also C.Van der Waal, 'The Continuity between the Old and New Testaments', *Neotestamentica* 14 (above, 21), (1-20) 11: 'The church is heir to Israel's promises... we nowhere find in the early writings (of the church) any indications of special expectations regarding Israel.' Van der Waal regards the patristic evidence as important. According to L.Goppelt (in connection with Rom.11, see below), 'unbelieving Israel is not the still unbelieving part of the community of God, not the counterpart of the church, but the counterpart of the old people of the covenant, the people which affirmed against Christ its divine covenant (Rom.9.4) that has been done away by Christ...' (*Christentum und Judentum im ersten und zweiten Jahrhundert*, Gütersloh 1954, 124 = ET, *Jesus, Paul and Judaism*, New York 1964; similarly also id., 'Israel und die Kirche, heute und bei Paulus', *LR* 1963, 429-52 = id., *Christologie und Ethik. Aufsätze zum Neuen Testament*, Göttingen 1968, [165-89]

180. – However, for Goppelt this does not yet finally settle the question of Rom.11.1, see below, 96f.). O.Semmelroth ('Die Kirche, das neue Gottesvolk', in *De Ecclesia*, ed. G.Barauna, Freiburg, Basle and Vienna 1966, 365-79) explicitly stresses that only the church is the new people of God. 'Certainly God's promises to his old people are not done away with. But that does not mean that God has two peoples who exist side by side, old and new, each with the same status. Rather, the abiding promise means a waiting on God's part until his old people of the promise enters into the new people of the fulfilment, which has indeed now taken the place of the old people of God' (378). For the popular view cf. also K.Hartenstein, *Israel im Heilsplan Gottes. Eine biblische Besinnung*, Stuttgart 1952, esp. the numerous references to Hebrews.

By contrast J.G.Mehl ('Kirche und Synagoge', in *Gottesdienst und Kirchenmusik* 5, 1961, 155-71 – similarly also Carli, *PalCl* 1965 [above, 72], 196ff. Carli defended his article against a press campaign which he provoked by making a second contribution to the debate, 'E possibile discutere serenamente della questione giudaica?', *PalCl* 44, 1965, 265-76) resolutely denies that contemporary Judaism has any special place in salvation history, repudiating the new reflection on the relation between the church and Judaism which emerged particularly clearly at the 1961 Berlin Kirchentag. In his eyes, reprehensible primitive antisemitism has now been replaced by an 'equally unbiblical theological philosemitism which in a primitive way, in the other direction, curtails and falsifies the message of holy scripture about Israel' (161). Above all, in his eyes it is 'not true that we praise the same God... *in common*. For the God whom today's Jews serve is not our God' (reference to John 8.19 – cf. also 162, reference to I John 2.23). There is only the one difference between those who believe in Christ and those who do not; even the Jews are no exception to this ('the Bible does not allow any theological weakening of the knees here', ibid.). Therefore there is no Christian Jewish brotherhood of a theological kind, but only one of a humanitarian kind with all men (Eskimos and Hottentots, 162); there is no Christian-Jewish collaboration in the religious sphere (that would be easier with Moslems, since these at least recognize Jesus as a prophet, 164). Since the repudiation of Christ all synagogues are no better than idolatrous pagan temples. 'What is at stake in our theme is nothing less than the quality of revelation and the claim of the gospel to absoluteness!' (ibid.). However, even Mehl does not say that the old people of God is fully rejected; but as a consequence of the abiding election, in accordance with Rom. 11, he no longer expects that many Jews will be converted to Christ and thus saved. Otherwise, though, the old Israel stands under God's special judgment because it rejected Christ. In America, T.Weiss-Rosmarin, *Judaism and Christianity: The Differences*, which saw nothing but differences between the two religions, went to five impressions: New York 1943, [5]1965.

Even when the view is put forward in a less crude form (cf. e.g. G.Jasper, 'Wie erklärt Israel seine leidvolle Führung?', *Jud* 21, 1965, 1-26, 68-100 [in controversy with H.J.Schoeps], a remnant remains, as Zimmerli similarly feels when he closes his comments with the consideration that if the promises whose fulfilment is seen in Christ were given to Israel, conversation with contemporary Judaism is unavoidable, and this must be about the claim of Israel to the Old Testament. 'Less and less will the church be able to avoid the question as to what is involved in this claim to be Israel, the question as to where its right, its limits, its temptations lie' ('Verheissung und Erfüllung' [above 18], 59/101 = ET, 121f.).

However, even in the light of the New Testament it is hardly possible to justify a simple 'substitution theory' (cf. Oesterreicher, *Unter dem Bogen*, 52ff.; also Klappert, *Israel und die Kirche* [above, 61], 14ff.) according to which the church has solely and completely taken over the role of the elect people. Many scholars discuss the (apparently) anti-Jewish sayings in the New Testament (cf. R.Kugelmann, 'Hebrew, Israelite, Jew in the New Testament', *Bridge* I, 1955, 204-24; G.Baum, *The Jews and the Gospel*, London 1960, new edition *Is the New Testament Anti-Semitic?*, New York 1965 – cf. also id., 'The Doctrinal Basis for Jewish-Christian Dialogue', in *Root and Branch. The Jewish/Christian Dialogue*, ed. M.Zeik and M.Siegel, New York 1973, 159-74 [however, he later expressed himself differently in his introduction to R.Ruether, *Faith and Fratricide*, above, 79, 1-22]; the collected volume *Antijudaismus im Neuen Testament?*, ed. W.P.Eckert, N.P.Levinson and M.Stöhr, Munich 1967; W.Wirth, 'Die "Verwerfung" Israels als polemische Aussage', in *Auf den Trümmern des Tempels*, ed. C.Thoma, Vienna, Freiburg and Basle 1968, 33-52; B.Vawter, 'Are the Gospels Anti-Semitic?, *JES* 5, 1968, 473-87; N.Lohfink, 'Methoden der Schriftauslegung unter besonderer Berücksichtigung der das Judentum betreffenden Schriftstellen', in *Judentum und christlicher Glaube*, ed.

C.Thoma, Klosterneuburg 1965, 19-41; K.H.Rengstorf, 'Das Neue Testament und die nachapostolische Zeit: I. Die Zeit des Neuen Testaments', in Rengstorf and Kortzfleisch, *Kirche und Synagoge* [above, 79], I, 23-50; K.Schubert, 'The People of the Covenant', *Bridge* V, 1970, 132-58; J.A.Grassi, 'Are the Roots of Anti-Semitism in the Gospels?', in *Root and Branch*, ed. Zeik and Siegel, 71-88; Ruether, *Faith and Fratricide*, 64ff.; S.Sandmel, *Anti-Semitism in the New Testament?*, Philadelphia 1978; S.Ben-Chorin, 'Antijüdische Elemente im Neuen Testament', *EvTh* 40, 1980, 203-14; id., *Theologia Judaica*, Tübingen 1982, 24-57; H.Thyen, 'Exegese des Neuen Testaments nach dem Holokaust', in *Auschwitz*, ed. Rendtorff and Stegemann [above, 63], 140-58; C. Thoma, 'Verhängnis, Missverständnis und Schuld beim frühen Eindringen der Judenfeindschaft in die christliche Botschaft', in *Gottesverächter*, ed. H.Goldstein [above 73], 13-27; E.Stegemann, 'Die Krise des christlichen Antijudaismus und das Neue Testament', in *Leben und Glauben nach dem Holokaust. Einsichten und Versuche*, ed. G.Wessler, Stuttgart 1980, 71-89; Mussner, F., 'Israel und die Entstehung der Evangelien', in *Jüdische Existenz und die Erneuerung der christlichen Theologie*, ACJD 11, Munich 1981, 48-57; W.Feneberg, 'Das Neue Testament – Sprache der Liebe. Zum Problem des Antijudaismus', *ZKT* 107, 1985, 333-40). In their view, in the earliest traditions that we can detect within the synoptic Gospels the apparently anti-Jewish sayings reflect thoroughly historically-conditioned polemic within Judaism (cf. O.Michel, 'Polemik und Scheidung', in *Basileia, FS W.Freytag*, Stuttgart 1959, [2]1961, 185-98) between Jesus and his first followers on the one side and their opponents on the other (according to K.Stendahl, 'Judentum und Christentum. Plädoyer für die Erneuerung ihres gegenseitigen Verhältnisses', *EK* 2, 1969, [73-8] 75, the church therefore 'has no right to use these prophetic sayings, since it has lost its identification with Judaism').

That Jesus was a Jew has been discovered by modern Judaism itself (there is a survey of recent Jewish views of Christianity in W.Jacob, *Christianity through Jewish Eyes*, Cincinnati 1974. For an earlier period cf.T.D.Walker, *Jewish Views of Jesus*, London 1931). The pioneering work here was done by J.Klausner with his book *Jesus of Nazareth* (Hebrew, Jerusalem 1922; ET London 1925; Jerusalem [3]1952 – for criticism cf. also G.Jasper, 'Stimmen aus dem neureligiösen Judentum in seiner Stellung zum Christentum und zu Jesus', *ThF* 15, Hamburg-Bergstedt 1958, 69-89). Cf. id., *From*

Jesus to Paul, Hebrew, Jerusalem 1939; ET London 1944; Jerusalem 1950. Cf. also E.R.Trattner, *As a Jew Sees Jesus*, New York 1931; L.Baeck, *Das Evangelium als Urkunde der jüdischen Glaubensgeschichte*, Berlin 1938. A series of Jewish literary figures has also taken up the theme: Scholem Asch, *The Nazarene, Mary, The Apostles*; M.Brod, *The Master*, and so on (cf. also Jasper, *Stimmen*, 90-120). Isaac introduced this as a then much-noted perspective into Christian-Jewish conversations: J.Isaac, *Jésus et Israël*, Paris 1948, ²1959 = ET *Jesus and Israel*, New York 1971. Cf. also H.Flannery, 'Jules Isaacs *Jesus und Israel*', *FrRu* 23, 1971, 10-16 = 'Jesus, Israel and the Christian Renewal', *JES* 9, 1972, 74-93. Cf. further G.Lindeskog, *Die Jesusfrage im neuzeitlichen Judentum*, Uppsala 1938 (Darmstadt ²1973); M.Buber, *Zwei Glaubensweisen*, Zurich 1950 = *Ges.Werke* I, Munich 1962, (651-782) 656f. = ET *Two Types of Faith*, London 1951; M.Goldstein, *Jesus and the Jewish Tradition*, New York 1950; S. Ben-Chorin, 'Das Jesus-Bild im modernen Judentum', *ZRGG* 5, 1953, 231-57 = id., *Im jüdisch-christlichen Gespräch*, Berlin 1962, 61-95 = Eckert and Ehrlich, *Judenhass* (above, 65), 139-72 = id., *Jesus im Judentum*, Wuppertal 1970, 7-46 = ET 'The Image of Jesus in Modern Judaism', *JES* 11, 1974, 410-30; id., 'Jüdische Fragen um Jesus Christus', in *Juden, Christen, Deutsche*, ed. H.J.Schultz, Stuttgart 1961, 140-50 = 'Jüdische Fragen um Jesus', in id, *Das Judentum im Ringen der Gegenwart*, EZS 22/23, Hamburg 1965, 14-23 = 'Jüdische Fragen um Jesu Sendung und Bedeutung', in id., *Jesus im Judentum*, 65-75; id., *Bruder Jesus. Der Nazarener in jüdischer Sicht*, Munich 1967, reprinted 1971, List Taschenbuch 1962, dtv 1253, 1976, ⁴1981, Ch.I, 'Die Gestalt Jesu', also in *Jesus im Judentum*, 47-64; id., 'Bruder Jesus', in *Theologia Judaica* [above 86], 1-13; J.Jocz, *The Jewish People and Jesus Christ*, London 1962; H.A.Wolfson, 'How the Jews Will Reclaim Jesus', *MenJ* 50, 1962, 25-31 = *Judaism and Christianity. Selected Accounts 1892-1962*, ed. J.B.Agus, New York 1973, without repagination; H.J.Schoeps, 'Jesus und das jüdische Gesetz', in id., *Studien zur unbekannten Religions- und Geistesgeschichte*, Göttingen 1963, 41-61 (cf. already *RHPR* 33, 1953, 1-20); S.Sandmel, *We Jews and Jesus*, New York 1965; Bokser, *Judaism* [above, 73], 181-209; D.Flusser, *Jesus. In Selbstzeugnissen und Bilddokumenten*, Reinbek 1968 (RoMo); id., 'The Son of Man. Jesus in the Context of History', in *The Crucible of Christianity*, ed.A.J.Toynbee, New York 1969, 215-34 = 'Der jüdische Ursprung der Christologie'; id., *Bemerkungen eines Juden zur christlichen Theologie*, Munich 1984, 54-65; id., *Die rabbinischen Gleichnisse und der Gleichniserzähler Jesus. I. Das Wesen der Gleichnisse*, Bern, Frankfurt am Main and Las Vegas 1981; C.Raphael, 'Jesus and the Jews', *Commentary* 49, 1970, 77-80; id., 'Jesus und die Synagoge', in *Der Mann aus Galiläa in Bildern dargestellt*, ed.E.Lessing, Freiburg, Basle and Vienna 1971, 21-37 = id., *Bemerkungen eines Juden zur christlichen Theologie*, Munich 1984, 10-34;G.Vermes, *Jesus the Jew: A Historian's Reading of the Gospels*, London 1973, reissued London and Philadelphia 1981 (cf. also the review by W.Horbury, *Theol* 77, 1974, 227-32); cf. id., *The Gospel of Jesus the Jew*, Riddell Memorial Lectures 48, Newcastle upon Tyne 1981 = id., *Jesus and the World of Judaism*, London and Philadelphia 1983, 1-57; id., 'Jesus der Jude', *Jud* 38, 1982, 215-28; R.Gradwohl, 'Das neue Jesus-Verständnis bei jüdischen Denkern der Gegenwart', *FZTP* 20, 1973, 306-23; P.Lapide, *Der Rabbi von Nazareth. Wandlungen des jüdischen Jesusbildes*, Trier 1974; id., *Ist das nicht Josephs Sohn? Jesus im heutigen Judentum*, Stuttgart and Munich 1976; H.Küng and P.Lapide, *Jesus im Widerstreit. Ein jüdisch-christlicher Dialog*, Stuttgart and Munich 1976 (²1981) = ET *Brother or Lord? A Jew and a Christian Talk about Jesus*, London and New York 1977 = 'Is Jesus a Bond or Barrier? A Jewish-Christian Dialogue', *JES* 14, 1977, 466-83 (abridged version); *Jesu Jude-Sein als Zugang zum Judentum*, ed. W.P.Eckert and H.H.Henrix, Aachen 1976 (with contributions by W.P.Eckert, E.L.Ehrlich, J.Maier, H.Jochum, H.H.Henrix, W.Wirth, F.J.Schierse); E.Fischer, *Faith* (above, 72), 30-53; P.Lapide, 'Eine jüdische Theologie des Christentums. Bausteine zum Brückenschlag', in *Was Juden und Christen voneinander denken*, ed. P.Lapide, F.Mussner and U.Wilckens (above, 81), (11-39), 15ff.; P.Lapide and U.Luz, *Der Jude Jesus. Thesen eines Juden. Antworten eines Christen*, Zurich, Einsiedeln and Cologne 1979; N.P.Levinson, 'Nichts anderes als Jude', in *Gottesverächter*, ed. Goldstein (above, 73), 44-57 (however, for a criticism of method, especially directed at P.Lapide, cf. H.Merkel, 'Jesus im Widerstreit', in *Glaube und Gesellschaft, FS W.F.Kasch*, ed. K.Wolf, Bayreuth 1981, 207-17); Volken, *Jesus* (above, 81), 129ff. For the understanding of Jesus in the earlier Jewish tradition cf. J.Maier, *Jesus von Nazareth in der talmudischen Überlieferung*, EdF 82, 1978 (bibliography). For Jesus' Jewishness see also H.Haag, 'Jesus von Nazareth und die Tradition seines

Volkes', *FrRu* 18, 1966, 45-50 = *Von der Kraft jüdischen Glaubens*, ed.E.Klausener, Berlin 1967, 45-67 = id., *Buch des Bundes* (above, 16), 94-108; P.Richardson, *Israel in the Apostolic Church*, Cambridge 1969, 48ff.; T.Suriano, 'The Jewishness of Jesus', *NCW* 217, 1974, 24-29 = *Jewish-Christian Relations*, ed.R.Heyer, New York 1975, 32-40; E.Schillebeeckx, *Jezus. Het verhaal van een levende*, Bloemendaal 1974 = ET *Jesus. An Experiment in Christology*, London and New York 1979; L.Swidler, 'The Jewishness of Jesus: Some Implications for Christians', *JES* 18, 1981, 104-13; E.P.Sanders, *Jesus and Judaism*, London and Philadelphia 1985. Cf. also the anthology by T.Weiss-Rosmarin (ed.), *Jewish Expressions on Jesus*, New York 1977.

One special problem is the question of the Pharisees and the relations Jesus may have had to this important group in the Judaism of his time. Both the characteristics of Pharisaism and the character of the sources – biblical and extrabiblical – which could inform us about Jesus' attitude to the Pharisees are uncertain and debated. For bibliographies on the Pharisees cf.e.g. R.A.Marcus, 'The Pharisees in the Light of Modern Scholarship', *JR* 32, 1952, 153-64; L.Finkelstein, *The Pharisees*, Philadelphia ³1962 (reprinted 1966), II, 905-15; A.Michel and J.LeMoyne, 'Pharisiens', *DBS* 39/40, 1022-1115. Additional literature: J.Massingberd Ford, 'The Christian Debt to Pharisaism', in *Brothers in Hope* (*The Bridge*, Vol.5), ed. J.Oesterreicher, New York 1970, 218-30; E.Rivkin, 'The Internal City: Judaism and Urbanization', *JSSR* 5, 1966, 225-40; id., 'Defining the Pharisees: The Tannaitic Sources', *HUCA* 67, 1970, 205-49; id., *The Shaping of Jewish History* (above, 78), 42ff.; id., 'The Pharisaic Background of Christianity, in *Root and Branch*, ed.M.Zeik and M.Siegel (above, 85), 47-70; id., *A Hidden Revolution: The Pharisees' Search for the Kingdom Within*, Nashville 1978; J.Neusner, *The Rabbinic Traditions about the Pharisees before 70*, 3 vols., Leiden 1971; id., 'The Use of Later Rabbinic Evidence for the Study of First-Century Pharisaism', in *Approaches to Ancient Judaism: Theory and Practice*, ed. W.S.Green, Missoula, Mont 1978, 215-25; R.Ruether, 'The Pharisees in First-Century Judaism', *Ecumenist* 11, 1972, 1-17. – On Jesus and the Pharisees: D.W.Riddle, *Jesus and the Pharisees; A Study in Christian Tradition*, Chicago 1928; A.Finkel, *The Pharisees and the Teacher of Nazareth*, AGSU 4, Leiden 1964; C.Thoma, 'Der Pharisäismus', in *Literatur und Religion des Frühjudentums*, ed.J.Maier and J.Schreiner, Würzburg and Gütersloh 1973, 254-72; W.E.Phipps, 'Jesus, the Prophetic Pharisee', *JES* 14, 1977, 17-31; M.Cook, 'Jesus and the Pharisees. The Problem as it Stands Today', *JES* 15, 1978, 441-60; J.T.Pawlikowski, *Christ* (above, 79), 76-107.

The whole problem also has a methodological aspect: the quest of the traditio-historical connection between early Christianity and Judaism; cf. especially K.Müller, *Das Judentum in der religionsgeschichtlichen Arbeit am Neuen Testament*, Judentum und Umwelt 6, Frankfurt am Main and Bern 1983. Cf. also below, 94ff.

However, even the overall view of the evangelists does not envisage a simple replacement of the old people of God by the church; the claim of the earliest community is that it embodies the 'true Israel'. (Cf. for the situation in New Testament times F.Grant, *Ancient Judaism and the New Testament*, New York 1959; for the Synoptics generally, J.Gnilka, *Die Verstockung Israels*, SANT 3, Munich 1961; for Matthew, W.Trilling, *Das wahre Israel* [Leipzig 1959, 1961], SANT 10, Munich ³1964; but cf. H.Frankemölle, *Jahwebund und Kirche Christi*, NTA NS 10, Münster 1974, esp.257ff., who stresses against Trilling the eschatological proviso [261 n.12; 263 n.23]: the church has certainly replaced Israel as the people of God, but it too is a *corpus mixtum* and continues until the βασιλεία τοῦ θεοῦ which is still to come and will only be attained through fulfilment of the will of God; also G.Künzel, *Studien zum Gemeindeverständnis des Matthäusevangeliums*, CThM A.10, Stuttgart 1978, esp. 259ff.; for Luke cf. G.Lohfink, *Die Sammlung Israels*, SANT 39, Munich 1975; cf.also R.A.D.Hare, 'The Rejection of the Jews in the Synoptic Gospels and in Acts', in *Antisemitism*, ed.A.T.Davies, 27-47; for Mark cf.M.Cook, *Mark's Treatment of the Jewish Leaders*, NT.S 51, Leiden 1978; for the so-called anti-Jewishness in John cf. R.Leistner, *Antijudaismus im Johannesevangelium?*, Berne 1974; also e.g. E.Grässer, 'Die Juden als Teufelssöhne in Johannes 8, 37-47', in *Antijudaismus im Neuen Testament?*, ed. W.P.Eckert, N.P.Levinson and M.Stöhr, Munich 1967, 157-70 = id., *Der Alte Bund im Neuen*, WUNT 35, Tübingen 1985, 135-67; C.K.Barrett, *Das Johannesevangelium und das Judentum*, FDV 1967, Stuttgart 1970 = ET *The Gospel of John and Judaism*, London 1975; Fischer, *Faith*, 54-75; Schram, T.L., *The Use of Ioudaios in the Fourth Gospel*, Diss. Utrecht 1974; M.Lowe, 'Who were the ΙΟΥΔΑΙΟΙ?', *NT* 18, 1976, 101-30; W.Trilling,

'Gegner Jesu – Widersacher der Gemeinde – Repräsentanten der Welt. Das Johannesevangelium und die Juden', in *Gottesverächter*, ed. Goldstein [above, 73], 190-210; J.T.Townsend, 'The Gospel of John and the Jews: The Story of Religious Divorce', in *Antisemitism*, ed.A.T.Davies [above, 61], 72-97; H.Thyen, ' "Das Heil kommt von den Juden" [Joh.4.22]', in *Kirche. FS G.Bornkamm*, ed. D.Lührmann and G.Strecker, Tübingen 1980, 163-84, and the literature mentioned there, and most recently F.Hahn, 'Die Juden im Johannesevangelium', in *Kontinuität und Einheit, FS F.Mussner*, Freiburg, Basle and Vienna 1981, 430-8; some of these are controversial. For the New Testament as a whole cf. K.H.Schelkle, *Theologie des Neuen Testaments* 2, Düsseldorf 1973, 156-85; id., 'Israel und die Kirche im Neuen Testament', in *Die Kirche des Anfangs, FS H.Schürmann*, ETS 38, Leipzig and Freiburg im Breisgau 1978, 607-14.) Many apparently anti-Jewish statements in the Pauline writings are in fact to be seen as arguments in the battle over the continued observance among Christian diaspora communities, which included an increasing number of non-Jews, of Jewish forms on which the 'opponents' insisted. That was diametrically opposed to the idea of justification, which was central for Paul. As O.Michel makes clear, 'His polemic serves to protect and further his mission', but it is not anti-Jewish: 'Paul is concerned with *the right way of being a Jew*' ('Polemik' [above, 86], 193f.). (For Paul see especially Parkes, *Judaism* [above, 77], 71-111; M.Barth, 'Paulus und die Juden', in id., *Jesus, Paulus und die Juden*, TS 91, Zurich 1967, 40-82; P.Richardson, *Israel* (above, 89), 70ff.; D.Zeller, *Juden und Heiden in der Mission des Paulus*, Stuttgart ²1976; id., 'Christus, Skandal und Hoffnung. Die Juden in den Briefen des Paulus', in *Gottesverächter*, 256-78; K.Stendahl, 'Paul among Jews and Gentiles', in *Paul among Jews and Gentiles and Other Essays*, Philadelphia 1976 and London 1977, 1-77; W.D.Davies, 'Paul and the People of Israel', *NTS* 24, 1977, 4-39; E.P. Sanders, *Paul and Palestinian Judaism. A Comparison of Patterns of Religion*, London and Philadelphia 1977; M.Barth, 'Das Volk Gottes. Juden und Christen in der Botschaft des Paulus', in M.Barth et al., *Paulus – Apostat oder Apostel?*, Regensburg 1977, 45-134 (cf. also the contributions by R.J.Z.Werblowski, ibid., 135-46, and J.Blank, 147-72; K.Haacker, 'Paulus und das Judentum', *Jud* 33, 1977, 161-77; J.Eckert, 'Paulus und Israel', *TTZ* 87, 1978, 1-13; L.Gaston, 'Paul and the Thora', in *Antisemitism*, ed.A.T.Davies, 48-71, and recently E.Stegemann, 'Der Jude Paulus und seine antijüdische Auslegung', in *Auschwitz*, ed. Rendtorff and Stegemann [above, 63], 117-39; P.Lapide and P.Stuhlmacher, *Paulus. Rabbi und Apostel. Ein jüdisch-christlicher Dialog*, Stuttgart and Munich 1981; F. Annen, 'Saulus, der Christenverfolger – Paulus, der Kritiker des Judentums', in *Kritik*, ed. Lauer, 37-66; G.Klein, 'Christlicher Antijudaismus', *ZTK* 79, 1982, [411-50] 433-50. For the history of the Jewish interpretation of Paul cf. W.Wiefel, 'Paulus in jüdischer Sicht', *Jud* 31, 1975, 109-15, 151-72). The dialectic pointed out by G.Harder ('Kontinuität und Diskontinuität des Volkes Gottes', in H.Gollwitzer and E.Sterling, *Das gespaltene Gottesvolk*, Stuttgart 1966, 267-82) of the two perspectives in the relationship between Israel and the church is worth noting (though in parts he still refers back to obsolete dogmatic contrasts like those between law and gospel, or ritual holiness and sacraments, or to central concepts like 'covenant' and 'messianic key figures' which no longer do justice to the Old Testament). Paul's remarks in Rom.9-11 still play a special role in more recent discussion of the fate of Israel.

Cf. especially Peterson, E., *Die Kirche aus Juden und Heiden*, Salzburg 1933; also in *Theologische Traktate*, Munich 1951, 239-92; Schrenk, G., *Der göttliche Sinn in Israels Geschick. Eine Erläuterung zu Röm 9-11*, Zollikon-Zurich 1943; Schmidt, K.L., *Die Judenfrage im Lichte der Kapitel 9-11 des Römerbriefes*, TS (B) 13, Zollikon-Zurich ²1943; Vischer, W., 'Étude biblique sur Rom 9-11', *FV* 46, 1948, 97-141 = 'Das Geheimnis Israels. Eine Erklärung der Kapitel 9-11 des Römerbriefes', *Jud* 6, 1950, 81-132; Munck, J., *Christus und Israel. Eine Auslegung von Röm. 9-11*, Copenhagen 1956 = ET *Christ and Israel*, Philadelphia 1967; cf. also id., *Paulus und die Heilsgeschichte*, Copenhagen 1954 = ET *Paul and the Salvation of Mankind*, London and Richmond, Va 1959 [²1977]; Lohse, E., *Israel* (above, 83), 24ff.; Goppelt, 'Israel und die Kirche', (above 83), 180ff.; Käsemann, E., 'Paulus und Israel', in *Juden, Christen, Deutsche*, ed. H.J.Schultz, Stuttgart 1961, 307-11 = Käsemann, E., *Exegetische Versuche und Besinnungen* II, Göttingen ²1965, 194-7 = ET 'Paul and Israel', in *New Testament Questions of Today*, London and Philadelphia 1969, 183-7; Müller, C., *Gottes Gerechtigkeit und Gottes Volk*, FRLANT 86, Göttingen 1964; Baum, G., *Is the New Testament Anti-Semitic?* (above, 85), 275-348; Vischer, W., 'Le

Mystère d'Israël', *FV* 6, 1965, 427-87; Bartsch, H.-W., 'Streit-schrift für Israel. Über den Römerbrief des Paulus', *Christlich-jüdisches Forum* 37, 1966, 1-7; Zerwick, M., 'Die Zukunft Israels nach dem Römerbrief', in *Von der Kraft jüdischen Glaubens*, ed. E.Klausener, Berlin 1967, 68-90; Luz, U., *Das Geschichtsver-ständnis des Paulus*, BEvTh 49, Munich 1968; Plag, C., *Israels Wege zum Heil*, AzTh I, 40, Stuttgart 1969; Cross, F.M., 'A Christian Understanding of the Election of Israel', in *The Death of Dialogue and Beyond*, ed.S.Seltzer and M.L.Stackhouse, New York 1969, 72-85; Cazelles, H., 'Israel, the Faith and Catholic Theology', *Bridge* V, 1970, 88-105; Marquardt, F.W., *Die Juden im Römerbrief*, TS (B) 107, Zurich 1971 (cf. Klein, G., 'Erbarmen mit den Juden', *EvTh* 34, 1974, 201-18; countered by H.Gollwitzer, M.Palmer and V.Schliske, 'Der Jude Paulus und die deutsche neutestamentliche Wissenschaft', in ibid., 276-304; retort by G.Klein, 'Präliminarien zum Thema Paulus und die Juden', in *Rechtfertigung, FS E.Käsemann*, Tübingen 1976, 229-43); Güttgemanns, E., 'Heilsgeschichte bei Paulus oder Dynamik des Evangeliums? Zur strukturellen Relevanz von Röm 9-11 für die Theologie des Römerbriefs', in *studia linguistica neotesta-mentica*, BEvTh 60, Munich 1971, 34-58; Stuhlmacher, P., 'Zur Interpretation von Römer 11, 25-32', in *Probleme biblischer Theologie, FS G. von Rad*, ed. H.W.Wolff, Munich 1971, 555-70; Zeller, D., *Juden und Heiden* (above, 91); id.,' Israel unter dem Ruf Gottes (Röm 9-11)', *IKaZ* 2, 1973, 289-301; Eichholz, G., *Theologie des Paulus im Umriss*, Neukirchen-Vluyn 1972, 284-301; Judant, *Jalons* (above, 83), 47ff.; Mussner, F., '"Ganz Israel wird gerettet werden." Versuch einer Auslegung', *Kairos* 18, 1977, 241-55; id., *Traktat* (above, 77), 45ff., 52ff.; id., 'Refle-xionen eines Neutestamentlers über das Heil Israels', *KatBl* 104, 1979, 974-6; Barth, M., 'Das Volk Gottes', 75ff.; Eckert, W.P., 'Israels Berufung', *LebZeug* 32, 1977, 7-14; Kümmel, W.G., 'Die Probleme von Römer 9-11 in der gegenwärtigen Forschungslage', in *Die Israelfrage nach Röm 9-11*, ed. L.de Lorenzi, Benedictine Monography series, Biblical Ecumenical section, 3, Rome 1977, 13-33 (discussion, 34-56) = id., *Heilsgeschehen und Geschichte 2*, MTS 16, Marburg 1978, 245-60 (bibliography); cf. also the other contributions to the collection, esp. C.K.Barrett, 99-121; F.Dreyfus, 131-51; J.Jeremias, 193-205; P.Benoit, 217-36. – O.Betz, 'Die heilsgeschichtliche Rolle Israels bei Paulus', *ThBeitr*

9, 1978, 1-21; Rengstorf, K.H., 'Das Ölbaumgleichnis in Röm 11.16ff. Versuch einer weiterführenden Deutung', in *Donum Gentilicium*... *D.Daube*, Oxford 1978, 127-64; Steiger, L., 'Schutzrede für Israel... Röm 9-11', in *Fides pro mundi vita. FS H.-W.Gensichen*, Gütersloh 1980, 44-58; cf. also Barth, M., 'Der gute Jude Paulus', in ibid, 107-37; Klappert, B., 'Traktat für Israel (Römer 9-11)', in *Jüdische Existenz und die Erneuerung der christlichen Theologie*, ed. M.Stöhr, ACJD 11, Munich 1981, 58-137; von der Osten-Sacken, P., *Grundzüge einer Theologie im christlich-jüdischen Gespräch*, Munich 1982, 39ff.; Volken, L., *Jesus* (above, 81), 206ff.; Hübner, H., *Gottes Ich und Israel. Zum Schriftgebrauch des Paulus in Römer 9-11*, FRLANT 136, Göttingen 1984. In addition also see the commentaries, esp. Käsemann, E., *An die Römer*, HNT 8a, Tübingen 1973, ⁴1980 = ET *Commentary on Romans*, Grand Rapids and London 1980, ²1982.

To some degree Rom.9-11 is the touchstone for deciding between two alternative understandings of Pauline theology: that in terms of existentialist theology and that in terms of salvation history. Those New Testament scholars who make an interpretation of the message of justification structured by existentialist theology the centre of what Paul says usually acknowledge that Rom. 9-11 has the apostle thinking from a perspective of salvation history. (Even P.Vielhauer, 'Gesetzesdienst und Stoicheiadienst im Galaterbrief', *FS Käsemann*, [543-55] 553f. = id., *Oikodome* [above, 23], 183-95. For E.Käsemann, 'Paulus und Israel', 310/197 = ET, 187, only 'the exemplary significance of Israel' explains the promise of salvation over all Israel in Rom.11, whereas elsewhere, in the light of the idea of justification he says that all human claims are shattered; Israel is exemplary, because 'real promise is always only for the broken'. Cf. also *An die Römer*¹, 298-304 = ET, 307-14). Here too G.Klein is an exception; he consistently brackets out Rom.11.25ff., and even in his most recent statements ('Präliminarien' [above, 93]; cf. also id., 'Predigtmeditation zum Reformationstag über Römer 3,21-28', *GPM* 68, 1980, [409-19] 417ff. – against this H.Gollwitzer, 'Kirche und Judentum. Alt-Bestimmung gegen Neu-Bestimmung', *epd-Dokumentation* 42/1980, 44-59), to be set against the background of an exclusively general and anthropological interpretation of the Pauline concept of the law, declares that the juxtaposition of Jews and Gentiles is soteriologically insignificant both in respect of a past salvation history which has been radically devalued and even more (as we must interpret his silence on this point) of a possible eschatological future for Israel (cf. also Güttgemanns, 54ff., who largely takes up earlier remarks of Klein's). E.Dinkler ('Prädestination bei Paulus', *FS G. Dehn*, Neukirchen 1957, 81-102 = id., *Signum Crucis*, Tübingen 1967, 241-69) gives a more sophisticated verdict. He sees a 'break' (251) and a 'decisive contradiction' (252) between Rom. 9.6-13 and 11.1f., 11-32: in 9.6ff. the promises do not relate to the empirical historical Israel but to 'eschatological' Israel (constituted in the election of individuals), while in ch.11 the role of historical Israel continues. However, its superiority lies only in 'historical priority' (254). Dinkler's approach cannot provide a satisfactory solution to the problem of a salvation-historical dialectic in Paul.

Given Paul's contradictory statements about the Jews, with M.Barth ('Das Volk Gottes' [above, 91], 60ff.), we can move on from just speaking in terms of a superficial juxtaposition of such passages as I Thess.2.15f.; Gal.4.30; I Cor.2.8; II Cor.3.4ff. down to Rom.9-11 (Eph.2.11ff.; 3.6; cf. also M.Barth, *Israel und die Kirche im Brief des Paulus an die Epheser*, ThExH NF 75, Munich 1959; id., *The Broken Wall*, Chicago 1959 and London 1960, 125-38, cf. 190f.; id., 'Was Paul an Anti-Semite?', *JES* 5, 1968, 78-104; O.Betz, 'Paulus als Pharisäer nach dem Gesetz. Phil.3.5-6 als Beitrag zur Frage des frühen Pharisäismus', in *Treue zur Thora, FS G.Harder*, Berlin ²1979, 54-64. M.Rese ['Die Vorzüge Israels in Röm 9.4f. und Eph 2,12', *TZ* 31, 1975, 211-22] differs from M.Barth in distinguishing the attitude of Ephesians from that of Paul in Rom.9; there Paul begins from the abiding faithfulness of God towards his people as the last word, whereas Eph.2.12 envisages a final passing of the promise from Israel to the church. P.von der Osten-Sacken, 'Gemeinsame Hoffnung von Juden und Christen', in *Deutscher Evangelischer Kirchentag Nürnberg 1979*, ed. H.Uhl, 616-22 = *Glaube und Hoffnung nach Auschwitz*, ed. P.von der Osten-Sacken and M.Stöhr, Berlin 1980, 83-9 = P.von der Osten-Sacken, *Anstösse* [above, 80], 145-51, also sees Ephesians in this sense as un-Pauline and therefore not normative). We may assume a theological development in Paul's views on Israel or may have to emphasize more strongly the individual situations of particular Pauline statements (cf. also Hübner, *Gottes Ich* [above, 94], 127ff.). His initial polemic against his former fellow-believers who stubbornly resist the Gospel gives way to an increasingly theocentric view (cf. Luz, *Geschichtsver-ständnis* [above, 93], 300), in which human behaviour (of Jews and Gentiles) becomes increasingly less important, compared with the abiding aim of God with his people (cf. also W.Schrage, 'Israel nach dem Fleisch' (I Kor 10.18)', in *FS H.J.Kraus* [above, 58], 145-51). G.Eichholz has convincingly integrated the Pauline sayings about Israel, esp. in Rom.9-11, into Paul's message of justification (287; similarly Zeller, 286; cf. also H.Spaemann, *Die Christen und das Volk der Juden*, Munich 1966, 37f.; J.B.Soucek, 'Israel und die Kirche im Denken des Apostels Paulus', *CV* 14, 1971, 143-54); the apostle describes 'God's action in terms of the incalculable mercy of God directed towards Israel' (293). Specifically in connection with the simile of the olive tree in Rom.11.16ff. (for the Old Testament model in Jer.11.16 and the method of rabbinic haggadah used by Paul, cf. recently Rengstorf) it becomes clear that for Paul there is only one people of God (cf. also M.Barth, 'Das Volk Gottes' [above, 91], 62; Baum, *Is the New Testament Anti-Semitic?* [above, 85], 314ff.; Volken, *Jesus* [above, 81]), 218f.) in which, whether Jew or Gentile, one is only accepted by faith in the justification of the sinner which has taken place in Christ (cf. also K.W.Clark, 'The Israel of God', in *Studies in New Testament and Early Christian Literature, FS P.Wikgren*, NT.S 33, Leiden 1972, 161-9). This olive tree lives from the living root of the old people of God, which has not died out because God cannot reject his people (11.1), and in which even the noble branches (Israelites) which have temporarily been broken off will again be grafted if they do not persist in unbelief (11.23f.). So the church is not a new people of God but the continuation of the old, albeit under the sign of the cross, which changes everything (cf. recently also E.Grässer, 'Zwei Heilswege? Zum theologischen Verhältnis von Kirche und Israel', in *FS Mussner* [above, 91], [411-29] 419-22 = id., *Der Alte Bund* [above, 91], 220-3; id., 'Christen und Juden', *PT* 71, 1982, [431-49] 438ff. = id., *Der Alte Bund*, 278ff.; Judant, *Jalons*, esp.82f., makes the same point on other [traditional Catholic] presuppositions). Of course, the real μυστήριον of Israel, of which Paul speaks in 11.25ff. (cf. also J.Bonsirven, 'Le mystère d'Israël', in de Lubac et al., *Israël* [above, 83], 121-50; H.Schlier, 'Das Mysterium Israels', *WuW* 7, 1952, 569-78 = H.Gross et al., *Die religiöse und theologische Bedeutung des Alten Testaments* [above, 49], 163-91; = id., *Die Zeit der Kirche*, Freiburg 1956 [³1962], 232-44; J.Blank, 'Das Mysterium Israel', in

Jüdische Hoffnungskraft und christlicher Glaube, ed. W.Strolz, Freiburg, Barcelona and London 1971, 134-90 = id., *Christliche Orientierungen* [above, 79], 11-57; Hübner, *Gottes Ich*, 109ff.) and the eschatological deliverance of all Israel which he foresees for the same reason, that God cannot repent of his demonstration of grace and his calling (v.29), goes far beyond this. According to Goppelt (*Israel und die Kirche* [above, 83], 185), this is to be expected only because of the faithfulness of God and not for any specific quality; here, however, the prophecy is also binding on us. (For the overall thought of Romans cf. also Bartsch and Zerwick.) There are two possible ways of understanding from 11.26 how this deliverance will take place, either through the eventual conversion of all Jews to Christ or by a special way (Zeller, *Juden und Heiden*, 245 – for the overall alternative cf. most recently Mussner, *Kairos* 1977; Hübner, *Gottes Ich*, 116); the second seems likely. For the present and the foreseeable future, however, that also means resignation; for the moment, no end can be seen to a Judaism which does not believe in Christ. Church and Judaism go through history side by side (cf. also K.H.Rengstorf, 'Das alte und das neue Gottesvolk', *PBL* 100, 1960, 409-19).

In modern discussions we find within Christian theology a series of different models for the relationship between church and Judaism (cf. also M.Barth, 'Das Volk Gottes' [above, 91], 65ff.; Davies, *Anti-Semitism* [above, 61], passim; Fleischner, *Judaism* [above, 77], 119ff.; Klappert, *Israel und die Kirche* [above, 61], 14-37). In addition to the substitution theory mentioned above and the related one, that a remnant of Israel (according to Rom.9.27; 11.1-7), the Jews who are converted, have entered into 'the new people of God', recently the idea of a schism within the one people of God existing between the church and Judaism (Klappert, *Israel und die Kirche*, 26-30, 'model of complementarity') has played a considerable role.

Cf. Grin, T., 'La Synagogue a-t-elle un bandeau sur les yeux?', *Le monde religieux*, V.10/11, *La résistance spirituelle. La lutte contre l'anti-sémitisme*, Lausanne 1945, (72-83) 82f.; Oehmen, *Le schisme* (above, 80); Demann, P., 'Israël et l'unité de l'Eglise', *CSion* 7, 1953, 1-24; id., 'Kirche und Israel in ökumenischer Sicht', in Marsch and Thieme, *Christen und Juden* (above, 78), 270-81; Lanne, E., 'Notes sur la situation d'Israël par rapport aux schisme dans l'Eglise chrétienne', in *L'Eglise et les églises*, FS L.Beauduin,

II, Chevetogne 1955, 67-86; Thieme, K., *Biblische Religion heute*, Heidelberg 1960, 149ff.; id., 'Ur-Diakonie als Heilmittel des Urschismas', *FrRu* 6, 1954, 13-21; Gollwitzer, H., 'Die Judenfrage – eine Christenfrage', ibid., 284-92; Jocz, J., *The Spiritual History of Israel*, London 1961, 159-65; Lambert, B., *Le problème oecuménique*, Paris 1962, II, 603ff. = *Ecumenism. Theology and History*, New York and London 1967, 450ff.; Richards, H., 'Vatican II and the Jews', *CleR* 49, 1964, 552-61; Lacoque, A., *Pérennité d'Israël*, Geneva 1964; Skydsgaard, K.E., 'Israel, Kirche und Einheit des Gottesvolkes', in Gollwitzer and Sterling, *Das gespaltene Gottesvolk* (above, 92), 294-7; Federici, T., *Israël vivant*, Paris 1965 (original *Israele vivo*, Turin 1962; also Spanish, *Israel Vivo*, Barcelona 1966), III, 6,207ff.; Pfisterer, *Juden, Christen* (above, 81), 35ff.; Spaemann, *Die Christen* (above, 96), 49f., 75ff.; Borchsenius, P., *Two Ways to God*, London 1968, esp.118ff., 200ff. (original *To Veje*, Copenhagen 1966); Davies, T., 'The Jews in an Ecumenical Context: A Critique', *JES* 5, 1968, 488-506; Henrix, H.H., 'Der Dialog mit dem Judentum als Aufgabe ökumenischer Theologie', *US* 31, 1976, 136-45; id., 'Ökumene aus Juden und Christen. Ein theologischer Versuch', in *Exodus und Kreuz im ökumenischen Dialog zwischen Juden und Christen*, ed. H.H.Henrix and M.Stöhr, Aachen 1978, 188-236; Flusser, D., 'Das Schisma zwischen Judentum und Christentum', *EvTh* 40, 1980, 214-39; cf. also Kremers, *Das Verhältnis* (above, 81), 23ff.; Löhrer, M., 'Kirche als Volk Gottes', *FS Oesterreicher/Ruckstuhl* (above, 81), (187-99) 192; Klappert, B., 'Die Juden in einer christlichen Theologie nach Auschwitz', in *Auschwitz*, ed. Ginzel (above, 65), 481-512, esp. 505ff.; above all Oesterreicher, J., '*Unter dem Bogen*' (above, 81). For criticism cf. Baum, 'Is the New Testament Anti-Semitic?' (above, 85), 324f. J. Daniélou, *Dialogue* (above, 78), 149ff., understands the 'schism' differently, as the separation of Israel which does not believe in Christ from the 'true people of God'.

From the Jewish side, as early as 1913 F.Rosenzweig had formulated in conversations and a correspondence with R.Ehrenberg (1913) and E.Rosenstock(-Huessy), which continued in 1916 out of the trenches of the First World War, the idea of a 'division of work in salvation history' between Jews and Christians (following Maimonides and S.Formstecher, 1841; F.Rosenzweig, *Briefe*,

Berlin 1935. Cf. especially the letter to R.Ehrenberg of 31.10.1913, 71ff.; the letters between Rosenzweig and Rosenstock in the appendix, 637-720. Cf. also the new editions: *Judaism Despite Christianity*, ed. E.Rosenstock-Huessy, Alabama 1969, 77-170; F.Rosenzweig, *Der Mensch und sein Werk, Gesammelte Schriften*, ed. R.Rosenzweig and E.Rosenzweig-Scheinmann, I, *Briefe und Tagebücher*, The Hague 1979, in each case under the relevant dates [extracts also in N.H.Glatzer, *Franz Rosenzweig: His Life and Thought*, New York, 1953, ²1961, 341-8]. Cf. also H.J.Schoeps, *Israel* [above, 78], 151-69; D.Clawson, 'Rosenzweig on Judaism and Christianity', *Jdm* 19, 1970, 90-8; W.Jacob, *Christianity* [above, 86], 122ff.; M.Bowler, 'Rosenzweig on Judaism and Christianity. The Two Covenant Theory', *Jdm* 22, 1973, 475-81; S.Talmon, 'Judaism and Christianity in Franz Rosenzweig's Perspective', in *De la Torah au Messie. Mélanges Henri Cazelles*, Paris 1981, 587-98; cf. also F.Rosenzweig, *Der Stern der Erlösung*, III, ³1954 = R.Rosenzweig and E.Rosenzweig-Scheinmann [eds.] II, ⁴1976, 293-472). Rosenzweig writes (alluding to John 14.6); 'Christianity acknowledges the God of Judaism not as God but as the Father of Jesus Christ... We are agreed in what Christ and his church in the world mean: no one comes to the Father but through him. No one *comes* to the Father – but it is different when someone does not need to come to the father because he already *is* with him. Now that is the case with the people of Israel (not the individual Jew). The people of Israel, elected by its Father, looks fixedly beyond the world and history to that last most distant point where this its Father will be all in all. At this point, where Christ ceases to be the Lord, Israel ceases to be elected...' (*Briefe*, 73 = ed. R.Rosenzweig/E.Rosenzweig-Scheinmann I, 134f.). The lines of salvation history – the church with its task of mission to the world, the synagogue turned inwards to preserve its identity as chosen people – therefore meet in the eschaton. This view was also put forward by Schoeps (*Israel*, 19f., 188ff.; cf. also id., 'Möglichkeiten und Grenzen jüdisch-christlicher Verständigung', in *Unterwegs* 3, 1948, 4-7; *TLZ* 79, 1954, 73-82 = id., *Studien* [above, 87], 184-96). But cf. the response by W.Dittmann, *Unterwegs* 3, 8-11. It is worth noting that S.Ben-Chorin once completely rejected this profound play on ideas because 'this represents a falsification of Christianity, whose message was in fact first addressed to Israel' ('Juden und Christen', in *Unterwegs* 12, 1960, 27 and note on 31; cf. also 43; cf. id., review of Schoeps,

Jüdisch-christliches Religionsgespräch [cf. above, 78], *Der Morgen* 13, 1939, 433-6), although he also said that Judaism and Christianity are 'parallels of faith, which meet in infinity' ('Juden und Christen', 10). But cf. more recently id., 'Ist im Christentum etwas von Gott her geschehen?', in id., *Theologia Judaica* (above, 86), (72-85) 80f. Ben-Chorin wants to see the present situation of the consolidation of Jews and Christians, under the challenge presented to them both by atheism, in terms of a reunion of the divided people of God (ibid., 83). Gollwitzer, in Gollwitzer, Rendtorff and Levinson, *Thema* (above, 77), 38, also rejects Rosenzweig's theory. Cf. already W.D.Davies, 'Torah and Dogma: A Comment', in *The Death of Dialogue* (above, 91), 120-44 = *HTR* 61, 1968, 87-105, for whom christology is the decisive obstacle for speaking of a schism between Jews and Christians; these are different religions.

The same thought-model also plays a role in the USA, among both Christian and Jewish thinkers, as conditioned by their particular confessional situation (for the involvement of three confessions in American society cf. W.Herberg, *Protestant, Catholic, Jew*, Garden City 1955 [²1960]; on consequences for the Jewish-Christian dialogue, cf. M.H.Tanenbaum, 'Major Issues in the Jewish-Christian Situation Today', *NCW* 217, 1974, 30-3 = *Jewish-Christian Relations*, ed. R.Heyer ([above, 89], 10-16; for the situation of Judaism, S.E.Rosenberg, *America is Different. The Search for Jewish Identity in America*, London, New York and Toronto 1964 [Garden City, NY 1965]; J.Neusner, *American Judaism: Adventure in Modernity*, Englewood Cliffs, NJ 1972; W.S.Berlin, *On the Edge of Politics: The Roots of Jewish Political Thought in America*, Westport, Conn. and London 1978; B.Martin (ed.), *Movements and Issues in American Judaism*, Westport, Conn. and London 1978), under the influence of e.g. M.Buber and F.Rosenzweig, and also of significant Christian theologians like P.Tillich (cf. e.g. 'Is there a Judaeo-Christian Tradition?', *Jud* 1, 1952, 106-9; also id., 'The Theology of Missions', *OBMRL* 5, 1954, 1-6 = *CaC* 1955/6, 35-8 and the numerous quotations which R.Eckardt [cf. below], cf. Index, also produces from Tillich's unpublished lecture manuscripts), R.Niebuhr (cf. Eckardt, *Brothers* [below] 89-95]) and Karl Barth (for a survey of the debate cf. L.A.Olan, 'Christian-Jewish Dialogue: A Dissenting Opinion', *RelLife* 41, 1972, 154-78 – for his special standpoint see below, 123). Cf. as Christian voices e.g. Parkes, *Judaism* [above, 77], 165ff., 182ff.; R.de Corneille, *Chri-*

stians and the Jews: The Tragic Past and the Hopeful Future, Toronto 1966; A.Roy Eckardt (*Christianity and the Children of Israel*, New York 1948; id., 'Christian Faith and the Jews', *JR* 30, 1950, 235-45; id., 'Can There Be a Jewish-Christian Relationship?', *JBR* 33, 1965, 122-30; id., 'End to the Christian-Jewish Dialogue', *CCen* 83, 1966, 393-5; id., *Elder and Younger Brothers*, New York 1967; cf. id., *Your People, My People*, New York 1974; id., 'Toward an Authentic Jewish-Christian Relationship', *JChS* 13, 1971, 271-82; J.C.Rylaarsdam, 'Common Ground and Difference', *JR* 43, 1963, 261-70; cf. also the collection *Jews and Christians. Preparation for Dialogue*, ed. G.A.F.Knight, Philadelphia nd. (1965); P.Kirsch, *We Christians and Jews*, Philadelphia 1975; M.Hellwig, *Proposal Towards a Theology of Israel as a Religious Community Contemporary with the Christian*, Diss. Catholic University of America 1968 (microfilm); id., 'Christian Theology and the Covenant of Israel', *JES* 7, 1970, 37-51; ead., 'Why We Still Can't Talk', *NCW* 217, 1974, 39-42 = R.Heyer (ed.), *Jewish-Christian Relations* (above, 89), 26-31; ead., 'Bible Interpretation: Has Anything Changed?', in *Biblical Studies. Meeting Grounds of Jews and Christians*, ed. L.Boadt et al., New York 1980, 172-89; P.van Buren, *Discerning the Way. A Theology of the Jewish-Christian Reality*, New York 1980; cf. also id., *The Burden of Freedom*, New York 1976, 57-85; for the perspectives for American Christianity see also M.Siegel, 'A Jewish Christianity?', in *Root and Branch*, ed.M.Zeik and M.Siegel [above, 85] 175-84, and, as a Jew, W.Herberg ('Judaism and Christianity. Their Unity and Difference', *JBR* 21, 1953, 67-78 = id., *Faith Enacted as History. Essays in Biblical Religion*, Philadelphia 1976, 44-64), who argues for a share of work in salvation history between Jews and Christians along the lines of Rosenstock and Schoeps (though Herberg stands on his own as a Jew; it is worth noting the episode in which Niebuhr dissuaded him from being converted to Christianity, which he had once considered, with the recommendation that he should first be a good Jew – cf. B.W.Anderson, 'Will Herberg as a Biblical Theologian' in Herberg, *Faith Enacted*, [9-28] 14 – similarly also Wyschogrod [above, 81] and, more recently, P.Lapide, in P.Lapide and J.Moltmann, *Israel und Kirche: ein gemeinsamer Weg? Ein Gespräch*, KT 54, Munich 1980, 43-78, 36f.; id., 'Eine jüdische Theologie...' [above, 88], 24-6; R.B.Brickner, 'Postscript', in de Corneille, *Christians* [above, 100], 134-47; Bokser, *Judaism* [above, 73]; J.Agus, *Dialogue and Tradition: The Challenges of Contem-*

porary Judaeo-Christian Thought, New York 1971, I, 3-129.) For the overall theme cf. also W.Jacob, *Christianity Through Jewish Eyes*, Cincinnati 1974; Pawlikowski, *What are they Saying...* (above, 73), 69ff. S.Talmon, 'Towards World Community: Resources and Responsibilities for Living Together', *ER* 26, 1974, 604-36, regards a world community between people belonging to different faiths (Jewish, Christian, Moslem) as being possible for the present time, because Judaism, too, has a universalistic expectation of the eschatological salvation of all who observe at least the Noachite commandments.

Though even the standpoints among Christian authors differ widely (Lambert, e.g. speaks of the 'tragic situation of the rest of Israel... which did not enter the Christian church', of the loss of substance in Jewish institutions and the 'religious value of the testimony' of their waiting, however wrongly, for the Messiah who is still to come, and E.Lanne sees the tragic basis of the schism in the fact that the Jews have rejected the salvation offered to them in Jesus Christ, while for Oesterreicher [and M.Barth] the unity of the people of God, divided and yet held up together by God's forgiveness and faithfulness, stands at the centre; A.Lacoque, 'Israël, pierre de touche de l'oecuménisme', *VC* 48, 1958, 331-4; Hruby [*Conc* 98, 87-92, see below, 103],speaks of a 'necessary permanent complementarity between Judaism and Christianity' up to the point of time envisaged in Rom.11.25b; by contrast K.Stendahl [*EK* 1969, above 86, 76] thinks: 'We are those who ask to be recognized as a special kind of Jew and it is for Judaism to decide whether that is possible'; cf. also id., 'Judaism and Christianity: Then and Now', *HDB* 18, 1963, 1-9 = *New Theology*, ed.M.E.Marty and D.G.Peerman, no.2, London and New York 1965, 153-64; id., 'Judaism and Christianity II: After a Colloquium and a War', *HDB* 32, 1967, 2-9, esp.5: 'We need to ask..., whether they are willing to let us become again part of their family...' – there is sharp criticism of a similar formula from the 1980 Rhineland synod by E.Käsemann, 'Aspekte der Kirche', in id., *Kirchliche Konflikte* I, Göttingen 1982, [7-36] 20ff.), but from this there follows a demand (emphasized for Catholic authors by Vatican II) for ecumenical conversation with Judaism (instead of evangelization aimed at conversion).

Cf. especially R.Smith, 'The Christian Message to Israel', in *Church*, ed. G.Hedenquist (above, 80), (189-200) 194; W.Strolz (editor's introduction to id. [ed.], *Jüdische Hoffnungskraft* [above, 97], 7-15) even says that the Declaration on the Jews has been put in the wrong place – in the Schema on the dialogue with other religions rather than in that on the church – thus already H.D.Leuner, 'Der Vatikan und die Juden', *Zeuge* 17, 1966, (1-8) 6f. [on Karl Barth, see above, 63]).

For the whole question cf. also 'Eine Diskussion über den Platz der Judenerklärung innerhalb der Konzilsdokumente', *FrRu* 18, 1966, 35-37; C.F.Pauwels, 'Ist das Mysterium Israels eine ökumenische Frage?', *FrRu* 12, 1959/60, 8-10; S.S.Schwarzschild, 'Judaism, Scriptures, and Ecumenism', *Judaism* 13, 1964, 259-73; E.L.Ehrlich, 'What Vatican II Means to Us Jews', *Bridge* V, 1970, 37-53; G.Harder, 'Christen vor dem Problem der Judenfrage', in *Christen und Juden*, ed.Marsch and Thieme (above, 78), 251-69; id., 'Das christlich-jüdische Gespräch im Verhältnis', in *Der ungekündigte Bund* (above, 80); id., 'Das christlich-jüdische Gespräch', *LR* 14, 1964, 413-26; W.Eckert, 'Der ökumenische Aspekt der christlich-jüdischen Begegnung', *FrRu* 15, 1964, 9-13; id., 'Jüdisch-christlicher Dialog heute', in *Jüdische Hoffnungskraft*, ed. W.Strolz, 244-79; Federici, *Israël* (above, 103), III.4, 157ff.; L.Althouse, *When Jew and Christian Meet*, New York 1966; P.Schneider, *Sweeter than Honey* (above, 78), esp. 154ff.; E.Flannery, 'The Church, the Synagogue, and the Ecumenical Movement', *PCTSA* 21, 1966, 315-22; A.Chouraqui and J.Daniélou, *Les Juifs*, Paris 1966 = ET *The Jews, Views and Counterviews*, New York 1967; G.Baum, 'The Doctrinal Basis for Jewish-Christian Dialogue', *Month* 224, 1967, 232-45; C.Thoma, 'Points of Departure', *Bridge* V, 1970, 159-70; K.Hruby, 'Israel, peuple de Dieu. Existe-t-il une théologie d'Israël dans l'Eglise?', *LV(L)* 18, 1969, 59-82; id., 'Reflections on the Dialogue', *Bridge* V, 1970, 106-31; id., 'The Future of Christian-Jewish Dialogue: A Christian View', *Conc* 98, 1974/75, 87-92; U.Tal, 'The Future...: A Jewish View', ibid., 80-6; H.Siegman, 'Dialogue with Christians: A Jewish Dilemma', *Jdm* 20, 1971, 93-103; J.T.Pawlikowski, 'The Contemporary Jewish-Christian Theological Dialogue Agenda', *JES* 11, 1974, 599-616 = 'The Theological Agenda of the Jewish-Christian Dialogue', *Christian Attitudes on Jews and Judaism* 42, 1975, 1-10 (abridged); the collection, *Speaking of God Today. Jews and Lutherans in Conversation*, ed.P.D.Opsahl and M.H.Tanenbaum, Philadelphia 1974;

D.Judant, *Jalons*, 7-32; *Jewish-Christian Dialogue. Six years of Christian-Jewish consultations. Published by the International Jewish Committee on Interreligious Consultations and the World Council of Churches' Subunit on Dialogue with the People of Living Faiths and Ideologies*, Geneva 1975; Fleischner, *Judaism* (above, 77), 105ff., 139ff.; Henrix, *US* 1976, above 98; id., 'Gedanken zur Nichtexistenz, Notwendigkeit und Zukunft eines Dialogs', *FrRu* 28, 1976, 16-27; R.Schaeffler, 'Das Gespräch zwischen Christen und Juden als Herausforderung an die Ökumene', in *Exodus und Kreuz*, ed. H.H.Henrix and M.Stöhr (above, 98) 166-87; *Christian-Jewish Relations in Ecumenical Perspective with Special Emphasis on Africa*, ed. F.von Hammerstein, Geneva 1978; J.Moltmann, in Lapide and Moltmann, *Israel und Kirche* (above, 101), (9-42) 9-15; cf. 97ff.; P.Lenhardt, *Auftrag und Unmöglichkeit eines legitimen christlichen Zeugnisses gegenüber den Juden*, Berlin 1980.

The change of view over the question of the mission to the Jews that is becoming evident in official declarations is also reflected in scholarly discussion. Immediately after the end of the war the Reformed Basle Pastor R.Brunner ('Judenmission nach dem zweiten Weltkrieg?', *Jud* 1, 1945, 296-319) felt that even after the horror of the annihilation of the Jews the only conceivable course for the church was now to resume with renewed effort the task of preaching the gospel to the Jews which it had so criminally neglected: 'The mission to the Jews should really be much closer to the heart of the Christian church than the mission among the Gentiles' (300). Of course so-called Christian culture had finally come into disrepute over what had been done, and in respect of 'what so-called Christian nations have done to Jews in recent years, without doubt a maximum of sin has come about' (302), so that repentance and reparation are the only appropriate attitude for the church. However, in the last resort the decisive factor is rather different – if penitence can lead to hopes for forgiveness and open up the prospect of forgiveness: 'But in asking whether mission should or should not, may or may not be carried on, the essential question is that of Christ. In other words, the question is whether Jesus is Christ or not' (301). Therefore: 'the relationship between Christians and Jews in principle continues now, as always, to be governed by Jesus Christ's command for mission and the promises given to the Jewish people and confirmed in Jesus Christ' (303). The church was also guilty towards the Jews before the war through its widespread neglect of the mission to the Jews. However, this mission must be exclusively concerned with the Word of God and nothing else (302). In 1947, for W.Holsten ('Deutsche Missionsaufgabe heute?', *EvTh* 7, 1947/48, [155-70] 158) 'the Jews and the East, which is more or less dominated by or infected by the Bolshevists', are the specific mission fields of the German church in its 'home situation'.

However, Brunner already pointed out that his view was not the only one prevalent in the church. He indicated groups in it which stood far too near to Jewish thought still to be able to understand the mission to the Jews (308). Some years later, in a report 'Kirche und Synagoge' (*LMJ* [B] 40, 1951/2, [156-66], 163, which described above all the declarations of Amsterdam 1948 and Berlin 1950 [above 69, 69f.]), G.Hedenquist felt the need to warn against a 'syncretism' in which 'the boundaries between the two religions are eliminated in such a way that the absoluteness of Christian faith is put in question' (the charge of syncretism also appears in E.Grässer, *PT* 1982 [above, 96], 446 = id., *Der alte Bund* [above, 91], 286). According to John 14.6 the church must also reflect on its obligation of mission towards the Jews. 'There is no second way of showing the Jews true love' (164 – similarly also M.Wittenberg, 'Begegnung mit dem Judentum', *JEM* 1963, [64-77], 71f., 75,77). In a later contribution, 'Judenmission und Heidenmission', *LM* 2, 1963, 22-6 = *Jud* 19, 1963, 113-26, W.Holsten continues to argue for the task of mission towards the Jews but stresses that in view of the continuity between the old and the new people of God, in which present-day Jews are also supported by the faithfulness of God, witness to Christ is to be shown to the Jews in a different way from that to the Gentiles (non-Jews). 'In mission the Gentiles are called out of their religions... into the people of God' (24/118). By contrast, Israel and the church are already in a situation of dialogue. Israel is (as Karl Barth put it) the 'older brother' (cf. also Eckardt, *Brothers* [above, 101]) which has a claim to service and testimony on the part of Christians. Neither is possible without the other; both are indispensable. Here Holsten can refer to the fact that S.Ben-Chorin also concedes to the church, 'in so far as it wills to be and remain the church of Christ', that especially to 'Israel, the people of salvation in the old covenant', it must put the question: 'Do you believe that

Jesus of Nazareth is the promised Messiah of Israel and the saviour of the world?' (cf. above, 100; quoted in Holsten, 25/123).

However, over against these comments have been raised the voices of those who have basic suspicions of any form of mission to the Jews (Holsten, 26/124, already concedes that this term is loaded, but sees no point in replacing it with 'conversation', since conversation cannot take the place of proclamation, 25/121).

Some authors go so far as to exclude *a priori*, as a possible aim of a conversation, any presentation of the message of Christ by the Christian partner to the individual and thus a possible conversion of the Jewish partner (thus especially H.Kremers, *Das Verhältnis* [above, 81], 25, cf. 14; id., *Judenmission heute?* [above, 81], passim, esp.78f.; id., 'Juden und Christen sind Zeugen Gottes voreinander', *FS H.J.Kraus* [above, 58], 237-46; cf. S.Schoon, *Nes Ammim – Een christelijk experiment in Israel*, Wageningen 1976 = *Nes Ammim. Ein christliches Experiment in Israel* [with H.Kremers], Neukirchen-Vluyn 1978, 73ff.; Kirsch, *We Christians* [above, 101], 124f.; R.Rendtorff, 'Alttestamentlicher Glaube und christliches Handeln heute', *Emuna* 1, 1966, [105-20] 108; cf. more recently also id., 'Judenmission nach dem Holokaust', *FS Gensichen* [above, 94], 173-83 = 'Judenmission nach Auschwitz', in *Auschwitz*, ed. Ginzel [above, 65], 539-56; P.G.Aring, 'Absage an die Judenmission', in *Umkehr*, ed. Klappert and Starck [above, 67], 207-14, is ambivalent; cf. also id., *Christliche Judenmission. Ihre Geschichte und Problematik dargestellt und untersucht am Beispiel des evangelischen Rheinlandes*, Neukirchen-Vluyn 1980, 255f.).

R.Eckardt has developed the most notable theological hypothesis (conceived from the perspective of the American form of the dialectical neo-Reformation school) of the possibility that any idea of converting Israel as a whole should be given up (he does not completely exclude the conversion of individual Jews, cf. *Christianity* [above, 101], 148n.; *Brothers* [above, 101], 155f.). The nub of his argument is that the existence of Judaism *alongside* Christianity accords with the divine will not only because the notion that it is the elect people must be maintained (cf. *Brothers*, esp. 141ff.) and because the concept of the elect people is the strongest insurance again any constantly recurring form of nationalism, even in the church (cf. *Christianity*, 39ff.), but above all because of the warning that it gives, derived from the central Reformation awareness that all men, even Christians, are sinners, against the all-too-easy assumption that conversion to Christ cannot mean anything other than conversion to Christianity, and thus to a form of life which is rated more highly, but which before God is only relative (cf. especially the section 'The Dilemma of the Missionary', *Christianity*, 145ff. A characteristic comment is that, 'If Jesus Christ is God's gift, He is not something we may *possess* or require other men to possess', 151). However, specifically against the background of these profound theological considerations Eckardt is much more cautious than many of his more recent successors: in some ways as a final conclusion from his reflections he remarks: 'These comments have not been made in order finally to deny the validity of the Christian mission to the Jews but instead to show that the problem is not as simple as often imagined. It is difficult to deal with this question in terms of a simple either-or and say that missions either are or are not fully justified.' In this connection mention might also be made of von der Osten-Sacken's view that it is the task of the church (in accordance with Rom.11.11,14) to *live out* the confession of Jesus Christ in such a way 'that the Jewish people may know – in whatever way – that God has also acted in favour of Israel in Jesus Christ' (*Grundzüge*, 121, cf. 112; on this see also recently id., 'Heil für die Juden – auch ohne Christus?', *FS H.J. Kraus* [above, 58] 169-82; id., 'Christen und Juden – Zukunftsperspektiven ihres Verhältnisses', *FÜI* 67, 1984, 98-110). This was still the focal point of the 1981 Hamburg Kirchentag ('Bist du, der da kommen soll? Jesus-Messias Israels?', *epd-Dokumentation* 31/81, [17-25] 24 = *Deutscher Evangelischer Kirchentag Hamburg 1981. Dokumente*, Stuttgart 1981, [568-77] 575f.): it is the task of the community to live out the fact that it is reconciled through Christ and thus also the fact that it is reconciled with the Jewish people.

From the Jewish side (like Schoeps, 'Möglichkeiten' [above, 99], 7; Herberg, *Faith Enacted* [above, 101], 61) before him, H.L.Goldschmidt, *Die Botschaft des Judentums*, Frankfurt am Main 1960, 157, requires that, 'From now on there may not be either mission to the Jews nor mission to Christians but only going over; not "organized" going over.' In America B.Brickner, 'Christian Missionaries and a Jewish Response', *Worldview* 21, 1978, 37-41, claimed a reawakening of missionary tendencies, especially in evangelistic Christian circles (and elicited an immediate answer: 'Christians' Challenge to Rabbi's Response', ibid., 42-6). For the discussion in Europe cf. recently also E.L.Ehrlich, 'Abschied von der Judenmission. Antwort an Arnulf Baumann' (cf. below, 114), *Jud* 38, 1982, 14-23. For Jews and Christians the task of world mission remains (cf. here also the Jewish self-understanding of the missionary task of Israel, articulated in different ways in B.Z.Bokser, 'Witness and Mission in Judaism', in *Issues in the Jewish-Christian Dialogue*, ed. H.Croner and L.Klenicki, New York and Ramsay, NJ 1979, 89-107, and M.A.Cohen, 'The Mission of Israel after Auschwitz', ibid., 157-80). The alternatives here are either to maintain (and consolidate) the schism up to the eschatological moment mentioned in Rom.11 (evocatively mentioned in Kremers, *Das Verhältnis* [above, 81], 25; F.von Hammerstein, 'Christlich-jüdischer Dialog in ökumenischer Perspektive' in *Richte unsere Füsse auf den Weg des Friedens. FS H.Gollwitzer*, Munich 1979, [329-48] 343, speaks of the Christian mission to the Jews who did not observe 'how little they took serious account of the faithfulness of God to his people, how strongly they threaten the Jewish people'. Similarly van Buren, *Discerning the Way* [above, 101], 64: '...special care must be exercised by the church... not to weaken the Jewish people.') That can even be assessed positively as collaboration between Judaism and Christianity in salvation history (thus the programmatical title [which takes up a former appeal by Goldschmidt, *Botschaft*, 135ff.] in H.L.Goldschmidt, *Weil wir Brüder sind. Biblische Besinnung für Juden und Christen*, Stuttgart nd [1975], 16), i.e. 'collaboration towards the kingdom of God, the consummation of which is still to come for Judaism as for Christianity!' (18). C.A.Rijk ('Das gemeinsame Band', *BiKi* 29, 1974, [42-44], 44) already sees a possible basis for a fruitful conversation between the two confessions in the positive tension between the 'now already' attested by the church and the 'not yet' attested by Judaism.

However it is Rosemary Ruether (*Faith and Fratricide* [above, 79]) who has put forward the most radical of all models for the relationship between Christianity and Judaism (and therefore the one in which the possible consequences of a revolution in traditional doctrine have become clearest; cf. also ead., 'Theological Anti-Semitism in the New Testament', *CCen* 85, 1968, 191-6; ead., 'Anti-Judaism is the Left Hand of Christology', *NCW* 217, 1974, 12-17 = *Jewish-Christian Relations*, ed.R.Heyer [above, 89], 1-9; for criticism cf. also J.Mejia, 'Problématique théologique des relations Judéo-chrétiennes. Analyse de quelques publications recentes', in

De la Torah au Messie. Mélanges H. Cazelles, Paris 1981, 599-616).
Her proposal reaches to the centre of Christian proclamation since
it is there that she clearly recognizes the key question for any
theological judgment on the relationship of Christianity to Judaism,
in christology (229ff.). Her solution is brilliant: a radical de-eschatologizing of christology which understands the resurrection that has
already taken place as exclusive only for the narrower group of those
who were affected by this experience, i.e. the first disciples of
Jesus and, in their complex of tradition, the church, the binding
interpretation of the eschatological experience ('Resting on a
particular salvific experience appropriated by a particular group
in a particular context..., Christianity confronts other cultural
heritages', 235), offers room within the provisionality of the unre-
deemed nature of man and history represented by the present
for several ways to the ultimately valid truth, in other words a
juxtaposition of religions and cultures (cf. 233ff.), including Judaism
and Christianity, which each in its own way lives from messianic
hope (cf. here also the offer to Israel contained in the argument of
von der Osten-Sacken [*Grundzüge*, 136], that the Coming One is
only to be greeted when he shows himself in the form in which he is
expected, without affecting the faith of the church in his identity
with the Crucified and Risen One).

J.B.Metz ('Ökumene nach Auschwitz. Zum Verhältnis von
Christen und Juden in Deutschland', *FrRu* 30, 1978, [7-13] =
E.Kogon and J.B.Metz et al., *Gott nach Auschwitz*, Freiburg,
Basle and Vienna 1979, [121-44] 9/130) calls for the recognition
of 'the messianic tradition of Judaism in its unsurpassed independence, as it were in its ongoing messianic dignity – without
Christianity betraying or deposing the christological mystery that
it represents' – and hopes for a kind of *coalition of messianic trust
between Jews and Christians* as an ultimate goal [11/144]. Cf. also
B.Klappert, 'Die Juden' (above, 98), 489ff.; id., 'Jesus Christus
zwischen Juden und Christen', in *Umkehr*, ed. Klappert and
Starck (above, 67), 138-66. Both in Metz and in Klappert implications for political action are on the horizon. Cf. also Klappert,
'Perspektiven einer von Juden und Christen anzustrebenden
gerechten Weltgesellschaft', *FrRu* 30, 1978, 67-82; M.Stöhr,
'Judenmission oder gemeinsamer Auftrag?', *Dü* 16, 1980, 54-7.
The proximity of this approach to the consistent eschatologizing

of christology in J.Moltmann, *Theologie der Hoffnung*, BEvTh 38, Munich 1964 ([10]1977) = ET *Theology of Hope*, London and New York 1967 ([7]1983) should be noted (cf. also Lapide, *Eine jüdische Theologie...* [above, 88], 25f. For criticism of Moltmann cf. H.Grass, *Christliche Glaubenslehre*, 2, Stuttgart 1974, 95f.; Pawlikowski, *Christ in the Light of the Christian-Jewish Dialogue* [above, 79], 42ff.). P.G.Aring ('Immer noch Judenmission', in *Auschwitz*, ed.Ginzel [above 65], 557-78), also speaks of a 'messianic-christological doctrinaire premise which so hinders Christian-Jewish dialogue even today' (564). A mission to the Jews is impossible after Auschwitz not only because of the guilt which has burdened Christians since then, but also 'because it has not yet been definitively proved, nor can it be, whether Jesus of Nazareth really was or was not the messiah of God. Christians believe that and confess it, but they do not know it. Jews do not know and believe it, but some consider it conceivable, not impossible' (574). McGarry, *Christology* (above 65), esp.10f., 103f., also argues that the Jewish-Christian dialogue must have consequences for christology. Similarly also D.J.Hall, 'Rethinking Christ', in *Antisemitism*, ed.A.T.Davies (above, 61), 167-87, and Pawlikowski, *Christ*, who develops proposals for an incarnational christology within the horizons of the Christian-Jewish dialogue. For Jewish messianism in the first centuries after Christ cf. J.Klausner, *The Messianic Idea in Israel from Its Beginning to the Completion of the Mishnah*, Jerusalem 1956; A.H.Silver, *A History of Messianic Speculation in Israel*, Boston 1959; C.Klick, 'Are You He Who is To Come?', *LuthQ* 24, 1972, 1-65; K.Schubert, 'Die jüdisch-christliche Ökumene – Reflexionen zu Grundfragen des christlich-jüdischen Dialogs', *Kairos* 22, 1980, (1-33) 18-23; Volken, *Jesus* (above, 81), 112ff.; for that of the Middle Ages e.g. G.D.Cohen, 'Messianic Postures of Ashkenazim and Sephardim', in *Studies of the Leo Baeck Institute*, ed. M.Kreuzberger, New York 1967, 117-56; for that of the present e.g. G.Scholem, 'Zum Verständnis der messianischen Idee im Judentum', *ErJb* 28, 1959, 193-239 = id., *Judaica*, Frankfurt am Main 1963, 7-74 = id., *Über einige Grundbegriffe des Judentums*, Frankfurt am Main 1970, 121-67; = 'Toward an Understanding of the Messianic Idea in Judaism', in id., *The Messianic Idea in Judaism*, New York and London 1971, 1-36; cf. also id., 'Jewish Messianism and the Idea of Progress', *Com* 25,

1958, 298-305 = 'The Messianic Idea in Kabbalism', in id., *Messianic Idea in Judaism*, 37-48; id., 'Die Krise der Tradition im Jüdischen Messianismus', *ErJb* 37, 1968, 9-44 = 'The Crisis of Tradition in Jewish Messianism', *Messianic Idea in Judaism*, 29-77; id., 'The Neutralization of the Messianic Element in Early Hasidism', *JJS* 20, 1969, 25-55 = id., *Messianic Idea in Judaism*, 176-202; E.Rivkin, 'The Meaning of Messiah in Jewish Thought', *USQR* 26, 1971, 383-406 = 'The Meaning of Messiah in Jewish Thought', in *Evangelicals and Jews in Conversation*, ed. M.H.Tanenbaum et al. (above, 22), 54-75; J.Petuchowski, 'Messianic Hope: 1.In Judaism', *Conc* 98, 1974/75, 56-61; id., 'Die messianische Dialektik im Judentum', *Kairos* 23, 1981, 66-74; A.I.Waskow, 'The Choice: Romanticism or True Messianism', in *Auschwitz*, ed. E.Fleischner (above, 79), 307-30. However, this line is in no way representative of Jewish theology as a whole. P.Lapide ('Der Messias Israels?', in *Umkehr*, ed. Klappert and Starck [above, 67] [236-46], 241f.; id., in Lapide and Moltmann, *Israel und Kirche* [above, 101], 58f.) emphatically stresses that at all events Jesus of Nazareth is not the messiah of the Jews, though he is possibly that of the Gentiles. H.Frankemölle, 'Jüdische Messiaserwartung und christlicher Messiasglaube', *Kairos* 20, 1978, 97-109; cf. id., 'Jewish and Christian Messianism', *TD* 28, 1980, 233-6, sees in the context of Mark 8.29 'a clear need for integrating Jewish-Christian perspectives into the Messiah/Christ concept' (*TD* 1980, 236). By contrast, U.Wilckens stresses the qualitative difference between Pauline christology and a (possible) Jewish messianism: 'Glaube nach urchristlichem und frühjüdischem Verständnis', in Lapide/Mussner/Wilckens, *Was Juden und Christen voneinander denken* (above, 81) (72-96), 84ff.; similarly H.Hübner, 'Der Messias Israels und der Christus des Neuen Testaments', *KuD* 27, 1981, 217-39. K.Kertelge, 'Der Jude Jesus – der universale Messias', in *Gottesverächter*, ed. H.Goldstein (above, 73), 58-78, sees in the universal aspect of Jesus' messiahship the deciding difference between the Jewish and the Christian view. For the topic cf. also C.Thoma, *Die theologischen Beziehungen* (above, 68), 135-49. For Jewish attitudes to Christian christology see S.Katz, 'Christology: A Jewish View', *SJT* 24, 1971, 184-200; for more recent christological outlines, E.B.Borowitz, *Contemporary Christologies: A Jewish Response*, New York and Ramsay, NJ 1980.

The christological approach is coupled with a massive criticism of the universalist claim of traditional Christianity, which is seen in close connection with its consequences – a cultural and power-political Western imperialism (238f.; G.Baum stresses this aspect in his introduction by the catchphrase 'symbolic imperialism', 14). Here there is an explicit connection with the new trend in wide areas of mission theology in which 'the dogma that all men and women must become Christians' is being reconsidered. 'Today missionaries try to be concerned for human solidarity and service, not for conversion' (235). In a commendably clear way it is said that a renunciation of the mission to the Jews is just one subsidiary instance of a renunciation of mission generally, to which according to Ruether only fundamentalists adhere(ibid.). Similarly, P.von der Osten-Sacken, in his postscript to the German edition ('Von der Notwendigkeit theologischen Besitzverzichts', ibid. [244-51], 246) defines the task as follows: 'Jesus is no longer to be defined in an absolutizing sense as the only way to the Father. This change would be to the benefit not only of Judaism as well as Christianity, but also of other (religious) communities, to whom the relativizing of the Christian claim to absoluteness and totality which is grounded in christology would allow room for an existence of their own.' (Similarly id., 'Rückzug ins Wesen und aus der Geschichte', *WPKG* 67, 1978, [106-22] 122. Cf. also id., 'Das paulinische Verständnis des Gesetzes im Spannungsfeld von Eschatologie und Geschichte', *EvTh* 37, 1977, 549-87. Here von der Osten-Sacken contrasts the message of the historical Jesus with the eschatological Pauline theology of the cross: the former was only for sinners, while for the righteous within Judaism the way of obedience to the law remained open as a way of salvation. Cf. also id., *Grundzüge*, 93: 'For sinners and publicans, for the impure in Israel and... for Gentiles, Jesus is... the mediator, who leads it to community with God. For Jews, who are on the way to God in the form of their life with the Torah, he does not have this function.'). The relativizing approach of J.Parkes, *Prelude to Dialogue: Jewish-Christian Relationships*, London 1969, esp 188f., arrives at similar results. Although he retains the basic Christian statements (the divinity of Christ, vicarious atonement, 198, 200) he can declare: 'All thought of a comparison claiming one to be better than the other vanishes before any objective consideration of the task which confronted each religion during the same formative centuries' (195). Certainly the Jews are in error if they do not recognize atonement, but Jews also possess things which Christians lack. 'What both sides can do is to accept the other side as an equal partner in the work of God in the world' (201). It is worth noting that in this approach historical revelation is said to be 'particular' and is therefore denied any general binding force outside the narrower group of those who belong to its tradition (are involved in it in a narrative sense), and instead of this the creation is raised to being a central theological statement: the (eschatological) 'point of unity now consists only in the transcendent universality of God and his real work as creator, which gives us grounds for confessing the universal brotherhood of man' (222; for the starting point in creation cf. also P.van Buren, *Discerning the Way* [above, 101], 184f.; id., 'Ein Modell systematischer Verhältnisbestimmung von Israel und Kirche', in *Jüdische Existenz*, ed. M.Stöhr [above, 94], [138-53] 149f.; M.Hellwig, *Proposal* [above, 101], 190). Parkes, *Prelude*, 202ff., cf.200, develops a trinitarian system of three channels in which the relationship between Judaism and Christianity is to be put: 'I believe that power flows from one unknowable Godhead through three equal channels... I believe that the first such moment was at Sinai. The second was at the Incarnation'(200). Both remain side by side in creative tension. The third is 'the channel of truth for man as seeker' (220). It is clear that here the claim of Judaism to bear binding witness to a historical revelation is as relativized as that of Christianity. – For criticism of Parkes cf.e.g.Pawlikowski, *Christ in the Light of the Jewish-Christian Dialogue* (above, 79), 19ff.

It is possible here only to indicate that this view is closely connected with more recent developments in the sphere of the theology of the history of religion and the consequences which follow from it in the field of mission (cf. also above, 76f.). In Roman Catholic theology these efforts are largely indebted to Karl Rahner, who in his lecture 'Christianity and the Non-Christian Religions' ('Das Christentum und die nichtchristlichen Religionen', in *Pluralismus, Toleranz und Christenheit, Veröffentlichungen d.Abendl.Akad.Nürnberg* 1961, 55-74 = *Schriften zur Theologie* V, Einsiedeln, Zurich and Cologne ²1964, 136-58 = ET *Theological Investigations* 5, London 1966, 115-34) gave the non-Christian religions a limited quality of revelation alongside Christianity. This attitude then also became established at the Second Vatican Council (cf. e.g. among others, H.Küng, *Christ sein*, Munich 1974 [⁹1977], 81ff. = ET *On Being A Christian*, London and New York 1976, paperback 1978, 89ff. The influence

of this view is also evident in other Roman Catholic authors, cf. e.g.
G.Baum et al, 'Doctrinal Basis' [above, 103]; P.Chirico, 'Christian
and Jew Today from a Christian Theological Perspective', *JES* 7,
1970, 744-62; J.T.Pawlikowski, *Christ in the Light of the Christian-
Jewish Dialogue* [above, 79], 148ff. – For Protestant views see the
report by P.Knitter, 'What is German Protestant Theology Saying
about the Non-Christian Religions?', *NZST* 15, 1973, 38-64. There
is a Jewish view in I. Maybaum, *Trialogue between Jew, Christian
and Muslim*, London 1973. Bokser, *Judaism* [above, 73], can
declare: 'The tensions between Judaism and Christianity – and all
other inter religious tensions – will dissolve when the validity of
pluralism is accepted in the religious realm as it is in all other realms
within a democratic society.')

Over against this, Lutheran statements in particular stress the
permanent task of mission even among the Jews (e.g. R.Dobbert,
'Das Zeugnis der Kirche für die Juden', in Becker, Dobbert and
Gjerding, *Das Zeugnis* [above, 67], [33-68] 39: 'The task that the
Lord Jesus Christ has given to his church necessarily entails the
proclamation of the gospel among the Jews. To refrain from this
special proclamation would be simply disobedience.' Cf. R.Becker,
'Gibt es ein Zeugnis der Kirche für die Juden?', ibid., 11-31, esp.30f.;
A.Baumann, 'Judenmission – gestern und heute', *EvMis* 9, 1977,
17-39; id., 'Evangelisch-lutherische Kirche und Mission unter
Israel', *FÜI* 62, 1979, 97f.; id., *Christliches Zeugnis und die Juden
heute*, Hanover 1981; id., 'Judenmission: Christliches Zeugnis unter
Juden, Bestandsaufnahme und Ausblick', *Jud* 38, 1981, 3-13; cf. also
'Niemand kommt zum Vater denn durch mich' [Podium speech],
Kirchentag 1981 [above 107], [588-607] 588-92; E.Bezzel, 'Christliches Zeugnis an Israel', *FÜI* 64, 1981, 147-53; cf. also the Festschrift
for the Centenary of the Lutheran Central Association for Mission
in Israel, *Zeugnis für Zion*, Erlangen 1971). The Lutheran attitude
over the question of the provisional juxtaposition of the church and
Judaism is essentially more matter-of-fact: thus for L.Goppelt (*Israel
und die Kirche* [above, 83], 188), contact between the church
and Judaism is 'not the salvation-historical presupposition of its
existence', nor even the fact that both participate in the same hope,
'but they can recognize one another as those who stand over against
the same revelation of God, a little way off' (189 – on the Jewish
side, the proposal of Zwi Werblowski, 'Trennendes und Gemeinsames', in *Handreichung* [above, 67], [29-43] = *FrRu* 31, 1979 [17-

23], 41f./22 that one can 'eschatologize the idea of the fulfilment of the task of mission [in accordance with Rom.11]' is not far from that). K.H.Rengstorf ('The Jewish Problem and the Church's Understanding of its Own Mission', in *Church*, ed. Hedenquist [above, 80], [27-46] 44) observes that according to the expectation expressed in Rom.9-11 God has reserved the conversion of all Israel for himself, but this should not keep the church from prayer for Israel and brotherly service. There has been no lack of protest against extreme abstinence from extending the message of Christ to Judaism already in view of the discussion at the 1961 Kirchentag. Cf. the discussion in *LM* 1, 1962, between G.Harder, P.Reinhardt and K.Wendtlandt, 76-81, 81-3, 95-9, 324-6, and Mehl, 'Kirche' (above, 84). According to P.Reinhardt, 'Kirche und Judentum' (*LM* 3, 1964, 249), the dispute over the mission to the Jews 'in the last resort betrays the deep uncertainty that the church has found itself in today over the task given it to bear witness about Jesus of Nazareth to Jews and Gentiles'. However, in the English and American discussion, too, there are voices which affirm the basic task of Christan mission even to the Jews, albeit under the conditions of 'fair partnership', which makes possible an authentic dialogue in faith. Cf. e.g. Peter Schneider, *Sweeter than Honey* (above, 78); J.R.Estes, 'Jewish-Christian Dialogue as Mission', *RExp* 68, 1971, 5-16. J.Jocz, *Christians and Jews: Encounter and Mission*, London 1966, also has firm views on this. Even from the Jewish side voices can occasionally be heard admonishing the church that it has a genuine missionary task, cf.e.g. Schwarzschild, 'Judaism' (above, 103), 262: 'It is inevitable and, from their point of view, perfectly legitimate and even spiritually necessary that the Roman Catholic approach to the Jews should be essentially missionary in character. And this is characteristic of Protestants as well.' The reasons given are: 'our understanding of and respect for the sincerity of Christianity..., the consideration that every monotheistic and, therefore, monistic truth must seek to persuade all men of its veracity and goodness' (263), and the expectation in Zech.14.9,16.

Especially in Germany, beyond question the experience of the 'holocaust' (or 'Auschwitz') has been a cause of this uncertainty. Thus e.g. G.P.Aring ('Immer noch Judenmission?' [above, 110], 578), says quite explicitly: 'After "Auschwitz" I no longer dare to say to my Jewish friends that Jesus is the Christ. I cannot even say it to my children and my congregation without blushing; I am no longer sure of myself' (cf. also id., *Christliche Judenmission* [above, 106], 8, 11, 259). There has even been a 'holocaust theology' in the USA which discussed the theological problem raised by 'Auschwitz' (cf. e.g. U.Simon, *A Theology of Auschwitz*, London 1967, paperback 1978; E.Fackenheim, *God's Presence in History*, New York 1970, 67ff.; E.Berkovits, *Faith after the Holocaust*, New York 1973; the symposium *Auschwitz: Beginning of a New Era* [cf. the conference report by G.Baum, *Ecumenist* 12, 1974, 65-80]; L.Rubinoff, 'Auschwitz and the Theology of the Holocaust', in *Speaking of God Today*, ed. P.D.Opsahl and M.H.Tanenbaum, Philadelphia 1974, 121-43; F.Sherman, 'Speaking of God after Auschwitz', *Worldview* 17, 1974, 26-30 = *Speaking of God*, 144-59; F.H.Littell, *The Crucifixion of the Jews*, New York 1975; cf. also id., 'Christians and Jews and Ecumenism', *Dialog* 10, 1971, 249-55; id., 'Christendom, Holocaust, and Israel', *JES* 10, 1973, 483-97; J.T.Pawlikowski, *Christ in the Light of the Christian-Jewish Dialogue* [above, 79], 136-47; A. and R.Eckard, 'Christentum und Judentum: Die theologische und moralische Problematik der Vernichtung des europäischen Judentums', *EvTh* 36, 1976, 406-26). Cf. also M.Dubois, 'Un regard chrétien sur l'Holocauste', in *Service International de documentation judéo-chrétienne* 7, 1974, 4-16, who sees parallels between the passion of the Jewish people in the Holocaust and the vicarious passion of Jesus for mankind on the cross. But is 'Auschwitz' a theological argument in respect of theodicy or even christology? There is legitimate criticism of this thought-pattern by G.B.Ginzel ('Christen und Juden nach Auschwitz', in id. [ed.], *Auschwitz* [above, 65], 234-76). Among his three questions on the 1980 Rhineland Theses the one about the justification for associating Christianity with 'Auschwitz' is particularly significant. He describes the question 'Why did God allow Auschwitz to happen?' as 'basically false' (as it seems, from an authentically Reformation approach; similarly also F.König, 'Nach Auschwitz andere Akzente setzen', ibid., [228-33], 228: God 'does not intervene in what is often fearful human history like a general, but with horror we note that human beings can become even more bestial than animals...' A.T.Davies, 'Response to Irving Greenberg', in *Auschwitz*, ed. E.Fleischner [above, 79], [57-64] 61, notes: 'most Christians are inclined to show much greater caution toward any attempt to decipher the presence of God in the events of history', and H.Seebass, *Der Gott der ganzen Bibel*, Freiburg,

Basle and Vienna 1982, 24, stresses 'that in the purely substantive question as to what biblical theology is, guilt feelings would be bad counsellors'; van der Waal, 'Continuity' [above, 83] comments: 'The Holocaust has boomeranged with the result that today an Israel cult has arisen' [9]. Cf. further M.Honecker, *KuD* 1981 [above, 68], 207-16; E.Grässer, *FS F.Mussner* [above, 91], 413ff. = id., *Der alte Bund*, 214ff.; G.Klein, *Antijudaismus* [above, 68], 414ff., 421ff.; Preuss, *Predigt*, 151f.; Thoma, *Beziehungen* [above, 68], 78ff.; and from the Jewish perspective Berkovits, *Faith*, esp.88ff.; E.Brocke, 'Der Holocaust als Wendepunkt?', in *Umkehr und Erneuerung*, ed. Klappert and Starck [above, 111], 101-10. For other Jewish comments cf. R.E.Willis, 'Christian Theology After Auschwitz', *JES* 12, 1975, [493-519], 494-500; I.Greenberg, 'Judaism and Christianity After the Holocaust', ibid., 521-51; also the Christian R.McAfee Brown, 'Die Massenvernichtung als theologisches Problem', in *Gott nach Auschwitz* [above, 109], 87-118 = *Dimensions of the Holocaust*, Evanston Ill, 1977, 47-63; id., 'The Holocaust as a Problem in Moral Choice', in *Dimensions of the Holocaust. Lectures at Northwestern University*, Evanson, Ill. 1977, 47-63; S.Schreiner, 'Jüdisch-theologisches Denken nach Auschwitz – ein Versuch seiner Darstellung', *Jud* 36, 1980, 1-13, 49-56. The interpretation of the Holocaust is also very much disputed in Judaism, a community with a stronger orientation on the theology of history; cf. e.g. D.Polish, 'Witnessing God After Auschwitz', in *Issues*, ed. Croner and Klenicki [above, 108], 134-56, esp.150: 'As we reflect on how to understand God after the *shoah*, then, I reject the proposition that we treat it as being of a different order of reality from anything that preceded it, thus needing theological responses of a wholly new order. I regard it as being different in magnitude, but not in kind, from cataclysms that the people had known before in its history.' R.L.Rubenstein, 'Some Perspectives on Religious Faith after Auschwitz', in *The German Church Struggle and the Holocaust*, ed.F.H.Littell and H.Locke, Detroit 1974 [reprinted 1975], resolutely refuses to accept the consequences of seeing God acting in all events of history, even in the holocaust. M.Stöhr, 'Erinnern, nicht vergessen', in M.Stöhr et al., *Erinnern, nicht vergessen. Zugänge zum Holocaust*, Munich 1979, [156-74] 168, stresses: 'One will not find a religious sense with Auschwitz, because every attempt at finding one leads to a blasphemy.' Cf. also id., 'Leben und Glauben nach dem Holokaust', in *Leben und Glauben nach dem Holokaust. Einsichten und Versuche*, ed. G.Wessler, Stuttgart 1980 [7-34], 29ff.). As Auschwitz 'was a human work', the question should really be, 'Why did human beings allow Auschwitz' (quotations, 272, similarly F.-W.Marquardt, 'Christsein nach Auschwitz', in F.-W.Marquardt and A.Friedländer, *Das Schweigen der Christen und die Menschlichkeit Gottes*, KT 49, Munich 1980, [7-34] 31). In fact 'Auschwitz' is one of the cruellest examples in the history of the world of racial hatred and the burden of human sin. It calls Germans in particular to the deepest penitence. It should not be forgotten that Christians above all incurred guilt because of their silence (that Christianity has become partly guilty of the holocaust by preparing for it in anti-Jewish ideology is a viewpoint stressed by several writers, cf.e.g. G.Baum, 'Catholic Dogma after Auschwitz', in *Antisemitism*, ed. A.T.Davies [above, 61], 137-50. The holocaust, therefore, reminds the Christian of a New Testament 'love of neighbour': E.A.Smith, 'The Christian Meaning of the Holocaust', *JES* 6, 1969, 419-22). However, equally important is the resolution with which Ginzel opposes the widespread view (251, cf. also W.Burghardt, 'Response to Rosemary Ruether', in *Auschwitz*, ed. Fleischner [above, 79], 93-5, and already Vawter, *JES* 1968 [above, 85], 487) which sweepingly makes 'Christianity' responsible for 'Auschwitz' (see e.g. B.Klappert, 'Die Juden' [above, 97], 484ff. Cf. C.Thoma, 'Theologie ohne Judenfeind-schaft', in *Jüdische Existenz* [above, 94], [13-31] 20: 'It is wrong to make the idea of the scapegoat, which was earlier directed e.g. by the church against the Jews, rebound against the church.' Cf. also his warning against generalizations, id., 'Kritik an heutigen Gesprächstendenzen bei Christen und Juden', *Jud* 38, 1982, [108-14] 111.) Not only Jews and foreigners but also Christians in Germany have suffered under the most violently anti-Christian National Socialist ideology. A witness to this who is above suspicion is the Jewish historian Y.H.Yerushalmi ('Response' [above, 80], 102f.), who (against R.Ruether) refers to the deep gulf between the predominantly tolerant attitude of the Christian Middle Ages towards Jewish fellow-citizens and the radically racist policy of the modern neo-pagan state: 'Between this and Nazi Germany lies not merely a "transformation" but a leap into a different dimension', 104. For the discussion cf. already K.Thieme, 'Der religiöse Aspekt der Judenfeindschaft', *FrRu* 10, 1957/58, 7-14; Baum, *Is the New Testament Anti-Semitic?* [above, 85], 328f. and n.40; also Fleischner,

Judaism [above, 77], 69ff. The contribution by G.Harder (*Der ungekündigte Bund*, ed. Goldschmidt/Kraus [above, 66], 145ff.) represents a notable balanced statement (similarly also id., *LR* 1964 [above, 103]), in which he requires on the one hand that the testimony to Christ in the New Testament should also be given to Judaism, but, on the other hand, stresses very clearly the points on which we Christians have to allow ourselves to be told something by our Jewish conversation-partners. (Similarly also A.de Quervain, *Judentum* [above, 81], esp.41f.; Flannery, 'The Church' [above, 103], esp.321f.; Schweikhart, *Dialog und Mission* [above, 64], passim, esp.240; cf. also G.Harder, 'Christen vor dem Problem der Judenfrage' [above, 103], 257ff.; J.Dijk, *Uw volk*, Wageningen 1975 [²1978], 82ff.; J.Moltmann, in Lapide and Moltmann, *Israel und Kirche* [above, 101], 99-101; Aring, *Christliche Judenmission* [above, 106], passim. R.L.Lindsay, 'Salvation and the Jews', *IRM* 61, 1972, 20-37, begins from the fact that the Jews and Christians are one people of God – 'Christendom is the extension of Jewry', 36, but that witness must be borne to Christ towards Jews and nominal Christians ['evangelism'], while addressing the Christian message to the Goyim is a special task ['Mission']. For 'Christian witness among Jews' as 'advocacy of the Jews in the church', cf. also Baumann, *Christliches Zeugnis*, 24ff.; id., *Jud* 1982, 7ff.)

The most important of these questions relate to the Old Testament (cf. also F.E.Greenspahn, ed., *Scripture in the Jewish and Christian Traditions: Authority, Interpretation, Relevance*, Nashville 1982 [contributions by S.H.Blank, A.Dulles, M.Fishbane, J.H. Gerstner, D.H.Kelsey, R.P.McBrien, J.Neusner, K.Stendahl, B.Vawter]): the question of the will of God made known there (all too often defamed by dogma by being described as the 'law' – cf. already F.Weber, *Jüdische Theologie auf Grund des Talmud und verwandter Schriften²*, ed. F.Delitzsch and G.Schnedermann, Leipzig 1897; also G.F.Moore, 'Christian Writers on Judaism', *HTR* 14, 1921, 197-254; cf. id., *Judaism in the First Centuries of the Christian Era: The Age of the Tannaim*, three vols., Cambridge, Mass. 1927-30 [⁹1962]; E.P.Sanders, [above, 91], Part I, 33-428; Bokser, *Judaism* [above, 73], 159ff.; R.J.Z.Werblowski, 'Thora als Gnade', *Kairos* 15, 1973, 156-63; Y.Aschkenasy and W.A.C.Whitlau, 'Jüdische Bibelauslegung', in *Juden und Christen lesen dieselbe Bibel* [above, 60], 46-61; C.Thoma, *Christliche Theologie des Judentums*, Aschaffenburg 1978; also G.M.Landes, 'The Canonical

Approach to Introducing the Old Testament: Prodigy and Problems', *JSOT* 16, 1980, 32-9; E.L.Ehrlich, 'Über die Thora', in
Wegweisung, ed. P.von der Osten-Sacken and M.Stöhr, Berlin
1978, 66-71; R.Rendtorff, 'Die jüdische Bibel und ihre antijüdische
Auslegung', in R.Rendtorff and E.Stegemann, *Auschwitz* [above,
63], 99-116; id., 'Die hebräische Bibel als Grundlage christlich-
theologischer Aussagen über das Judentum', in *Jüdische Existenz*,
ed. M.Stöhr [above, 94], [32-47] 40ff.; also F.Crüsemann, 'Tora
und christliche Ethik', in ibid., 159-77; M.Cohen, 'Record and
Revelation: A Jewish Perspective', in *Biblical Studies*, ed. L.Boadt
et al. [above, 101], 147-71; F.-W.Marquardt, *Die Gegenwart des
Auferstandenen bei seinem Volk Israel. Ein dogmatisches Experiment*, Munich 1983, 54-9; cf.A.Wittstock, *Toraliebe im jüdischen
Volk. Theologische Grundlegung und Ausarbeitung einer Unter-
richtsreihe für Sekundarstufe II*, Berlin 1981) which the Jew is
concerned to observe (cf.e.g. Mussner, *Traktat* [above, 77], 37ff.;
Ruether, *Faith and Fratricide* [above, 79], 222ff.), the praise of
Israel, its burning eschatological hope, but also the problem how
far the church is justified in relating to itself the election in which
Israel has gained a share. Mehl had asserted: 'We Christians have
only the external wording of the Old Testament, its "shell", in
common with the Jews' ('Kirche' [above, 84], 162). By this he means
that the right to the Old Testament and its legitimate interpretation
has passed over completely to the church (M.H.Woudstra, 'The
Old Testament in Biblical Theology and Dogmatics', *CTJ* 18, 1983,
[47-60] 59 n.47, makes a similar point from the standpoint of
Reformed dogmatics: 'The Old Testament as such is not a Jewish
book. One may say also: the Jews do not have the Old Testament
in common with the Christians.') By contrast Harder stresses:
'Christianity does not want to take the OT from Judaism' ('Das
christlich-jüdische Gespräch im Verhältnis zum christlichen Zeugnis
an Israel' above, 103], 157). The extreme position in the opposite
direction is again taken by R.Ruether (and, following her, P. von
der Osten-Sacken). One of her requirements runs: 'Christian biblical
scholarship must learn and teach the Jewish line of commentary
on and interpretation of Hebrew scriptures in the "Midrash",
questioning there by the treatment of Judaism as something fulfilled
and made obsolete by Christianity, to which the Hebrew scriptures
are assigned as "Old Testament"' (*Faith and Fratricide*, 259. P.von
der Osten-Sacken is rather more restrained in his Postscript to the

German edition [above, 79], 247f., as he is referring to the 'historical' exegesis of Paul). According to Ruether, in theological terms this means that 'Christians must recognize the "oral Torah" as an authentic, alternative route by which the biblical past was appropriated and carried on' (*Faith and Fratricide*, 257; cf. also von der Osten-Sacken, *Grundzüge*, 186: 'Jews and Christians walk in the name of the one God, the former in hearkening to the word of the Torah, the latter in their bond with Jesus Christ').

Here historical interest and theological postulates go side by side without being related. In so far as it is important to demonstrate that Jesus and even Pauline theology and other forms of New Testament thought are rooted in contemporary Judaism, a more thorough knowledge of Pharisaic and rabbinic thought is in fact needed, even among Christian theological students (Ruether, 258; von der Osten-Sacken, Postscript, 247). C.Thoma, 'Theologie ohne Judenfeindschaft' (above, 118), 15, goes further and calls for the auxiliary discipline of 'theological Judaistics' as an academic aid both in biblical studies and in systematic, historical and practical 'theology', 'which makes possible a Christian theology which is free of antisemitism and is bound up with Judaism'. U.Wilckens ('Glaube nach urchristlichem und frühjüdischem Verständnis' [above, 111]) stresses that the theology of the early church and especially Pauline theology are to be seen as being in continuity with the tradition of Old Testament and early Christian faith (cf. e.g. for the Our Father as a Jewish prayer H.Haag, 'Jesus von Nazareth und die Tradition seines Volkes', in *Von der Kraft*, ed. E.Klausener [above, 93], 45-67 = *FrRu* 18, 1966, 45-50 = ET 'Jesus and His People's Tradition', *Bridge* V, 1970, 171-89; A.Vögtle, 'Das Vaterunser – ein Gebet für Juden und Christen', in *Das Vaterunser. Gemeinsames im Beten von Juden und Christen*, ed.M.Brocke, J.J.Petuchowski and W.Strolz, Freiburg 1974, 165-95; for Paul e.g. P.von der Osten-Sacken, 'Paulus und das Gesetz', in *Kirchentag 1977* [above, 67], 609-16 = von der Osten-Sacken and Stöhr, *Wegweisung* [above, 67], 59-66 = von der Osten-Sacken, *Anstösse* [above, 80], 60-7; G.Baumbach, 'Der christlich-jüdische Dialog – Herausforderung und neue Erkenntnisse', *Kairos* 23, 1981, 2-16, and also the literature mentioned on 92ff. above). However, von der Osten-Sacken recognizes clearly enough that more is involved: 'What all the parts of Ruether's investigation are concerned with can be summed up under the heading of the need for theological renunciation of possessions on the part of theology and the church for the salvation of Jews and Gentiles' (Postscript, 246). If such a renunciation is thought to be theologically irresponsible (for criticism cf. also E.Grässer, 'Antijudaismus bei Bultmann?', *WPKG* 67, 1978, [419-29] 420-3 = id., *Der alte Bund* [above, 91], [201-11], 201-4), the discussion with Judaism must be over the legitimacy of the two-sided interpretation of scripture.

Clearly the theological dialogue with Judaism over Holy Scripture has hardly started. H. Schmid ('Die christlich-jüdische Auseinandersetzung um das Alte Testament in hermeneutischer Sicht', *Jud* 26, 1970, [129-77: published separately, SJK 1, Zurich 1971], 176f./52f.) points out that so far a common basis has been found only in the philological-historical sphere: this would be the foundation only for a 'solidarity of scholars' (similarly M.Stone, in 'Bibelinterpretation und der Nahe Osten. Eine Konsultation zwischen Juden und Christen in Jerusalem', in *Von Vorurteilen zum Verständnis*, ed. F.von Hammerstein, Frankfurt am Main 1976, [76-121] 78-87, 86 – For the theme cf. also S.Sandmel, 'Jewish and Christian Biblical Scholarship', in *Torah and Gospel*, ed.Scharper [above, 78], 63-79; R.E.Murphy, 'Present Biblical Scholarship as a Bond of Understanding', in ibid., 81-96). Of course it is to be regretted that Judaism itself has not yet even begun to develop a 'theology of the Old Testament' in the real sense (cf. M.H.Goshen-Gottstein, 'Christianity, Judaism and Modern Bible Study', *Congress Volume Edinburgh 1974*, SVT 28, Leiden 1975, 69-88; id., 'Jewish Biblical Theology and the Study of Biblical Religion', *Tarbiz* 50, 1980/81, 37-84 [in Hebrew; English summary, IIf.] – the theme was recently the subject of a symposium at the opening of the Eighth Jewish World Congress, Jerusalem 1981). Henrix ('Ökumene' [above, 98], 222ff.) also points out that for a Jew, dialogue with Christianity can usually be of interest, if at all, not from a theological, but exclusively from a cultural perspective (cf. also M.Vogel, 'The Problem of Dialogue between Judaism and Christianity', *JES* 4, 1967, 684-99; S.Talmon, 'Der interkonfessionelle Dialog in Israel. Rückblick und Ausblick', *Imm*, special series 1973, 9-20 [there is an English version of *Immanuel*, published in Jerusalem, of which the German is a translation] – *FrRu* 26, 1974 [140-6], 142; H.Siegman, 'A Decade of Catholic-Jewish Relations: A Reassessment', *JES* 15, 1978, 243-60; Schaeffler, 167f.; Thoma, *Beziehungen* [above, 68], 45, has as a title for one section 'Inhibitions among present-day Jews over the dialogue with Christians'). Within the complex entity that comprises 'Judaism' (cf. also R.Becker, 'Gibt es ein Zeugnis' [above, 114], 14ff.), it is the orthodox circles which are least ready for a conversation. Thus the clear references to divisive factors, which Z.Werblowski presented to the 1980 Rhineland Synod ('Trennendes', *Handreichung* [above, 67], 35ff. = *FrRu* 31, 1979, 20f. [cf. already S.Ben-Chorin, *Das brüderliche Gespräch. Ein Beitrag zum Gespräch zwischen Juden und Christen nach dem Zweiten Vatikanischen Konzil*, Trier 1967, 19ff. = 'Fraternal Dialog', *Bridge* V, 1970, (54-68) 60ff. – His criticism, that this attitude does not serve the truth, 21/62, is more that of an outsider as far as the Jewish side is concerned]), are a warning that sobriety is needed. He makes abundantly clear how strange the Jews find it to think in terms of taking account of Christianity at all (Lenhardt, *Auftrag* [above, 104], 21ff., 77, 130, etc., points to the 'asymmetry' of the relationship of faith as a background to the impossibility of a real dialogue: Jewish faith is not interested in the content of Christian faith, while Christian faith seeks to include Jewish faith. (L.A.Olan, 'Christian-Jewish Dialogue' [above, 100], has a similar standpoint. J.J.Petuchowski, 'A Jewish Response to "Israel as a Theological Problem in the Christian Church"' [by H.Berkhof, cf. above, 71], *JES* 6, 1969, [348-53], 348, can even confess: 'I am still of a divided mind on the question whether a special concern with the Jews on the part of the Church would necessarily be desirable.') However, there is Jewish criticism of this attitude in P.Lapide, *Juden und Israel*, *ThMed* 42, Zurich, Einsiedeln and Cologne 1976, 31ff.). M.Stone (op.cit., 87), notes: 'The extreme, pro-Israeli attitude of some Protestant Christians is alien to Judaism, not because of their eschatology but because the Jewish self-understanding is not apocalyptic. The basic attitude is different.'

Thus the conversation with Judaism over the Old Testament is not free from serious burdens. It remains open how far they can be lessened in the future. Earlier statements on the group of problems (H.W.Wolff, 'Das Alte Testament, die Juden und die Christen', in id., *Wegweisung*, Munich 1965, 47-53; S.Amsler, *Jud* 1961 [above, 13], 24-39) essentially begin from a christocentric hermeneutic which consistently makes the church the sole legitimate heir to the Old Testament. S.Ben-Chorin ('Juden und Christen' [above, 99], 36) rightly observes that the testimony of the Old Testament to Christ becomes visible only to a pneumatic exegesis, i.e. one whose judgments are in the light of Christian faith: 'The substance of the faith of the Jew... is never touched on by a christological exegesis of the Old Testament.' On the other hand, W.Zimmerli ('Wir Christen und die Juden', in *Der Auftrag der Kirche in der modernen Welt. FS E. Brunner*, Zurich 1959, 325-31 = *Deutscher Evangelischer Kirchentag München 1959. Dokumente*, Stuttgart 1959, 707-13 = id., *Israel und die Christen. Hören und Fragen*, Neukirchen 1964 [²1980], [9-16] 13) speaks of a community of hearers which binds us together as a community of brothers because God addresses us from the Old Testament in the same way – though otherwise the name of Jesus Christ separates us. Whereas in 1961 G.Harder (*Christen vor dem Problem der Judenfrage*, 255ff.) was still predominantly thinking in terms of points of controversial theology with specifically soteriological content, avant-garde theologians (like R.Rendtorff) have more recently come to envisage discussions of specifically Old Testament themes that are theologically topical, like creation, environment, social ethics and personal piety. Rendtorff ('Das "Ende" der Geschichte Israels', in *Gesammelte Studien zum Alten Testament*, Munich 1975, 267-76) sees a 'twofold outcome' of the Old Testament in history (275, cf. also id., in Gollwitzer, Rendtorff and Levinson, *Thema* [above, 77], 29: 'a double sequel'), i.e. in Christianity and in Judaism. Only a *theological* decision could be made about the legitimacy of one or other historical course, and that would also have to take seriously the Jewish understanding of the Bible ('Die jüdische Bibel' [above, 120], 115). In this connection it cannot be ignored that the Talmudic interpretation of the Bible is an integral part of Jewish tradition which has to be included in any Christian-Jewish discussion of Holy Scripture (cf.e.g.Schwarzschild, 'Judaism', 1964 [above, 103], 269f.). F.Hesse, *KuD* 1981 (above, 55) criticizes biblical theology which is orientated on the history of tradition for having to leave open the legitimacy of the two 'connecting traditions' (194); according to him it is only the break in the history of tradition brought about in the Christ event (196) that produces the decision. We cannot expect that there will be partners for such a conversation available within Judaism outside a narrow circle which is prepared for dialogue (like S.Ben-Chorin [see his bibliography in *FS Ben-Chorin*, above, 82, 195-202], D.Flusser and P.Lapide [for him cf. P.Höffken, 'Der Dialog wird immer intensiver. Lapides Impulse zum christlich-jüdischen Gespräch', *LM* 20, 1981, 562-65; cf. most recently on the whole subject

P.Lapide, 'Das christlich-jüdische Religionsgespräch', in *FS Gollwitzer* [above, 108], 40-8). – For the possibilities and also the difficulties of a Christian-Jewish dialogue on scripture see also the Jewish statement by M.Greenberg, 'On Sharing the Scriptures', in *Magnalia Dei. The Mighty Acts of God. In Memoriam G.E.Wright*, Garden City, NY 1976, 455-63 (cf.also id., 'Can Modern Critical Bible Scholarship have a Jewish Character?', *Imm* 15, 1982/3, 7-12), the collected volume *Juden und Christen*, ed.H.Kremers (above, 60), especially the contribution by Kremers himself (cf. ibid.), and Y.Aschkenasy and W.A.C.Whitlau, *Jüdische Bibelauslegung*, 46-61, with their widely divergent basic hermeneutical presuppositions.

Cf. further J.Jocz, *Theology of Election* (above, 80), esp.52ff.; id., *Spiritual History* (above, 98); H.-J. Kraus, *Begegnung mit dem Judentum*, Hamburg 1963; id., 'Jüdisches und christliches Verständnis der Hebräischen Bibel', *Chr.-jüd. Forum* 52, 1980, 1-12; W.Wirth, 'Der ökumenische Aspekt der Begegnung mit dem Judentum', in *Judentum*, ed. C.Thoma, (above, 85), 143-60; S.Herrmann, 'Die Schlüsselfunktion des Alten Testaments im ökumenischen Dialog', *US* 31, 1976, 109-17; N.P.Levinson, 'Das "Alte" Testament als Heilige Schrift der Juden', ibid., 118-24; R.Rendtorff, 'Wie neu ist das Alte Testament? Partnerschaftliche Zuwendung zur gemeinsamen Bibel', *LM* 15, 1976, 253; M.Brocke, 'Von jüdischer Weise, die Schrift auszulegen', *LebZeug* 32, 1977, 109-25; M.Wyschogrod, 'Judaism and Evangelical Christianity', in *Evangelicals and Jews in Conversation*, ed.M.H.Tanenbaum (above, 22), 34-52; B.Martin, 'Scriptural Authority, Scriptural Interpretation and Jewish-Christian Relations', ibid., 206-12 (for a liberal critical Jewish view of Scripture); the collected volume *Biblical Studies* [above, 101], ed. L.Boadt et al.: not only the introduction by Boadt, 1-15, but also especially the contributions of S.D.Sperling, 'Judaism and Modern Biblical Research', 19-44; A.Lacoque, 'The "Old Testament" in the Protestant Tradition', 210-46; J.Blenkinsopp, 'Tanach and the New Testament: A Christian Perspective', 96-119; cf. also id., 'Old Testament Theology and the Jewish-Christian Connection', *JSOT* 28, 1984, 3-15; H.Schmid, 'Erwägungen zur christlichen Hermeneutik des Alten Testaments unter

Beachtung der "bleibenden Erwählung Israels'", *Jud* 37, 1981, 16-30; Preuss, *Predigt* (above, 10), 146ff.

Exeler ('Verhältnis' [above, 65], 246ff.) has summarized some consequences for theological reflection which would follow from beginning a serious conversation with present-day Judaism: 1. 'God did not revoke the covenant with his people' (247). In reflecting on the statements in the Old Testament which relate to the connection between the unfaithfulness of the people and God's punishment of his people on the one hand and the faithfulness of God and his guarantee that the promise will remain in force on the other, it is important to take into account the corresponding texts in the New Testament, especially those in Paul, and from there reflect on the relationship between the church and Judaism in the context of God's universal will for salvation against the background of the Christ event. 2. If (according to Eph.2.14-16) the Christians from the Gentiles are 'an extension of Israel and not a replacement for it' (255), an important starting point follows both for the relationship of the Testaments and for conversation with present-day Judaism. 3. However, this conversation (which may in no way bracket off the testimony to Christ) must also put in proper proportion the popular understanding of the theological content of the Old Testament, which in many respects is still distorted (say in the matter of the 'law', where more recent exegetical theological insights about the interconnection of gift and task, justification by faith, which is already known to the Old Testament, and so on, need to be taken fully into account; cf. here especially R.Rendtorff, 'Die hebräische Bibel als Grundlage christlich-theologischer Aussagen über das Judentum', in *Jüdische Existenz* [above, 94], ed. M.Stöhr, 32-47); similarly, on the other side, the Christian caricature of the nature of modern Jewish piety (cf. on this C.Klein, *Theologie und Antijudaismus. Eine Studie zur deutschen theologischen Literatur der Gegenwart*, ACJD 6, Munich 1975 = ET *Anti-Judaism in Christian Theology*, Philadelphia and London 1978; D.Flusser, 'Bemerkungen eines Juden zur christlichen Theologie des Judentums', *CiW*, 6.ser.4 a/b, Aschaffenburg 1978, 6-32). In all this we are only just at the beginning.

If one chose a middle way, in which justice was done both to what separates Christians and Jews and to what they have in common, it would be possible to introduce R.Rendtorff's comment (*Emuna*

1966 [above, 106]) that the really decisive starting point for such a conversation must be that by the appearance of Jesus, participation in Israel's experiences of God has become possible also for us non-Jews (M.Barth, *Broken Wall* [above, 95], takes things a little further: 'As [younger] brothers of the Jews, Christians enter an unchangeable constitution and order. They are incorporated into the God-given way in which the house of God is ordered'), just as Christians can regard this experience of God as having reached its goal only by the one way of Jesus Christ. (Thus e.g. Harder, *LR* 1964 [above, 103], 413-26: 'If Judaism is still... God's people, then its cult is worship of the living and true God.' However, 'conversation with Judaism cannot pass over the one through whom alone we Christians have found access to the living God as a partner in this conversation, namely Christ' [417]. Similarly also M.K.Hellwig, [above, 101]). During the last years there were several, more or less speculative, but at all events stimulating attempts at a new form of christology including the Old Testament heritage and open to a dialogue with contemporary Judaism; cf. especially F-W.Marquardt, *Die Gegenwart des Auferstandenen* (above, 120); the works of J.T.Pawli-kowski (esp. *Christ in the Christian-Jewish Dialogue* [above, 79]); E.Schillebeeckx, *Jezus* (above, 89; cf. also R.Schreiter, 'Christology in the Jewish-Christian Encounter: An Essay Review of Edward Schillebeeckx' *Jezus. Het Verhaal van een Levende*', *JAAR* 44, 1976, 693-703; H.Dickerhoff, *Wege ins Alte Testament und zurück*, EHS.T 211, Frankfurt am Main, Berne and New York 1983, 98ff.) – By contrast Jewish voices speak only of a 'Jesuology' (Lapide, *ThMed* 42 [above, 123], 63ff. S.Ben-Chorin, 'Jüdische Fragen' [above, 87], 142/16/67, puts it this way: 'the faith *of Jesus*... unites us but belief *in* Jesus divides us.'). Rendtorff also stresses as a common feature the fact that this is the experience, or the tradition, 'of the *one* God who is really God' (*Emuna* 1966, 108; similarly e.g. Lapide, *ThMed* 42, 35. L.Klein, introduction to S.Ben-Chorin, *Judentum und Christentum im technologischen Zeitalter*, Freising, etc. 1972, 7, speaks in this context of a 'monotheistic oecumene'). This corresponds precisely to the opening thesis of the 1975 German Protestant church study and is also reflected in other statements about the foundations of a possible Christian-Jewish dialogue (cf. e.g. the programmatic preface by J.J.Dougherty to *The Bridge*: 'The One God', *The Bridge* 1, 1955, 15-19 – cf. also J.C.Schoonefeld, 'Israel and the Church in Face of God: A Protestant Point of View', *Imm* 3, 1973/4,

80-3, for whom 'God who is in search of man' is the only common background for both religions. However, here too there are serious problems which go back to the incarnatory christology and doctrine of the Trinity in the early church, the foundations for which were already laid in the New Testament and which indicate a difference even extending to the understanding of God (cf. e.g. G.Lindeskog, 'Jüdischer und christlicher Monotheismus – ein dialogisches Problem', in *Der Herr ist einer*, ed. K.-J.Illmann and J.Thuren [above, 87], 66-80 [with bibliography]; P.Lapide and W.Pannenberg, *Judentum und Christentum. Einheit und Unterschied*, KT, Munich 1981; C.Thoma, 'Theologie ohne Judenfeindschaft' [above, 118], 22ff.; cf. id., *Christliche Theologie* [above, 119], esp.186-96; also W.Schrage, 'Ja und Nein – Bemerkungen eines Neutestamentlers zur Diskussion von Christen und Juden', *EvTh* 42, 1982, [126-51] 137; id., in *'Niemand kommt zum Vater...' Kirchentag 1981* [above, 107], 597, 601f. – N.P.Levinson, 'Eine Entgegnung', in Gollwitzer, Rendtorfff and Levinson, *Thema*, 94f., makes it clear that christology is the decisive, unbridgable point of difference between Judaism and Christianity. See also Lenhardt, *Auftrag* [above, 104], 130; Volken, *Jesus* [above, 81], 184ff., stresses the aspects of the christology of Chalcedon which mention Jesus the man and the Jew. Similarly already B.Dupuy, 'What Meaning has the Fact that Jesus was Jewish for a Christian?', *Conc* 98, 1974, 73-9. If one follows von der Osten-Sacken, *Grundzüge*, 72f. and passim, esp.182f., in deliberately advocating an adoptionist christology, the difference would be lessened – but can that be justified?). So the Christian-Jewish conversation, too, ends up in biblical theology, or rather, it is a perspective within it which cannot be abandoned. Many wrong verdicts on the relationship between the Testaments in fact rest on an inadequate knowledge of Judaism in the New Testament period and also of present-day forms of Jewish piety (for the picture of Jews as an 'outside group' in American confessional teaching cf. B.E.Olson, *Faith and Prejudice*, New Haven and London 1963, 168ff.). Indirectly they have also led to numerous misinterpretations of the Old Testament itself brought about by dogmatic factors (cf. also Schaeffler [above, 104] and as a Jewish voice: N.Fuchs-Kreimer, 'Christian Old Testament Theology: A Time for New Beginnings', *JES* 18, 1981, 76-92). Henrix (*Ökumene aus Juden und Christen* [above, 98]) rightly observes: 'The adoption of the Christian-Jewish dialogue corrects the unconscious "Marcionitism" in ecumenical theology.'

The possibility that the biblical promise of land continues to be valid is a particularly difficult area here (for the Old Testament perspectives cf. A.Ohler, *Israel, Volk und Land*, Stuttgart 1979). So, in particular, is the existence of the state of Israel (for this cf. e.g. S.Ben-Chorin, *Die Antwort des Jona*, Hamburg 1956, esp.45ff.; id., 'Die heilsgeschichtliche Komponente Israels im Lichte des christlich-jüdischen Dialogs', in *Jahrbuch der Evangelischen Akademie Tutzing* 14, 1964/5, 22-39 = id., *Jüdische Existenz heute*, Trier 1967, 39-58). For some believing Jews it is central (cf. e.g. I. Greenberg, 'Cloud of Smoke, Pillar of Fire: Judaism, Christianity, and Modernity after the Holocaust', in *Auschwitz*, ed. E.Fleischner [above, 79], [7-55] 48ff.; P.Lapide, *ThMed* 42 [above, 123], 12f.), others reject it, while secularized Jews and atheists welcome the modern democratic state or steer clear of it (S.Ben-Chorin [*Das brüderliche Gespräch*, above, 123, 11f., cf. 29] points to the lack of an awareness of election among many present-day Jews). The dispute in Judaism itself, which is accentuated by present-day controversies involving parties and groups in everyday Israelite politics (cf. e.g. the discussion reported in *FrRu* 27, 1975, 175-81, between Y.Leibowitz and Z.Yaron on the one hand and Y.Amital on the other, over the eschatological significance of the Yom-Kippur war) commends restraint on the Christian side (cf. also R.Rendtorff, 'Hat sich unser Israel-Engagement gewandelt?', in *FS Gollwitzer* [above, 108], 155-66). Christian authors show the same breadth of opinions between the extremes: they hold either that the Old Testament promise of land is transcended in a higher fulfilment through the universalism of the Christian message and that the modern state of Israel is a purely secular construction, or that the promise continues unchanged and is already beginning to be realized in the foundation of the state in Palestine.

Bibliography

Faccio, G., 'Sionismo e Sacre Scritture', *TS (I)*, March 1950, 78-86; Demann, P., 'Le rassemblement des dispersés d'après la Bible', *CSion* 4, 1950, 92-110; id., 'Signification de l'Etat d'Israël', *CSion* 5, 1951, 32-43; Muñoz Iglesias, S., 'Origen de la creencia vulgar en las pretendidas profecías sobre la no restauración política de Israel', *EstB* 10, 1951, 403-33; Macanna, R.C., 'The Emergence of the State of Israel and its Significance for the Christian Church', in *Church*, ed. Hedenquist (above, 80), 77-90; Flannery, E.H., 'Theological Aspects of the State of Israel', *Bridge* III, 1958, 301-24; Stamm, J.-J., *Der Staat Israel und die Landverheissung der Bibel*, Zurich and Frankfurt ²1961; Harder, G., *Christen vor dem Problem* (above, 124), 264-6; Hertzberg, H.W., 'Theologische Bemerkungen zum Israelproblem', *GWU* 10, 1959, 162-74 = id., *Beiträge zur Traditionsgeschichte und Theologie des Alten Testaments*, Göttingen 1962, 134-47; Kraus, H.-J., *Begegnung* (above, 125), 80-95; Marquardt, F.-W., *Die Bedeutung der biblischen Landverheissungen für die Christen*, ThExH 116, Munich 1964; id., *Die Juden und ihr Land*, Siebenstern-Tb 189, Hamburg 1975; Zimmerli, W., 'Das heutige Israel', *Die Sammlung* 8, 1953, 107-81 = id., *Israel und die Christen* (above, 124), 31-46; id., 'Der Staat Israel – Erfüllung biblischer Verheissungen?', in *Israel und die Christen*, 71-91; Spaemann, H., *Die Christen* (above, 81), 7f., 20f.; Molinski, W. (ed.). *Unwiderrufliche Verheissung* (above, 81); Lüthi, L., 'Die biblische Botschaft vom Heiligen Land in ihrer aktuellen Bedeutung für die Christenheit', in C.Thoma, *Auf den Trümmern* (above, 85), 15-31; Duvernoy, C., *Le prince et le prophète*, Jerusalem 1966 (²1967) = ET *The Prince and the Prophet* (T.Herzl and W.Hechler), Fleurier, Switzerland 1979, ch.1; Heschel, A.J., *Israel: An Echo of Eternity*, New York 1967 (³1969); Diamond, M.L., 'Christian Silence on Israel: An End to Dialogue?', *Jdm* 16, 1967, 411-22 = *The Death of Dialogue*, ed.Seltzer and Stackhouse (above, 93), 19-39; Frutiger, S., et al., 'Israël. Un dossier sur diverses options exégétiques et théologiques', *FV* 5, 1967, 51-84; Agus, J., 'Israel and the Jewish-Christian Dialogue', *JES* 6, 1969, 18-36; Berkhof, H., ibid., 329 (above, 71); Petuchowski, J.J., ibid., 348-53 (above, 71); Stendahl, K., *EK* 1969 (above, 86), 77f.; Thoma, C., *Kirche aus Juden und Heiden. Biblische Informationen über das Verhältnis der Kirche zum Judentum*, Konfrontation no.8, Vienna, Freiburg and Basle 1970, 117-55; Eckert, W.P., Levinson, N.P. and Stöhr, M., *Jüdisches Volk – gelobtes Land. Die biblischen Landverheissungen als Problem des jüdischen Selbstverständnisses und der christlichen Theologie*, ACJD 3, Munich 1970 (from this F.-W.Marquardt, *Christentum und Zionismus*, 241-74 = *EvTh* 28, 1968, 629-60 = id., *Verweg-*

enheiten, Munich 1981, 165-201); Petuchowski, J.J., 'The Dialectics of Salvation History', *Bridge* V, 1970, 69-78, esp.76f.; Eckardt, A.R. and A.L, *Encounter With Israel: A Challenge to Conscience*, New York 1970, esp.241ff.; Oesterreicher, J.M., 'The Theologian and the Land of Israel', in *Brothers in Hope (The Bridge* V), 1970, 231-43; Weber, H.R., 'The Promise of the Land. Biblical Interpretation and the Present Situation in the Middle East', *StEnc* 7, No.4, 1971, 1-16; U.Tal, 'Jewish Self-Understanding and the Land and State of Israel', with responses by J.J.Petuchowski, R.L.Rubenstein and A.Hertzberg, *USQR* 16, 1971, 351-81; Marquardt, F.-W., 'Gottes Bundestreue und die biblischen Landverheissungen', in *Jüdische Hoffnungskraft*, ed. W.Strolz (above, 97), 80-133 = id., *Verwegenheiten*, 202-45; id., 'Israel, Judentum, Zionismus als Fragen an die Kirche', in id, *Verwegenheiten*, 281-310; Finn, J., 'Christians, Jews and Israel', in *Root and Branch*, ed. M.Zeik and M.Siegel (above, 85), 133-47; Klein, C., 'The Theological Dimensions of the State of Israel', *JES* 10, 1973 ,700-15; Rendtorff, R., 'Der Staat Israel und die Christen', *ZW* 45, 1974, 183-96 = *Chr.-jüd.Forum* 47, 1975, 1-14; Davies, W.D., *The Gospel and the Land. Early Christianity and Jewish Territorial Doctrine*, Berkeley, Los Angeles and London 1974; Neher, A., 'Die Haltung Israel gegenüber: Staat, Land und Volk. Ein jüdischer Standpunkt', *Conc* (German ed.; at this time not all *Conc* issues were translated into English) 10, 1974, 580-4; Davies, A., 'Die Haltung... Ein christlicher Standpunkt', ibid., 585-9; von Waldow, H.E., 'Israel and Her Land: Some Theological Considerations', in *A Light unto My Path. FS J.M.Myers*, Philadelphia 1974, 493-508; Fleischner, E.M., 'The Religious Significance of Israel: A Christian Perspective', *NCW* 217, 1974, 18-23 = *Jewish-Christian Relations*, ed.R.Heyer (above, 89), 17-25; Hals, R.M., 'The Promise and the Land', in *Speaking of God*, ed. Opsahl and Tanenbaum (above, 116), 57-72; Werblowsky,Z., 'The People and the Land', in ibid., 73-80; Rendtorff, R., *Israel und sein Land. Theologische Überlegungen zu einem politischen Problem*, ThExH 188, Munich 1975; Judant, *Jalons*, 41ff., 65ff., 96f., 115f.; Kirsch, *We Christians* (above, 101), 112-21; Hammerstein, F.von (ed.), *Von Vorurteilen* (above, 122), 87-105; Osten-Sacken, P. von der (ed.), *Zionismus. Befreiungsbewegung des jüdischen Volkes*, Berlin 1977; Brueggemann, W., 'Tiefe dogmatische Verhärtungen. Zum Stand des

Dialoges zwischen Juden und Christen', *LM* 18, 1979, 654-7 = *Chr.-jüd. Forum* 52, 1980, 25-30 = 'Vom Nutzen des Judentums für die Kirche', in id., *Anstösse* (above, 80), 139-44; id., *The Land*, Philadelphia 1977; Gollwitzer, H., Rendtorff, R. and Levinson, N.P., *Thema: Juden -Christen – Israel* (above, 77), 56-79; Mosis, R. (ed.), *Exil – Diaspora – Rückkehr. Zum theologischen Gespräch zwischen Juden und Christen*, Düsseldorf 1978; Mayer, R., 'Leiderfahrung in der Diaspora – Heilserfahrung im Israelland', in *FS Ben-Chorin* (above, 82), 183-93; Mussner, *Traktat* (above, 77), 26ff.; Stöhr, M. (ed.), *Zionismus*, Munich 1980; Pawlikowski, *What are They Saying...?* (above, 73), 109ff.; id., *Christ in the Light of the Christian-Jewish Dialogue* (above, 79), 127ff.; Haag, H., 'Die Auferstehung Israels und der christliche Glaube', in id., *Buch des Bundes* (above, 16), 275-88; J.Moltmann, in Lapide and Moltmann, *Israel und Kirche* (above, 68), 38-40; Lapide, ibid., 75-7; Honecker, M., *KuD* 1981 (above, 68), 207-11; Pfisterer, R., 'Grundvoraussetzungen der Begegnung zwischen Juden und Christen', *ThG (B)* 24, 1981, 1-13, esp. 8ff.; Grässer, E., *FS Mussner* (above, 96), 415 n.13 = id., *Der alte Bund* (above, 90), 216 n.13; Pawlikowski, *Christ in the Light*, 127-33; Westermann, C., 'Die Landverheissung im Alten Testament und ihre Bedeutung für die Gegenwart', *US* 38, 1983, 91-8 = id., *Erträge der Forschung am Alten Testament. Gesammelte Studien III*, TB 73, Munich 1984, 88-95.

7. The Problem of the Canon

The theological significance of the Old Testament canon poses a special problem within Old Testament theology, but it has only been brought into greater prominence in recent times. (The question of the canon already became the centre of interest at a consultation of the Faith and Order Commission in Boldern in 1968, cf. the report by J.Barr, 'The Authority of the Bible. A Study Outline', *ER* 21, 1969, [135-50] 141). This heightened attention is connected with the growing interest in a revival of biblical theology, with the problems of which the question of the canon clearly has a close connection.

First of all there is a historical dimension to the question of the Old Testament canon, which at times has been the focus of controversy in recent years. In some respects the accepted view about the origin and completion of the Old Testament canon which has prevailed over a long period (cf. e.g. R.Meyer, 'Κρύπτω C. Beilage: Kanonisch und apokryph im Judentum', *TWNT* III, 979-87 = 'Supplement on Canon and the Apocrypha', *TDNT* III, 978-87; id., 'Bemerkungen zum literargeschichtlichen Hintergrund der Kanontheorie des Josephus', in *Josephus-Studien. FS O.Michel*, Göttingen 1974, 285-99; O.Eissfeldt, *Einleitung in das Alte Testament*, Tübingen ³1964, 765-73 = ET *The Old Testament. An Introduction*, Oxford 1965, 560-70) has been put in question. The deep-seated and extremely important theological difference between the rabbinic canon (which was later taken over by the Reformers) and the canon of the early church (finally established as binding on the Roman Catholic church at the Council of Trent), which was enlarged by the addition of the so-called Apocrypha, was explained by two historical hypotheses, both of which have proved questionable. The first of these hypotheses was that the Hebrew canon was still open in the New Testament period and at a synod arranged in Jabneh (Jamnia) by the rabbinic authorities about AD 100 was officially limited to the books which are now contained in the Massoretic Bible (this was also a defensive measure against Christian claims to the Old Testament). After that, doubt remained over the canonical worth of just a few books, but this gradually died away. Since J.P.Lewis ('What Do We Mean By Jabneh?, *JBR* 32, 1964, 125-32 = *The Canon and Masorah of the Hebrew Bible*, ed. S.Z.Leiman, New York 1974, 115-41) cast substantial doubts on the existence of such an assembly (cf. recently also R.C.Newman, 'The Council of Jamnia and the Old Testament Canon', *WTJ* 38, 1975, 319-50; P.Schäfer, 'Die sogenannte Synode von Jabne', *Jud* 31, 1975, 54-64, 116-24), such an event has proved improbable. By contrast, T.N.Swanson (*The Closing of the Collection of the Holy Scriptures*, Diss. Vanderbilt University, Nashville 1970, University Microfilms) has produced good reasons for supposing that the Masoretic canon was fixed at the latest among the Pharisees in Palestine round about AD 50, along with a normative form of the text: probably even before the appearance of Jesus. S.Z.Leiman, *The Canonization of Hebrew Scripture: The Talmudic and Midrashic Evidence*, 1976, esp. 125ff., produces convincing material to support the theory that the inspired canon was already closed at the time of the Maccabees (for the difference between 'canonical' and 'inspired' see ibid., 127ff.). If the hypotheses put forward by Swanson and Leiman are correct, this also does away with the second hypothesis, about the origin of the form of the canon, expanded by the so-called apocrypha, which was taken over by the Western church. The traditional view here (which can already be found in J.S.Semler, *Abhandlung von freier Untersuchung des Canons* I, Halle 1771) was that the canon goes back to the Alexandrian canon of Hellenistic Diaspora Judaism. Against this, A.C.Sundberg (*The Old Testament of the Early Church*, Cambridge, Mass. 1964; cf. id., 'The Old Testament in the Early Church', *HTR* 51, 1958, 206-26; id., in 'A Symposium on the Canon of Scripture', *CBQ* 28, 1966, [189-207] 194-203; id., 'The Old Testament: A Christian Canon', *CBQ* 30, 1968, 143-55 = *The Canon*, ed. Leiman [above, 133], 99-111) had claimed that the early church found in Palestine a Jewish canon which was still open, with the insertion of some books which were later declared apocryphal; thus the canon of the Western church originated in primitive Palestinian Christianity (for a discussion see e.g. the review by R.A.Kraft, *JBL* 85, 1966, 258f.; L.Harris, 'Was the Law and the Prophets Two Thirds of the Old Testament Canon?', *JETS* 9, 1966, 163-71; N.L.Geisler, 'The Extent of the Old Testament Canon', in *Current Issues in Biblical and Patristical Interpretation. Studies... M.C.Tenney*, ed. F.Hawthorne, Grand Rapids, Mich 1975, 31-45). In contrast to the relatively early completion of the Jewish canon, the formation of the Western canon (cf. A.Jepsen, 'Kanon und Text des Alten Testaments', *TLZ* 74, 1949, 65-74) was a relatively lengthy process (for the whole complex of problems and the following discussion see the further contributions by Leiman, op.cit., and J.K.West, 'Rethinking the Old Testament Canon', *RelLife* 45, 1976, 22-33; also the stimulating theory of A.Lemaire, *Les écoles et la formation de la Bible dans l'ancien Israël*, OBO 39, Göttingen 1981, who argues that the canonical Bible originated from old Israelite school practice).

Dogmatic decisions on the extent of the canon were only made at a relatively late stage: first of all at the Council of Florence in 1441 in favour of the expanded canon (confirmed at Trent, cf. *EnchB* 57-60); and by Luther in favour of the Massoretic canon for the Reformation (although the so-called Apocrypha only disappeared slowly from editions of the Bible, a process lasting into the twentieth century). In theological terms, that means that the canon (and the same is true of the New Testament) came into being first in ancient Israel as a result of the practical use of certain books containing sacred tradition (S.Sandmel, 'Symposium', 205, speaks of a 'logical development, but also as determined by fortuitous circumstance') and then in the early church; so far ecumenical agreement as to its limits has yet to be achieved. (Geisler, op.cit., 31, regrets that Vatican II also again indirectly confirmed the decision of Trent.)

The significance of the canon as being also a central factor for theology was recently discovered above all in the American discussion (cf. [as also for what follows] J.Mays, 'Historical and Canonical: Recent Discussion about the Old Testament and Christian Faith', in *Magnalia Dei* [above, 125], 510-28); J.K.West even thinks that in recent years it has attracted most attention (op.cit., 22). The most significant factor in this development was the call issued by B.S.Childs in his book *Biblical Theology in Crisis* ([above, 2] 99ff.) that biblical theology, which in his view was now in a state of crisis, should make a new beginning on the basis of the canon of the Old and New Testament seen as having been not so much *created* by a church authority, as having been *recognized* (105) as a *normative* basis by the church in the light of the divine authority of its scriptures (cf. also id., 'The Old Testament as Scripture of the Church', *CTM* 43, 1972, 709-22; id., 'The Exegetical Significance of Canon for the Study of the Old Testament', *SVT* 29, 1978, 66-80; id., 'The Canonical Shape of the Prophetic Literature', *Int* 32, 1978, 46-55; cf. also G.T.Sheppard, 'Canon Criticism: The Proposal of Brevard Childs and an Assessment for Evangelical Hermeneutics', *SBT* 4, 1974, 3-17; similarly R.E.Murphy, 'The Old Testament as Word of God', in *FS Myers* [above, 52], 367-74; cf. more recently also R.Rendtorff, 'Zur Bedeutung des Kanons für eine Theologie des Alten Testaments', in *'Wenn nicht jetzt, wann dann?'*, FS H.-J.Kraus, Neukirchen-Vluyn 1983, 3-11). Here he was deliberately opposing the older school, represented above all at that time in the USA by G.E.Wright (*The Old Testament and Theology*, New York 1969, 166-85), which had looked for a 'canon in the canon' or a 'centre' of scripture (cf. *Problems of Old Testament Theology*, 125ff.) and precisely in so doing had found themselves in what Childs believed to be the crisis about which he was complaining.

This demand did not come out of the blue. It had been prepared for above all by observations made by exegetes, especially in redaction criticism. In contrast to the efforts of earlier schools of literary and tradition criticism, who had attached importance to working out the earliest literary strata of the text and the most basic units which underlay it, together with the way in which they had been used in theology, this approach had taken into consideration the 'Nachgeschichte' (cf. H.W.Hertzberg, 'Ist Exegese theologisch möglich?', in id., *Beiträge zur Traditionsgeschichte* [above, 130], [101-17] 110) or 'relecture' (the term goes back to A.Gelin, cf. especially 'Comment le peuple d'Israël lisait l'Ancien Testament', in id., *L'Ancien Testament et les Chrétiens*, Paris 1951, 117-31 = id., *Bible et communauté*, in id., *Problèmes d'Ancien Testament*, Lyons 1952, 93-110; id., 'Les quatre lectures du psaume 22', *BVC* 1, 1953, 31-9; id., 'La question des "relectures" bibliques à l'interieur d'une tradition vivante', *Sacra Pagina* I, Paris and Gembloux 1959, 303-15; cf. also A.Robert, 'Littéraires (Genres)', *DBS* V, [405-21] 411ff. However, according to H.Cazelles, 'Une relecture du psaume XXIX?', in *Mémorial A.Gelin*, Le Puy 1961, [119-28] 119 n.1, in verbal communications Gelin made known his preference for the term 'réinterprétation') of the literary units and whole New Testament books as they moved towards the way in which they are used in the present (for this cf. M.Fishbane, 'Revelation and Tradition: Aspects of Inner-biblical Exegesis', *JBL* 99, 1980, 343-61; the catchword 'comparative Midrash' has become a popular term for this in the light of investigations into the methods of rabbinic exegesis: cf. R.Bloch, 'Midrash', *DBS* V, 1955, 1263-81; A.G.Wright, 'The Literary Genre Midrash', *CBQ* 28, 1966, 105-38, 417-57; R.Le Deaut, 'A propos d'une définition du midrash', *Bibl* 50, 1969, 395-413 = ET *Int* 25, 1971, 259-82; M.P.Miller, *JSJ* 1971 [above, 22]; B.S.Childs, 'Psalm Titles and Midrashic Exegesis', *JSS* 16, 1971, 137-50; G.Vermes, 'Bible and Midrash: Early Old Testament Exegesis', *CHB* 1, 199-231). Here attention had also come to be devoted to the use of the Bible in the worship of the synagogue and the early church. This was an academic evaluation of an aspect which seemed to have been eliminated once and for all by historical criticism in its struggle against the dogmatic authority of the Bible and the traditional dogma of inspiration. Thus as early as 1963 P.R.Ackroyd (*Theol* 1963 [above, 1]) had already spoken out against the view that academic exegesis was concerned only with discovering the original view of the individual biblical author: 'The words of a prophet, the narrating of a story, the reciting of a psalm, are all mediated to us through the life and experience of a religious community with a continuity of life, a changing situation and appropriation of the nature of God. The meaning of a passage is limited only by the widest bounds within the real and living context'

(50; cf. also id., 'Original Text and Canonical Text', *USQR* 32, 1977, 166-73, esp. 169ff.). W.C.Smith ('The Study of Religion and the Study of the Bible', *JAAR* 39, 1971, [131-40] 134) sees the real task of those studying religion by means of historical criticism as being the study of the process of synthesis, in the case of the Bible the way in which it became canon and its effect, rather than the exclusively analytical method which had been long dominant. However, an interest with a centrally theological concern sees itself pointed in the same direction; here we should recall A.Jepsen who, as early as 1958 (*Wissenschaft* [above, 27], esp. 29f./31f.), stressed the canon as an important frame of reference for all theological evaluation of the Old Testament, even in its relationship to the New (cf. also above, 134). Finally, on the Catholic side the notion of a 'social' character of the inspiration of scripture has been considered (J.McKenzie, 'Social Character of Inspiration', *CBQ* 24, 1962, 115-24; D.J.McCarthy, 'Personality, Society and Inspiration', *TS* 24, 1963, 553-76); the limitation of inspiration to the final author (or redactor) of the biblical books was transcended in favour of an inclusion of all those who were involved in the process of its origin (cf. P.Benoit, 'Les analogies de l'inspiration', *Sacra Pagina* I, 86-99; id., 'L'inspiration', in *Initation Biblique*, ed. Robert and Tricot [above, 31], 6-45, esp. 25f.) and the canon as a whole was related, in terms of being 'the book of the church', to the community of the earliest church, constituted according to the divine will (cf. K.Rahner, 'Über die Schriftinspiration', *ZKT* 78, 1956, 137-68). In his lecture on 'Inerrancy' ('Die Irrtumslosigkeit' [above, 46]), N.Lohfink asserts that the idea of inspiration and thus inerrancy cannot be related either to the individual writer or to individual books but only to scripture as a whole; here the Christian canon is only brought to a close by the New Testament as the 'last sacred writing' ('Siegeslied' [above, 22], 63) of the Old Testament. To be dogmatically correct one can only speak of an 'inerrancy of the Bible' (65). There is also a consequence for academic exegesis: 'A further process of exegesis must be developed over and above the investigation of the most basic statement, which manages to be a total expression of scripture' (78). This important observation would have to be developed further in the context of a biblical hermeneutics; Lohfink himself stresses, rather, the difficulties in such a course (78ff.). As N.Fuchs-Kreimer, *JES* 18, 1981 (above, 128), 84ff., stresses, a new evaluation of the canonical tradition, especially in its post-exilic stages, would also further the Jewish-Christian dialogue on scripture.

However, Childs had combined his general call to treat the canon as a whole as the basis for a biblical theology with a specific methodological proposal which was soon justifiably criticized (cf. e.g. the review by G.F.Hasel, *AUSS* 10, 1972, 179-83, esp. 182f.): his view was that scholars should start from the Old Testament texts quoted in the New Testament and define their functions in the context of a biblical theology from there. His basic position that the canon as a whole had to serve as the framework for any form of biblical theology was also taken over by J.A.Sanders (*Torah and Canon*, Philadelphia 1972 [²1974], esp. XVf.): in his own way Sanders repeated the statement, 'It is the nature of canon to be contemporized', i.e., 'it is not primarily a source book for the history of Israel, early Judaism, Christ, and the early church, but rather a mirror for the identity of the believing community...'(XV). But he himself called for a new form of canonical criticism (returning to the 'canon in the canon' method, cf. XV), which undertakes to investigate the function of the canon and its parts in the course of the history of its influence (cf. also E.Jacob, 'Principe canonique et formation de l'Ancien Testament', *SVT* 18, 1974, [101-22] 103f.). For Sanders the Torah (the Pentateuch) is the real nucleus of crystallization here, around which the other main parts of the canon, like the prophetic canon and the writings, are to be arranged (for discussion see the review by B.S.Childs, *Int* 27, 1973, 88-91; cf. further Sanders, 'Torah and Christ', *Int* 29, 1975, 372-90; id., 'Adaptable for Life: The Nature and Function of Canon', in *Magnalia Dei* [above, 125], 531-60; id., 'Biblical Criticism and the Bible as Canon', *USQR* 32, 1977, 157-65; id., 'Torah', *IDB.S*, 1976, 909-11; id., 'Torah and Paul', in *God's Christ and his People, FS N.Dahl*, ed. W.Meeks and J.Jervell, Oslo 1977, 132-40; id., 'Bible as Canon', *CCen* 98, 1981, 1250-5; id., *Canon and Community. A Guide to Canonical Criticism*, Philadelphia 1984; cf. also F.W.Spina, 'Canonical Criticism: Childs versus Sanders', in *Interpreting God's Word for Today: An Inquiry into Hermeneutics from a Biblical Theological Perspective*, ed. W.McCown and J.E.Massey, Anderson, Indiana 1982, 165-94; R.P.Carroll, 'Canonical Criticism: A Recent Trend in Biblical Studies', *ExpT* 92, 1980, 73-8. A somewhat different position is to be found in R.E.Clements, 'Covenant and Canon in the Old Testament', in *Creation, Christ and Culture, FS T.F.Torrance*, ed. R.A.McKinney, Edinburgh 1976, 1-12. The Torah as a nucleus for crystallization is also rejected by J.C.Lebram, 'Aspekte der alttestamentlichen Kanonbildung', *VT* 18, 1968, 173-89; J.Conrad, 'Zur Frage nach der Rolle des Gesetzes bei der Bildung des alttestamentlichen Kanons, *ThV* 11, 1979, 11-19. J.D.G.Dunn, 'Levels of Canonical Authority', *HBT* 4, 1982, 13-60, distinguishes four levels of canonical authority which follow one after the other: (*a*) the traditio-historical [the way in which the law books, individual prophetic sayings and so on were regarded as authoritative in an early period]; (*b*) the level of the final composition of individual writings of the OT or NT; (*c*) the level of the canon itself as the real norm [36]; (*d*) the level of the church [the use and interpretation of the canon in synagogue and church]). This produces the view of a canonical process which is characterized by adaptability and stability ('Adaptability and stability. That is canon', in 'Adaptable', 551). According to this, canonical criticism (which according to Sanders, *USQR* 1977, 162, cf.also id., *Canon and Community* [above, 138], 8ff., should be a supplementary exegetical sub-discipline which determines the setting of the Bible in the Christian and Jewish community) would be an extended form of tradition history, not stopping at the individual text but taking account of the canon as a whole (first of all the Old Testament and then the New, since the New Testament cannot be Holy Scripture for Christians without being related to the whole of the canon) – here he goes beyond even the redaction-critical level for the individual books of the Bible. G.T.Sheppard, 'Canonization: Hearing the Voice of the Same God through Histori-cally Dissimilar Traditions', *Int* 36, 1982, 21-33, finds the 'hermeneutical construct' for a total understanding of the canon over and above all the differences of content in (the Torah for the Jewish understanding of the Old Testament and) the Gospel of Jesus Christ for the Christian understanding of the New Testament, whereas the external limitations are only of secondary importance here (P.Beauchamp, *L'un et l'autre Testament*, Paris 1976, has recently put forward an interesting overall programme along these lines on the basis of the principle of 'relecture' [above, 136]). In his review, Childs repeats his assertion that the theologically significant factor is not the history of the origin of the canon and its historical background (which Sanders seeks to elucidate; c.f also D.N.Freedman, 'Canon of the OT', *IDB.S*, 130-6; for J.Blenkinsopp, *Prophecy and Canon*, Notre Dame and London 1977, the prophetic character of the canon, which is intrinsic to the process of its formation, is decisive) but its final form: 'I believe that the witness of the Old Testament lies in the historical shape which the Jews gave their Scriptures and not in the historical processes which gave them a shape' (review, 90; cf. also *SVT* 1978, 67, 68f.).

Childs went on to test his position by actually carrying through the exegesis of a book of the Bible in his Exodus commentary (*The Book of Exodus*, OTL, Philadelphia and London 1974; for the prophetic canon see id., *Int* 1978 [above, 135]) and has also recently presented detailed theoretical justification for it in his *Introduction to the Old Testament as Scripture* (London and Philadelphia 1979; cf. esp. I, II-IV for his theoretical justification of the canon as the basis of a theological exegesis; II, V-X for the implementation of Pentateuchal criticism orientated on the canon. There has recently been discussion of this book in *JSOT* 16, 1980, with contributions by B.Kittel, J.Barr, J.Blenkinsopp, H.Cazelles, G.M.Landes, R.E.Murphy, R.Smend, and a response by B.S.Childs; also in *HBT* 2, 1980, 113-211, with contributions by B.C.Birch, D.A.Knight, J.L.Mays, D.P.Polk, J.A.Sanders and a response by Childs. There are also reviews e.g. by J.F.Priest, *JAAR* 48, 1980, 259-71; W.Harrelson, *JBL* 100, 1981, 99-103; for criticism of Childs see also S.E.McEvenue, 'The Old Testament, Scripture or Theology?', *Int* 55, 1981, 229-43; R.N.Whybray, 'Reflections on Canonical Criticism', *Theol* 84, 1981, 29-35; H.M.Barstad, 'Le canon comme principe exégétique. Autour de la contribution de Brevard S.Childs à une herméneutique de l'Ancien Testament', *StTh* 38, 1984, 77-91).

It is notable that the same contrast recurs in the recent Dutch discussion between the supporters of F.H.Breukelman (who adopts Miskotte's approach) on the one hand and those of the traditional historical-critical school on the other (cf. the report 'Een geschil over de uitleg van het Oude Testament' [above, 57, where the most important literature is also cited]). The trend introduced by Breukelman sees the canon in its final form, on the basis of which the word of proclamation addresses its Christian hearers, as the starting point for all theological and exegetical concern with the Old Testament (historical investigation of the way in which the text came into being is not rejected completely, but it is thought to be of secondary importance); the traditional historical-critical approach wants to retain the usual analytical stages as a presupposition for any theological evaluation. In terms of method the first approach is also influenced by structuralism.

As J.K.West rightly stresses (*RelLife* 1976 [above, 134], 31), it is difficult to choose between the positions of Childs and Sanders. West recalls in this context a comment by G.E.Wright (cf.29) that in any period those parts of the canon are preferred which come nearest to the theological needs of the time, and others are neglected (cf. also D.Ritschl, 'A Plea for the Maxim: Scripture and Tradition', *Int* 25, 1971, [113-28] 124f.) Such a process is even explicitly claimed as legitimate in the approach of R.B.Laurin to the problem ('Tradition and Canon', in *Tradition and Theology in the Old Testament*, ed. D.A.Knight, Philadelphia 1976, [261-74], 272): in ✗ his view any stage in the process of canonization can be authoritative for us, and the final stage, even if it is the New Testament, need not necessarily be more authoritative than, say, the Yahwist, if it comes closer to our Sitz im Leben. However, such an attitude leaves suspiciously open the question as to how far the canon has binding character. Nevertheless, since it represents a fixation of the total tradition of the church, the canon makes it impossible for the ongoing stream of theology through history to push the biblical truth permanently to one side, and constantly enables new corrections to be made in the light of a 'centre', which, if we are to understand the canon as a whole as having a unitary meaning, will in some way remain indispensable. Conversely, the ultimate meaning of an individual text will only be exhausted when it is put against the overall horizon of the canon (cf. Jacob, 'Principe' [above, 138], 120). Here one aspect should not be forgotten to which G.Östborn (*Cult and Canon. A Study in the Canonization of the Old Testament*, UUÅ 1950, 10) has drawn attention (albeit following an approach which has been stamped by the Scandinavian 'cultic pattern' model): the canon has its *Sitz im Leben* in the worship of the Old and New Testament people of God in whom it makes God's words and actions present (cf. also R.C.Leonhardt, *The Origin of Canonicity in the Old Testament*, Diss.Boston University Graduate School, Boston 1972 [University Microfilm], though he assumes the 'covenant renewal festival' as the setting for its elements). Alongside this it must also be remembered (cf. here the remarks of N.W.Porteous, 'Probleme biblischer Theologie' [above, 3], [417-27], 425f.) that the human side of scripture must not be overlooked, either. J.Barr also stresses this human side in his book *The Bible in the Modern World* (above, 9; for criticism cf. also J.A.Sanders, 'Reopening Old Questions about Scripture', *Int* 28, 1974, 321-30). For him the biblical tradition is 'an account of a *human* work. It is *man's* statement of his beliefs, the events he has experienced, the stories he has been told, and so on' (120). The significance of the canon is closely connected with the inadequacy of a pure 'event' theology: the Bible is in a comprehensive sense a source of information in which the interpretations and 'theologies' of the biblical authors are just as significant (75-88). But if the Bible is understood in this way as the living tradition of a variety of witnesses (115 – for canonical pluralism, cf. also Sanders, *CCen* 1981 [above, 138], 1253ff.), the foundation of the canon and its authority in the church and theology follows from the recognition achieved at a specific point that these particular books (and no others) are to be regarded as normative, especially in view of the fact that the decisions were human and therefore also fallible (117ff.). Nevertheless, the thought of the biblical witnesses serves as a model, and therefore has to some degree a binding character, which can be described in terms of the 'spirit' (132). Since in this way a general framework of binding tradition is offered, a 'canon in the canon' which would again restrict this is ruled out (161; cf. more recently also id., *Holy Scripture. Canon, Authority, Criticism*, Oxford 1983, 49ff.; id., *Escaping from Fundamentalism*, London 1984, 41ff.).

On the whole the question of the canon can only be assessed in the context of the problem of a biblical theology generally; the reawakened interest in the canon is closely connected with the revival of the discussion of this comprehensive aspect. Childs's proposal that the starting point should be the Old Testament texts cited in the New Testament, in order to demonstrate by means of a practical example the harmony between the original Old Testament passage and its later interpretation in the New Testament, is as much evidence for this as the opposite proposal by G.E.Wright ('History and Reality: The Importance of Israel's "Historical" Symbols for the Christian Faith', in *The Old Testament and Christian Faith*, ed. B.W.Anderson, New York and London 1963, 176-99), that the starting point should be an Old Testament canon treated as 'dynamic' (187) and considered primarily in historical terms (184f.), and that an answer to the question 'whether the God of Israel is the God and Father of Jesus Christ and our God' (189) should be found in the events reported in the Old Testament, i.e. the history of Israel. At all events, the relationship between the two Testaments remains a key question for all Christian exegetes, even when it comes to discussing how the problem of the Old Testament canon is to be treated. The same also goes for J.Bright (*Authority* [above,2]), who in other respects is still to be counted among the representatives of the old 'biblical theology movement' with his stress on the Israelite understanding of history (130), the structure (137) of the Old Testament which is open to a future in a hope that is still unfulfilled (134), and on salvation history and a permanent identity which becomes visible in the faith of Israel (126). In the last resort, for Bright the significance of the Old Testament can only be determined in the light of the New, which is the 'final arbiter' (52). Here, he argues, it should be noted that the relationship between the two Testaments is complex (197); they are both bound together (by an ongoing unitary structure of faith and the one salvation history) and separated (by the radical newness of the Christ event). In the canon, continuity and discontinuity are interconnected (201).

This new stress on the canon as a decisive aspect of any theology of the Old Testament and indeed of the Bible as a whole which is to do justice to its content has also recently found a way into general accounts like that of R.E.Clements (*Old Testament Theology. A Fresh Approach*, London 1978, 15ff.). Clements stresses the decisive importance of the whole of the Old Testament in its present form, along with its elements, like the Pentateuch, particularly if one recognizes that each of these parts contains very different individual material, which has come into being over the course of many centuries. He refers in particular to the liturgical use of the Bible as an area the theological significance of which so far has been wrongly neglected (18f. – Cf. also B.S.Childs, 'Some Reflections on the Search for a Biblical Theology', *HBT* 4, 1982, [1-12] 7f.). C.Westermann's *Theologie des Alten Testaments in Grundzügen*, Göttingen 1978 represents an attempt to make the canonical structure of the Old Testament as a whole the basis for a 'theology of the Old Testament': according to Westermann, the historical books record the action of God, saving and blessing, in the history of his people, of the individual and of creation as a whole; the prophetic books record the word which enters into this history; and the psalms the human response (however, commandments and law, along with the sphere of wisdom, cannot be fitted into the scheme, which shows its limitations). W.Brueggemann, *The Creative Word: Canon as a Model for Biblical Education*, Philadelphia 1982, also sees the tripartite canon (Torah, prophets and writings) as an appropriate model for biblical instruction.

Finally, mention should also be made of the collected volume *Canon and Authority* (*Essays in Old Testament Religion and Theology*, ed. G.W.Coats and B.O.Long, Philadelphia 1977), in which a series of articles (1-87) deals with the preliminary stages in the development of the canon and a second part (89-175), with the title 'Aspects of a Canonical Hermeneutics', summarizes a number of different kinds of individual ventures in exegesis (though these are only loosely connected with the theme). Nevertheless, this volume too testifies to the popularity of the concept at present (cf. further B.Vawter, 'History and Kerygma in the Old Testament', in *FS Myers* [above, 52], 485ff.; M.G.Kline, 'The Correlation of the Concepts of Canon and Covenant', in *New Perspectives on the Old Testament*, ed. J.B.Payne [above, 11], 265-79).

Still, supporters of a consistent tradio-historical view must remain sceptical about any restriction to the canon (thus e.g. J.Barr [cf. above, 150]). For the role of the problem of the canon above all in Gese and Stuhlmacher, cf. also below, 150f., 170f.

III

New Approaches to a Biblical Theology

Anyone seeking to give an account of the most recent attempts to re-establish a 'biblical theology' which have been undertaken in the last few years, above all in the German-speaking world (cf. also H.Seebass, 'Biblische Theologie', *VF* 27, 1982, 28-45) must begin systematically with the description of the tasks in this specific area given by G.Ebeling a quarter of a century ago: 'In "biblical theology" the theologian who devotes himself specially to studying the connection of the Old and New Testaments must give account of his understanding of the Bible as a whole, that is, above all of the theological problems that arise from the variety of the biblical witness considered in relation to its inner unity' ('Was heisst "Biblische Theologie"?', in ibid., *Wort und Glaube*, Tübingen [1960] ³1967, [69-89] 88 [original ET = 'The Meaning of Biblical Theology', *JTS* NS 6, 1956, [210-25] 224 = L.Hodgson et al, *On the Authority of the Bible*, London 1960, [49-67] 66 = id., *Word and Faith*, Philadelphia and London 1963, [79-97] 96). Ebeling believes that such a task – which has to take account of both the Old and the New Testaments – can only be accomplished by an intensive collaboration between Old and New Testament scholars: systematic theologians must also be involved because of the hermeneutical problems in question. Of the two alternative possibilities of understanding the term which he sees, either 'the theology contained in the Bible', 'the theology of the Bible itself', or 'theology in accordance with the Bible, scriptural theology' (69 = ET, 210/49/79; this understanding, applied to all theological disciplines, has recently also appeared in C.Westermann, 'Aufgaben einer zukünftigen Biblischen Theologie', *DtPfrBl* 81, 1981, 2-6 = id., TB 73 [above, 132], 203-12), only the first is discussed – here it seems obvious to Ebeling that in accordance with the presuppositions laid down by Gabler we have to do with a historical discipline (cf. *Problems of Old Testament Theology*, 3f.).

Even the most recent phase of the discussion over 'biblical theology' is therefore confronted with the old questions – to which, as we have seen, a wealth of answers had already been given in the course of the history of research. But theology cannot be done independently of the presuppositions and even the possibilities of the thought of the time. And here in particular, a considerable change has taken place over the last ten years. Especially after the 'crisis of biblical theology' (cf. above, 8f.) which could be traced not only in America but similarly also in Europe, the most recent attempts to arrive at a biblical theology (of the whole Bible) are to be regarded as a new approach, even if the old models, like the approach from salvation history or the pattern of 'promise and fulfilment', are not thrown overboard. It is already important that individual pioneers – since for the moment we have no more than these (the formation of the 'biblical theology project group' within the 'Wissenschaftliche Gesellschaft für Theologie' at Bethel in 1976 can be seen as one encouraging sign of a co-operation which extends beyond them; cf. my report 'Aus der Arbeit der Projektgruppe "Biblische Theologie" der Wissenschaftlichen Gesellschaft für Theologie', *TZ* 39, 1983, 65-7; id.,'Die Arbeit der Projektgruppe "Biblische Theologie" in den Jahren 1976-1981', in *Schriftauslegung als theologische Aufklärung*, ed.O.Merk, Gütersloh 1984, 94-102) – are venturing on such a new beginning. Here (in accordance with Ebeling's insight) the co-operation between Old and New Testament specialists which is becoming evident is decisive – however, considerable hesitation over all attempts of this kind can be seen especially among New Testament scholars. Thus according to O.Merk (*Biblische Theologie des Neuen Testamentes in ihrer Anfangszeit. Ihre methodischen Probleme bei Johann Philipp Gabler und Georg Lorenz Bauer und deren Nachwirkungen*, MTS 9, Marburg 1972, 270f.), separate work on Old and New Testaments is a necessary consequence of Gabler's methodological approach, so that the demand for a 'biblical theology' embracing both the Old and New Testaments represents a 'retrograde tendency which largely surrenders the insights of Gabler and G.L.Bauer' (id., 271 n.193; cf. also id., 'Biblische Theologie II', *TRE* 6, [455-77] 470; similarly E.Grässer and G.Strecker, see below. Also bound up with this fundamental scepticism is the proposal by H.Hübner ['Biblische Theologie', above, 21] that a first step to such an account should be an account of the use of scripture in the New Testament). Even

Gerhard von Rad, who in the concluding part of the second volume of his *Old Testament Theology* pointed out the strength of the lines in the Old Testament running towards the New Testament, was much more sceptical in the 'Retrospect and Prospect' which was added at the end of the fourth edition (it does not appear in the ET). He wondered whether the distant goal of a biblical theology 'in which the dualism of a theology of the Old Testament and a theology of the New Testament, each keeping within all too narrow boundaries' could be overcome in the foreseeable future. 'It is still very hard to see what form such a biblical theology could then take' (*Theologie* II[6], 447).

However, for a long time there had already been a call for a biblical theology (cf. already H.Schlier, 'Über Sinn und Aufgabe einer Theologie des Neuen Testaments', *BZ* NF 1, 1957, [6-23] = id., *Besinnung auf das Neue Testament. Exegetische Aufsätze und Vorträge* II, Freiburg 1964, [7-24] 19f./20 = *Das Problem der Theologie des Neuen Testaments*, ed.G.Strecker, WdF 367, Darmstadt 1975, [323-44] 339f.; for further similar voices see K.Haacker, 'Die Fragestellung der Biblischen Theologie als exegetische Aufgabe', in Haacker et al, *Biblische Theologie heute*, BTS 1, Neukirchen 1977, [9-23], 9f.), and this demand at the same time contained the expectation that its concern would in due course produce fruits which would lead beyond the historical and descriptive restrictions laid down by Ebeling and Merk. In his presidential address to the International Congress of Old Testament Scholars at Strasbourg in 1956, R.de Vaux summed up these expectations in the thought that the ultimate goal of a Christian scholar must be a biblical theology of both Testaments, since both contained the word of God; such a theology was more than a history of Old Testament religion, but rather 'une science de Dieu et de l'homme élaborée à la lumière de la foi'; it included not only reason but also faith ('A propos de la Théologie Biblique', *ZAW* 68, 1956, [225-7] 226; cf.also id., 'Peut-on écrire une "Théologie de l'Ancien Testament"?', in *Mélanges M.Chenu*, Paris 1967, 439-49 = *Bible et Orient*, Paris 1967, 59-71 = ET 'Is it Possible to Write a "Theology of the Old Testament"?', in *The Bible and the Ancient Near East*, London 1972, 70; id., 'Science et Foi dans l'étude de la Bible', *VS* 117, 1967, 531-52). In a similar way N.W.Porteous ('The Theology of the Old Testament', *PCB*, London 1962, reprinted 1967, 151-9 (151 [= Sections 120a-128g]) also defined biblical theology (and Old Testament theology taken by itself) as a *normative* discipline [sections 120a-c]) which has to develop the biblical witness to the acts of God in and with the human response to these acts (cf. already id., 'Semantics and Old Testament Theology' [above, 3]) and includes the participation of the theologian in faith (cf. also id., 'Some Theological Thought Forms' [above, 3], esp.44f.).

Of course both statements come from a time before the crisis in biblical theology – but they do indicate an inner impulse which is also alive in the latest phase of the movement (cf. e.g. R.E.Clements, *Theology* [above, 143], 6f.; cf. also H.Seebass's programme of an 'Initiation into the Bible' as an 'Initiation into Christianity', *Der Gott* [above, 116], 32f.; cf. also the preface, 7ff.) and at the same time forms the background to the debates which developed in it above all over methods and hermeneutical approach. H.H.Schmid has recently commented to a similar effect in observing that the project of 'biblical theology' covers three basic problems in theological work: in addition to the relationship between the Old Testament and the New and that between exegesis and systematic theology there is 'the question of the theological function of historical-critical interpretation of the Bible in particular. Or, to put it another way: exegesis as a theological problem is being debated under the catch-word of "biblical theology"' ('Unterwegs zu einer neuen biblischen Theologie?', in K.Haacker et al., *Biblische Theologie*, [75-95], 75. Also according to G.F.Hasel, 'Biblical Theology: Then, Now and Tomorrow', *HBT* 4, 1982, [61-93], 74, biblical theology is 'not a purely historical enterprise but a theological-historical undertaking'.)

Among the most recent attempts to regain a theology of the whole of the Bible (cf. also Hasel, 'Biblical Theology') one can distinguish three particular models (which partly overlap): 1. The traditio-historical approach which has been developed above all by H.Gese (cf. his collected volumes *Vom Sinai zum Zion. Alttestamentliche Beiträge zur biblischen Theologie*, BEvTh 64, Munich 1974; *Zur biblischen Theologie* = ET, *Essays on Biblical Theology* [above, 48]; also recently 'Tradition and Biblical Theology', in *Tradition and Theology*, ed.D.A.Knight [above, 141], 301-26 = 'Tradition und biblische Theologie', in *Zu Tradition und Theologie im Alten Testament*, BTS 2, Neukirchen 1978, 87-111) and supported on the New Testament side by P.Stuhlmacher (K.Müller, *Das Judentum* [above, 90], cf.esp.198, defends a similar position: 'The aim of "biblical theology" should be a coherent description of Israel's tradition history, of early Judaism and primitive Christianity'). 2. The attempt to discover a particular concept or central idea as a connecting link between the two Testaments or as their 'centre', around which a biblical theology can be built up. A variant of this is the collection of a number of concepts which in their totality are then meant to form a bridge between the Testaments; 3. To use the idea of world order as a starting point, an approach developed by H.H.Schmid and supported on the New Testament side by U.Luck (the former 'Bethel model').

On 1:

H.Gese developed his ideas of a biblical theology as early as in a programmatical article published first in 1970, which he put at the head of the collection *Vom Sinai zum Zion*: 'Erwägungen zur Einheit der biblischen Theologie' (*ZTK* 67, 1970, 417-36 = *Vom Sinai*, 11-30). The programmatical article of the second collection, 'Das Biblische Schriftverständnis' ('Zur biblischen Theologie, 9-30 = ET 'The Biblical View of Scripture', in *Essays*, 9-33) again summarizes some main perspectives, and the contribution to the collection edited by Knight does not produce any essential progression in thought. This is also in accord with the character of Gese's model, which to a large degree represents a closed system.

The traditio-historical approach forms the real foundation of this system. To this degree (and in the way in which he keeps to kerygmatic theology in principle) Gese stands in the succession of the previous generation of German Old Testament scholars (the so-called Alt school) and especially G.von Rad. One new development even over against von Rad is, however, the assumption of a closed complex of tradition which leads without interruption from the Old Testament and only finds its conclusion with the New Testament. One fundamental thesis is: 'the Old Testament arises through the New Testament; the New Testament forms the conclusion of a process of tradition which is in essential a unity, a continuum' ('Erwägungen', 420/14: cf. 'Schriftverständnis', 11,14 = ET, 11,14; 'Tradition', 322/106f.). Gese wants to retain this process of tradition, with no prior determination of its content, as the starting point of a biblical theology; this runs counter both to von Rad's presupposition that the Old Testament kergyma is inherently related to history (Gese rightly points out that a large part of the Old Testament traditions, and especially wisdom, is left aside ['Erwägungen', 425/19]), and to attempts to establish the content of a 'centre' of the Old Testament ('Tradition', 304/90) or a 'canon in the canon' (cf. 'Schriftverständnis', 29 = ET, 32) – though he is himself well able to define a 'nucleus' of the Old Testament, albeit in terms of tradition history: it is the revelation on Sinai ('Erwägungen', 427/21; 'Schriftverständnis', 23 = ET, 25; cf. already 'Bemerkungen zur Sinaitradition', *ZAW* 79, 1967, 137-54 = *Vom Sinai*, 31-48; also 'Das Gesetz', in *Biblische Theologie*, [55-84] 59 = ET 'The Law', *Essays*, [60-92] 64f.), which (and here he follows Zimmerli) is shaped by the self-revelation of the 'I am YHWH' in content as well as form ('Schriftverständnis', 23 = ET, 25; cf. 'Gesetz', 59f. = ET, 65; 'Tradition',310/95). However, in the course of the development of the tradition of the Torah a second centre comes to be formed: Gese thinks that he can discover a sapientalizing and de-eschatologizing of the Torah in the late period where no longer Sinai but Zion is the place of revelation, and accordingly distinguishes between the 'Sinai torah' and the 'Zion torah' ('Gesetz', 74f. = ET, 80f.)

For Gese, the essence of the tradition consists in its nature as kerygma: organic terms like the 'growth' ('Schriftverständnis', 18 = ET, 19; 'Tradition', 314f./99f.) of the kerygma in the course of a process of development ('Erwägungen', 425f./19) issuing in 'permanent reinterpretation, selection and actualization' ('Erwägungen', 425/18), from which 'the testimony to the history of revelation as it developed in the living process of tradition history' proceeds ('Schriftverständis', 29 = ET, 32) underline this approach: this is the 'organon of the biblical testimony' (ibid.). 'The traditio-historical process corresponds to a process in the history of revelation' ('Schriftverständnis', 16 = ET, 18). Gese can also attempt to portray the tradition, which he can describe in biological terminology as a 'totality of growth' ('Tradition', 316/101) by what he calls an 'analysis of the ontological structure which underlies the text (a particular text)' ('Erwägungen', 429/23); e.g. in Jeremiah he can establish 'alterations in structure' which are to be noted (432/26). Here he is treading on dangerous ground in terms of terminology and thought. In order to counter possible objections (which immediately follow), he stresses (431/25) that this has nothing to do either with a 'history of the spirit' or with a history of development understood in Hegelian terms; as there is no metaphysical or static ontology in the background, the history of tradition has, rather, the dynamic of a development which constantly discloses new areas: 'In objective terms it is a matter of a dawning, a manifestation, of new reality' (ibid.). Most of the objections to his approach relate to this conceptuality (cf. especially the review by H.-J.Kraus, 'Theologie als Traditionsbildung?', *EvTh* 36, 1976, 498-507 = Haacker et al., *Biblische Theologie* [above, 148], 61-73, who objects that here 'theology is turned into a phenomenology of the history of tradition' [502/66], and Schmid, who accuses Gese and Stuhlmacher of 'understanding the ontological process which they depict basically as the history of a biblical special ontology' ['Unterwegs?', above, 148, 84]). It is in fact open to misunderstanding, but this could have been avoided had Gese had a more adequate philosophical background, and is at all events intended to describe a situation for which he had found no more appropriate terminology. With J.G.Janzen ('The Old Testament in "Process" Perspective: Proposal for a Way Forward in Biblical Theology', in *Magnalia Dei* [above, 125], 480-509), one might ask whether Whitehead's 'process' philosophy, which is very common in America (and which led to a similar 'process' theology, cf. *Problems of Old Testament Theology*, 153f.) would not work as a more suitable model for thought and terminology. More important is Schmid's objection relating to the substance of Gese's approach ('Unterwegs?', 79ff.), to the effect that he begins from a unilinear and straight-line development of tradition in the Old Testament of a kind that cannot be found there; what one in fact sees in the Old Testament are its many strands, its contradictions, and even a multiplicity conditioned by local circumstances (cf. already Ebeling, 'Biblical Theology' [above, 146], 221/83 = ET 61/92; cf. recently also S.Wagner, ' "Biblische Theologien" und "Biblische Theologie"', *TLZ* 103, 1978, [786-98] 787ff.; W.H.Schmidt, 'Vielfalt und Einheit alttestamentlichen Glaubens', in *'Wenn nicht jetzt, wann dann?' FS H.J.Kraus*, Neukirchen-Vluyn 1983, 13-22; P.D.Hanson, *The Diversity of Scripture*, Philadelphia, 1982 [he proposes a 'dynamic view of scripture', founded on its diversity]; for the New Testament, E.Käsemann, 'Begründet der neutestamentliche Kanon die Einheit der Kirche?', *EvTh* 11, 1951/2, 13-21 = id., *Exegetische Versuche und Besinnungen* I, Göttingen 1960, 214-23 = id. [ed.], *Das Neue Testament als Kanon*, Göttingen 1970, 124-33 – but cf.also E.Lohse, 'Die Einheit des Neuen Testaments als theologisches Problem', *EvTh* 35, 1975, [139-54] 154: 'The unity of the New Testament... is to be found only in the diversity of proclamation of primitive Christianity... In the preaching by which the church was founded, which has been handed down in the canon of the New Testament scriptures, Jesus Christ as the one Word of God is proclaimed.' Cf. also W.Schrage, 'Zur Frage nach der Einheit und Mitte neutestamentlicher Ethik', in *Die Mitte des Neuen Testaments. FS E. Schweizer*, Göttingen 1983, 238-53). Moreover in the tradition we find not only progress, but often also interruptions and retrogression. Of course Gese ('Tradition', 316/101) defends himself against this by pointing out that it is the nature of a living development of tradition to 'replace what has fallen out, compensate for incomplete developments, and eliminate the insignificant, the disruptive, and false developments'. All that matters is the context as a whole, if the formation of the tradition is understood in this sense as a response to the demands of history, and in no way issues in a chance result.

However, this does not remove the basic objection of H.-J.Kraus that in reality this is a kind of phenomenology (Gese himself speaks of 'structural analysis', 'Erwägungen', 430/24), and not theology. The fact that it seems plausible, at least for the present, is evidently connected with Gese's continued retention of the definition of biblical theology as a *historical* discipline ('Tradition', 303/88): i.e., he claims that it fulfils a descriptive task. Things would only be otherwise if F.Mildenberger were right ('Systematisch-theologische Randbemerkungen zur Diskussion um eine Biblische Theologie', in *Zugang zur Theologie. FS W.Joest*, Göttingen 1979, [11-32] 14) 'to adopt Gese's description of the process of tradition as a description of what faith perceives.' Mildenberger thinks that he can discover two features in Gese: as a theologian the exegete 'so to speak enters into the process of tradition and continues it in an interpretative way' (12), while on the other hand he has the detachment of the historical observer. We shall have to return to this problem.

Gese also has an Achilles heel in a historical question, relating to his verdict on the problem of the canon. The assumption of an unbroken complex of biblical tradition calls urgently for a revision of the Reformers' decision only to recognize the Massoretic canon of the Old Testament. The exclusion of the intertestamental literature, above all most of the apocalyptic writings, opens up a great gap between the Testaments, and in Gese's eyes this breaks apart the living stream of tradition which, in particular, also contains apocalyptic. Whereas K.Koch, who turned against the 'prophetic connection theory' at the same time as Gese (*Ratlos vor der Apokalyptik*, Gütersloh 1970, 180 = ET *The Rediscovery of Apocalyptic*, London 1972, 129), which attaches the New Testament kerygma directly to Old Testament prophecy, lamented the restriction of the object of serious biblical scholarship to the narrow sphere of the canon (114f. = ET, 56; Ebeling, 'Biblische Theologie' [above, 145], 221/84 = ET, 61/92, had already done the same thing. Cf. also E.H.Scheffler, 'Die Verhouding tussen die Ou en Nuwe Testament', *Theologia Evangelica. Journal of the Faculty of Theology, University of South Africa*, Pretoria, 16, 1983, 38-52) and instead of this called also for non-canonical material to be taken into consideration in determining the historical context of Christianity (cf. also J.Barr, 'Den teologiska värderingen av den efterbibliska judendomen', *SEÅ* 32, 1967, 69-78; id., 'Le judaisme postbiblique et la théologie de l'Ancien Testament', *RTP* III, 18, 1968, 209-17; id., 'Judaism – its Continuity with the Bible, Montefiore Memorial Lecture, Southampton University 1968; id., 'Biblical Theology' [above, 2]; for the post-exilic period generally see J.J.Blenkinsopp, 'Tanach and the New Testament' [above, 125], 76-93), Gese seeks to keep to the framework of the canon and transcend the break in tradition between the Testaments by declaring that the process of the formation of the canon was still open in the New Testament period and was first closed by the New Testament. Hence the thesis 'The Old Testament arose through the New Testament (above, 150; cf. further 'Schriftverständnis', 9ff. = ET, 9ff.; 'Tradition', 317ff./102f.). Here he is particularly concerned with the so-called Apocrypha, above all with the apocalyptic literature and the sphere of late wisdom, which for him is the real breeding-ground of the message of the New Testament (cf. recently 'Die Weisheit, der Menschensohn und die Ursprünge der Christologie als konsequente Entfaltung der biblischen Theologie', *SEÅ* 44, 1979, 77-114). Hence the explicit demand that the Reformation decision in the matter of the canon should be withdrawn; it is to be declared an illegitimate 'reduction of the canon' ('Tradition', 324/108. 'It must be pointed out that the Reformation church, by separating out the Apocrypha, did not render a service to a total view of the biblical tradition with its exclusion of the apocrypha' ('Schriftverständnis', 13 = ET, 14).

Evidently here Gese is following Sundberg's position (above, 134), but this has become increasingly shaky since the hypothesis of a 'synod of Jamnia' has lost probability (above, 134f.) and there are increasing indications that the Massoretic canon already existed in its present extent by the middle of the first century AD (cf. Swanson, above, 133). In that case Kraus's requirement ('Theologie' [above, 151], 500/64) that Christianity must come to terms with the given canon, behind the formation of which there are dogmatic decisions, even if they are bound up with the situation of the time, again becomes important. Here questions also have to be asked about the theological content of the early Jewish writings which did not find a place in the rabbinic canon, a problem which is also important for ecumenical dialogue. Of course the biblical tradition, the people of the Old and New Testaments who are its bearers, and the canon (fixed within certain limits), in which the people established what for them would be the binding content of the tradition which supported them, are inter-related entities. Thus Gese's concern deserves the closest attention, but must be taken up in a broader hermeneutical approach.

On 2:

With the works of P.Stuhlmacher, who in other respects is Gese's most faithful supporter, we already enter the sphere of the second group of attempts at a biblical theology. Here a particular central notion or content is promoted to being the 'centre' of both Testaments and thus becomes an axis to bind them together. In Gese himself this already was, as we saw, the divine self-revelation on Sinai (for a criticism cf. H.H.Schmid, 'Unterwegs?' [above, 148], 84f.) as the nucleus of the whole tradition of salvation history, though this has now been broken apart, and at the same time completed and 'transcended' with the realization of salvation in Jesus Christ in the here and now ('Erwägungen' [above, 149],434ff./28ff.). This 'transcending' is at the same time both a consummation and a surpassing; the surpassing is achieved in the event of the resurrection (for the transcending of the Old Testament tradition in the event of incarnation, cross and resurrection cf. also Gese, '*Natus ex virgine*', in *FS von Rad*, 1971 [above, 93], 73-89 = id., *Vom Sinai* [above, 149], 130-46). Stuhlmacher (who in his investigation *Gerechtigkeit Gottes bei Paulus*, Göttingen ²1966 had already investigated a central concept of the New Testament against the background of its antecedents in the Old Testament – cf. also M.Barth, 'Rechtfertigung. Versuch einer Auslegung paulinischer Texte im Rahmen des

Alten und Neuen Testaments', in M.Barth et al., *Foi et salut selon S.Paul*, AnBib 42, Rome 1970, 137-97) is even more convinced in his Tübingen inaugural lecture of 1973, 'Das Bekenntnis zur Auferweckung Jesu von den Toten und die biblische Theologie' (*ZTK* 70, 1973, 365-403 = id., *Schriftauslegung auf dem Wege zur biblischen Theologie*, Göttingen 1975, 128-66) that the confession of the resurrection of Jesus and the event of the resurrection itself is not only the oldest theme of primitive Christianity but also forms its central content ('Auferweckung', 377ff./140ff.). At the same time, the fact that the idea of resurrection was already on the way to becoming an expectation of resurrection in the Old Testament, an expectation which like the so-called Easter faith relates to the action of God and therefore can be further defined as faith in the God who raised the Crucified One ('Auferweckung', 383/146), ultimately resting on trust in the power of Yahweh, which cannot stop even at the gates of death ('Auferweckung', 383ff./146ff.), seems to him to be the starting point for a possible biblical theology. Here Stuhlmacher sees 'the climactic Jewish confesssion of Yahweh' ('Auferweckung', 388/151) as having taken place. His ultimate conclusion follows from this: 'The Christian confession of resurrection makes more precise in christological terms the Israelite confession of God which has been formed in an ongoing process of tradition' ('Auferweckung', 388/151). In other words, 'In the Christian confession of resurrection... the Israelite belief in God reaches its goal and consummation' (ibid.). In methodological terms, for Stuhlmacher that means that 'a biblical theology of the New Testament must be sketched out which is open to the Old Testament' ('Auferweckung', 388f./151f – in his review of the work [*TZ* 33, 1977, 172-5], H.-W.Bartsch argues rather that equal value should be attached to both Old and New Testaments [175]). The New Testament scholar Stuhlmacher comes half-way to meet the Old Testament scholar Gese, who moves from an Old Testament open towards the New Testament.

Not only have doubts been expressed as to whether the resurrection hope can in fact be termed the 'climactic confession of Yahweh' in this way ('Unterwegs?' [above, 148], 82; cf. also J.Becker, 'Das Gottesbild Jesu und die älteste Auslegung von Ostern', in *Jesus Christus in Historie und Theologie. FS H.Conzelmann*, Tübingen 1975, [105-26], 107, 118; also G.Strecker, ' "Biblische Theologie"? Kritische Bemerkungen zu den Entwürfen von Hartmut Gese und

Peter Stuhlmacher', *FS Bornkamm* [above, 91], [425-45] 440 n.67);
Schmid has criticized Stuhlmacher on the grounds that he only
mentions texts 'which belong to the prehistory of the *conception* of
the resurrection' ('Unterwegs?', 88). Behind this lurks the old
criticism of a biblical theology along the lines of L.Köhler, orientated
on 'ideas, thoughts and concepts' (cf. *Problems of Old Testament
Theology*, 48). However, in terms of content Stuhlmacher probably
means more. Still, criticism has also been made of his assumption
that the confession of the *resurrection* in particular has a central
significance (cf. Schmid, 'Unterwegs?', 81f.). Stuhlmacher has
recently proposed other themes to provide a link between the Old
Testament and the New. Already in his 1975 Augsburg lecture
('Evangelische Schriftauslegung heute', in *Schriftauslegung* [above,
155], 167-83) he mentioned 'the gospel of Jesus Christ, the reconciler
and Lord', as the central message of the New Testament (177) and
at the same time as the 'really powerful focal point in the formation
of all Christian confessions' (179); above all he asserted: 'In the
proclamation of Jesus Christ as the reconciler a quite decisive
feature, if not the whole intention of the Old Testament, comes to
consummation' (78 – cf. already 'Jesus als Versöhner. Überlegungen
zur Darstellung Jesu im Rahmen einer biblischen Theologie', *FS
Conzelmann*, 87-104 = id., *Versöhnung, Gesetz und Gerechtigkeit*,
Göttingen 1981, 9-26). In the 1976 Bethel lecture 'Zum Thema:
Biblische Theologie des Neuen Testaments' (Haacker et al., *Biblische Theologie* [above, 147], 25-60), he once again terms 'the proclamation of the *reconciliation* of God with Jews and Gentiles initiated
in the mission, death and resurrection of Jesus' as 'the kerygmatic
centre of the New Testament'. In his hermeneutic text book *Vom
Verstehen des Neuen Testaments* (GNT 6, Göttingen 1979) he gives
the closing section which sums up his basic position (§15) the title
'Das Evangelium von der Versöhnung in Christus', 'The Gospel of
Reconciliation in Christ', and traces the idea of reconciliation
through the individual writings of the New Testament. He maintains
this standpoint in his most recent article on the theme (P.Stuhlma-
cher and H.Class, *Das Evangelium von der Versöhnung in Christus*,
Stuttgart 1979, 13-54 = ET 'The Gospel of Reconciliation in Christ',
HBT 1, 1979, 161-90): the concept of reconciliation is not only pre-
eminently suitable for denoting the 'centre' of the New Testament;
the whole message of the New Testament can be summed up in it:
'In the New Testament we have the testimony of a wide-ranging,

historically differentiated proclamation of reconciliation, elevated to the status of the canon of the church' (44). In an introductory letter ([5-11] 9) he makes it clear how K.Koch and H.Gese have shown him that 'atonement and reconciliation are one of the great themes in the Old Testament'. The Old Testament provides the 'exposition' for the New in that it presents 'hope for reconciliation and peace with God as the consummation of creation' (44) and thus the language which first makes possible the message of the New Testament. P.Pokorny (*TLZ* 1981 [above, 14], 6) has recently made the criticism that this is not a central concept for the New Testament. However, this reflection on talk of reconciliation as a 'centre' which links the two Testaments is evidently not meant in an exclusive sense. In the Bethel lecture, Stuhlmacher explained that undertaking an overall theology of the Bible is a matter of 'working out a systematic summary of the essential content of the proclamation and faith-content of the New Testament' (a task which an individual New Testament scholar is unable to accomplish), which took into account the fact 'that all decisive proclamatory statements of the New Testament have been formulated in the light of their connection of the language and experience of the Old Testament and Judaism' ('Zum Thema: Biblische Theologie', 25f.). Accordingly, not only this one conceptual 'centre' but also yet other centres of the Bible as a whole can be derived from the Old Testament in the sense of a 'linguistic theory of faith' (for the precedents for the language of christology, reconciliation and justification in the Old Testament cf. also Stuhlmacher and Class, 'Evangelium', 45; Pokorny, op.cit., 6, makes the same point). Stuhlmacher himself has done the same thing recently in an article, taking up Gese's distinction between the provisional Sinai Torah and the eschatological Zion Torah in connection with the New Testament understanding of the Law ('Das Gesetz als Thema biblischer Theologie', *ZTK* 75, 1978, 251-80 = id., *Versöhnung, Gesetz und Gerechtigkeit*, Göttingen 1981, 136-65) in which he describes the theme of the 'law' as 'an open fundamental problem of a biblical theology which binds together the Old Testament and the New' (279; cf. already G.Siegwalt, *La loi, chemin du salut*, Neuchâtel and Paris 1971; H.Hübner, 'Das Gesetz als elementares Thema einer Biblischen Theologie?', *KuD* 22, 1976, 250-76; also the discussion between G.Klein, 'Präliminarien' [above, 93], and H.Seebass, 'Zur Ermöglichung biblischer Theologie', *EvTh* 37, 1977, 591-600). In addition, most recently a whole series of further proposals for a 'centre' of the whole of the Bible has been discussed. One traditional proposal (and open now in an even more intensive way to the criticisms that were already made of Eichrodt's *Theology*) is the proposal that the idea of the covenant should be taken as the main connecting link between the Testaments (R.Campbell, *Israel and the New Covenant*, Philadelphia 1954; thus recently again F.C.Fensham, 'The Covenant as Giving Expression to the Relationship between Old and New Testament', *TynB* 22, 1971, 82-94; cf. already id., 'Sacrifice and Meal in the Forming of the Covenant in the Old and New Testament', *TGW* 5, 1965, 77-87; id., 'Covenant, Promise and Expectation in the Bible', *TZ* 23, 1967, 305-22 – In contrast to this E.Grässer, *Der alte Bund* [above, 90], [1-134] 130, denies the possibility of using the term 'covenant' as a link between the Testaments: 'The eschatological *kainotes* of the New Covenant gets in the way. *Diatheke* is not suited to be the catalyst of a biblical theology'). Other similar themes are election (e.g. F.Lang, 'Christuszeugnis und biblische Theologie',*EvTh* 29, 1969, [523-34] 531f.); the rule of God, the final dawning of which, as expected in the Old Testament, is announced by Jesus (Mark 1.14 par.) and brought in by him (H.Seebass, 'Der Beitrag des Alten Testaments zum Entwurf einer biblischen Theologie', *WuD* 8, 1965, 20-49; cf. also J.Gray, *The Biblical Doctrine of the Reign of God*, Edinburgh 1979); 'the movement of God towards humanity and the movement of humanity towards God' (H.Haag, 'Das Problem einer biblischen Theologie heute', in *Bibel und zeitgemässer Glaube*, ed. K.Schubert, Klosterneuburg 1965, [287-310] 291); 'life' (OT) and 'new life' (NT) (H.Klein, 'Leben – neues Leben. Möglichkeiten und Grenzen einer gesamtbiblischen Theologie des Alten und Neuen Testaments', *EvTh* 43, 1983, 91-108 = *Schriftauslegung als theologische Aufklärung* [above, 146], 76-93) or the community under the will of God realized by Christ (J.L.McKenzie, *Geist und Welt des Alten Testaments*, Lucerne 1962, 363); the people of God which participates in God's salvation in the continuity of Israel and the church (R.C.Dentan, *ATR* 1945 [above, 2], 26; H.Cazelles, 'The Unity of the Bible and the People of God', *Script* 18, 1966, 1-10); the 'primal confession' in which both Old Testament Israel and the church in the New Testament have attested their experience of the mighty help of God which has a corresponding structure (H.Lubsczyk, 'Die Einheit der Schrift', in *Sapienter ordinare. FS E.Kleineidam*, Leipzig 1969, 73-104 = also published separately, Stuttgart 1970); or 'law and promise' as basic concepts which already hold the Old Testament together (Clements, *Theology* [above, 143], 186). Christoph D.Müller (*Die Erfahrung der Wirklichkeit*, Gütersloh 1978) seeks the experience of reality which binds the two Testaments in the twin concepts *qds – hagios*, by means of a hermeneutical investigation. A.Schenker (*Das Abendmahl Jesu als Brennpunkt des Alten Testaments*, BiBe NF 13, Fribourg 1977) represents a remarkable attempt to collect various Old Testament themes in a New Testament field of reference.

In principle it is also possible to argue that a central concept should not be postulated as a 'centre' of the two Testaments, but rather that a number of connecting links in thought or conceptuality should be sought between them (thus H.Haag, ' Biblische Theologie', *MySal* I, Einsiedeln 1965 [440-59], 454: 'It is manifest that the biblical proclamation can be derived from a relatively small number of key concepts which run through the whole of Holy Scripture in various forms. If it should prove possible to collect together the precious content of the biblical message in these concepts as in golden shells, then it should also be possible to arrive at a biblical theology...' But Haag, too, then arranges all these concepts round a centre: 'life from God and before God, for God and with God... is in the last resort the one and only theme of the whole of Holy Scripture' (455f.). According to R.P.C.Hanson and B.Harvey (*The Loom of God* [above, 2], 72ff.), there are four truths on which the Bible rests: the existence of God, God as creator of a good world, the fall of mankind and the fact of election. The connection between the two Testaments can be seen in a series of 'key concepts'. Similarly F.F.Bruce, *This is That. The New Testament Development of some Old Testament Themes*, Exeter 1968 (paperback 1976) sees in the rule of God, in salvation, the victory of God, his people, in the 'son of David', the 'Servant Messiah' and the 'the Shepherd King' connecting links between the two Testaments within the framework of salvation history.

Instead of this, H.J.Kraus, who (also in the light of J.Barr's criticism of such conceptual investigations, *The Semantics of Biblical Language*, Oxford 1961) has suspicions about the wisdom of limiting biblical theology to the developments of concepts (*Die biblische Theologie. Ihre Geschichte und Problematik*, Neukirchen 1970, 371f. and n.12; id., 'Probleme und Perspektiven Biblischer Theologie', in Haacker et al., *Biblische Theologie* [above, 147], [97-124] 108), proposes a procedure in the sphere of 'theme-orientated complexes of texts' ('Probleme', 109f.); here a search is to be made by 'themes' for connections in the history of the reception of texts between texts with related themes, especially their historical perspectives as summed up in the kerygma ('Probleme', 116). The proposal by W.Bindemann, *Röm 8,18-27 und die Frage einer Theologie der Befreiung von Mensch und Natur*, MTS 14, Neukirchen 1983, 122, aims in a similar direction, seeking to discover common thought-structures in the Old and New Testament which have grown out of experiences with the one God. But it is probably right to follow Kraus (*Biblische Theologie*, 371) in modestly terming these individual investigations 'pre-investigations', which also show that we are still far removed from the goal of an extended biblical theology (for criticism cf. also B.S.Childs, review, *Int* 26, 1972, [20-9] 27f.).

Finally, the thought has also been expressed that there is a structural analogy between the two Testaments (cf. Gunneweg, *Verstehen* [above, 16], 178ff., 195ff. = ET 196ff., 212ff.; Preuss, *Predigt* [above, 10], 120ff. with further literature). Such structural analogies are seen between the construction of the canon of the two Testaments, and above all also between the 'disclosure situation' of the biblical texts in the relationship of the Testaments to each other, which at the same time reflect analogies in the action of God. Here, however, existential models are also provided (say for existence in faith in the relationship between the individual and the community), or basic references, like the relationships between revelation and history, and history and eschatology, which are helpful for understanding the action of God in the present. There is a broad field of possible interpretations. On the other hand, how far the structural models found here are binding is markedly dependent on subjective assessments.

Still, there is also a centre on which a variety of exegetes seem capable of agreement. O.Eissfeldt already raised the question 'Is the God of the Old Testament also the God of the New?' (id., 'Ist der Gott des Alten Testaments auch der Gott des Neuen Testaments', in id., *Geschichtliches und Übergeschichtliches im Alten Testament*, ThStKr 109,2, Berlin 1947, 37-54), but as here he began, with an approach in terms of the history of piety, from the conception of God or the experience of God among the faithful of the Old Testament, which for the Christian could only be a partial encounter with God, he gave a divided answer to the question. Since then, this approach has largely been recognized as inappropriate and obsolete (but cf. below, 163f. on Gunneweg, Strecker and Grässer). However, a great variety of instances make it clear that Eissfeldt's question continues to be asked and is now often answered positively. Cf. e.g. J.Lindblom, 'The Old Testament in the Christian Church', *ExpT* 51, 1940, 374-9; C.-H.Ratschow, *Der angefochtene Glaube*, Gütersloh 1957, 67-90. H.Wildberger (*EvTh* 1959 [above 17], 81) can stress (over against a directly christological interpretation of the Old Testament along the lines taken by W.Vischer), that the Old Testament is in fact an indirect testimony to Christ 'because it bears witness to the God who has acted decisively and finally in Christ'. A. Jepsen (*Wissenschaft* [above, 27]) bases his positive answer, first (18/21) on the New Testament itself, for which the God of the Old Testament is clearly the Father of Jesus Christ (on the other hand, however, something decisively new has happened in Jesus Christ over against the Old Testament); secondly, with the recognition of the Old Testament by the church as canon, derived from this New Testament attitude, because in it 'the same God speaks and acts who is the Father of its Lord Jesus Christ' (30/32); similarly e.g. B.-E.Benktson, 'Gamla testamentets prinzipiella betydelse för dogmatiken', *TAik* 69, 1964, [284-300] 295ff.; W.Zimmerli, 'Biblical Theology', *HBT* 4, 1982 [above, 82] 97ff.; J.Moltmann, *Theologie der Hoffnung* [above, 110], 127 = ET, 141: 'It was Yahweh...who raised Jesus from the dead'). H.-J.Kraus (*Biblische Theologie* [above, 159], 384f.) sees as its main task: 'That first and above all it must ask questions about the "self-identity" or the "selfhood" of God in Jesus Christ, in other words about the faithfulness of his promise to the creation disclosed in Israel...'

Now some people may perhaps find such answers too dogmatic and assertive. There are also indirect attempts to relate the christological centre of the New Testament and the theocentrism of the Old, as for example the interesting one made by D.J.A.Clines ('God in Human Form: A Thesis in Biblical Theology', *Journal of the Christian Brethren Research Fellowship* 24, 1973, 24-40) to connect together Old Testament anthropomorphic manifestations and hypostases of God, the conception of man as the 'image' of God, and the New Testament notion of incarnation; there is a more extended parallel to this in the book by U.Mauser (*Gottesbild und Menschwerdung*, BHT 43, Tübingen 1971); here an anthropomorphic conception of God, the prophet involved through suffering in the fate of his people as the image of God, and the incarnation of God in Christ are brought out as the central divine-human analogy connecting the Testaments. Or there are the theses of M.Saebø (' "Kein anderer Name". Sieben Thesen zur christologischen Ausschliesslichkeitsforderung aus dem Horizont des alttestamentlichen Gottesglaubens', *KuD* 22, 1976, 181-90), which open up the formula in Acts 4.12 relating to the exclusiveness of Christ in the direction of the requirement of an exclusive faith in Yahweh, and thus bring in the question of God in a wider sense (see esp. Thesis 7, 189). E.Otto, 'Schöpfung als Kategorie der Vermittlung von Gott und Welt in Biblischer Theologie', *FS Kraus* (above, 58), (53-68) 65ff., sees the negative experiences of the failure of life being transcended existentially by God in the incarnation and event of the cross against the background of the creation traditions of the Old Testament, as the transcendent nature of man. For more detail cf. id., *'Impleta est haec scriptura*. Zum Problem einer christologischen Interpretation des Alten Testaments im Anschluss an Traugott Kochs Christologie-kritik', in *Die Gegenwart des Absoluten*, ed. K.M.Kodalle, Gütersloh 1984. H.Clavier ('Variétés' [above, 20]) sees the most different lines emerging from the multiplicity of the Old Testament (cf. esp. 362ff.) and coming together within the multiplicity of the New in Jesus and his message. This message is nevertheless unprecedented and revolutionary in its newness, since it is the message of the unlimited love of God, in which Jesus has conquered even death, on the cross (cf. esp.341ff.) – though in nucleus (365) this message already shone out in a variety of places in the Old Testament (371); cf. also id., 'Les données bibliques et leur interprétation: principes de théologie biblique', *Studia Biblica 1978, I, Papers on Old Testament and Related Themes*, ed. E.A.Livingstone, *JSOT.S* 11, 1979, 65-81. For S.Terrien (*The Elusive Presence*, RPS 26, New York 1978 – cf. also the review by W.Brueggemann, *JBL* 99, 1980, 296-300 = *God and his Temple*, ed. L.E.Frizzel and S.Orange, New York 1981, 30-4, and E.Jacob, *RHPR* 60, 1981, 461-4), with a slight variant on Luther's formula, the *Deus Absconditus atque Praesens* (cf. esp. 470ff.) represents the real centre of the Bible (cf. also W.Brueggemann, 'The Crisis and Promise of Presence in Israel', *HBT* 1, 1979, 47-86). Alongside Terrien's book, H.Seebass, *Der Gott* (above, 116f.), already represents the second detailed attempt at an overall account of a biblical theology (F.Hahn, 'Auf dem Weg zu einer biblischen Theologie? Werkstattbericht Neues

Testament', *Nachrichten der Evangelisch-Lutherischen Kirche in Bayern* 35, 1980, [281-7] 287 still thinks that this is impossible). Starting from the so-called 'covenant formula', which he believes to be an adequate description of the understanding of God among the people of Israel (35f.; cf. already *Problems of Old Testament Theology*, 127f.), here the new understanding of God disclosed in Jesus Christ (II Cor.5.19: 'God was in Christ') is made the real foundation for a biblical theology which includes both Testaments. Further themes are then attached to this (resurrection, messianism, the people of God and the kingdom of God, creation, suffering from God). God's 'identity of function' through all the traditio-historical and redaction-critical disparities in the Bible as stressed by S. Wagner (*TLZ* 1978 [above, 151], 794) formalizes the same approach, the content of which is also to be filled in (E. Jacob, 'Possibilités et limites d'une théologie biblique', *RHPR* 46, 1966, [116-30] 121, speaks similarly of the 'dynamisme de la révélation, c'est-à-dire de la lutte toujours renouvelée pour degager Dieu de son image pour le faire saisir dans sa réalité et sa vérité').

The doubt expressed at one time as to whether the God of the Old Testament and the God of Jesus Christ are one and the same God seems to have become quite rare. As Eissfeldt once did at an earlier stage (above, 160) Gunneweg (*Vom Verstehen* [above, 16], 186 = ET, 165) finds a basis for the doubt in the discrepancy in the *image of God* even within the Old Testament itself: 'This God has so many names and such different characteristics that to speak of *the* God of the Old Testament runs the risk of being an empty formula' (similarly still Strecker, 'Biblische Theologie' [above, 155f.], 435 n.41, who similarly seeks to reject the notion that God is the same by referring to the difference in character between the Old Testament and the New Testament '*image* of God'; cf. also E. Grässer, ' "Ein einziger ist Gott" [Röm 3.30]. Zum christologischen Gottesverständnis bei Paulus', in *'Ich will euer Gott werden'. Beispiele biblischen Redens von Gott*, SBS 100, 1981 [²1982], [177-205] 193 n.48 – but cf. also 196. A similar rejection of Old Testament tradition on the basis of Jesus' completely different *image* of God in a psychological context can be found in H. Wolff, *Neuer Wein – Alte Schläuche*, Stuttgart ²1983). The consequences of such an approach become evident when e.g. N. K. Gottwald (*The Tribes of Yahweh* [above, 9], esp. 701-9) seeks to understand faith in Yahweh only as a symbol which helped early Israel to a particular form of social evolution. At other places in his textbook, however, Gunneweg starts directly without further ado from this very sameness of God in both Testaments (cf. *Vom Verstehen*, 37, 196f. = ET, 37, 179f.). Here we can see considerable obscurity (which has recently also been noted by W.Zimmerli, 'Von der Gültigkeit der "Schrift" Alten Testamentes in der christlichen Predigt', in *Textgemäss. FS E.Würthwein*, Göttingen 1979, [184-202], 195ff.). Another problematic proposal is that made by M.Oeming, *Gesamtbiblische Theologien* (above, 10), 226ff., that each text of the Old Testament should be taken on its own merits and be valued in accordance with a value system (analogous to the value theory of the Neo-Kantian, H.Rickert) derived from the New Testament or 'Christian' thinking. Here the continuity of God's acting on his people through the periods of both Testaments completely disappears from view.

On 3:

H.H.Schmid and U.Luck (and in part also E.Brandenburger) have made their own independent contribution to biblical theology in close co-operation (above all during their work together at Bethel). In the article on 'Creation, Righteousness and Salvation' included in Schmid's collected papers *Altorientalische Welt in der alttestamentlichen Theologie* (Zurich 1974; first published as 'Schöpfung, Gerechtigkeit und Heil', *ZTK* 70, 1973, 1-19) the programme appears as a sub-title: ' "Theology of Creation" as the Overall Horizon of Biblical Theology'.

In it, Schmid has sought to extend to the whole Bible his view that creation faith in the form of the general Near Eastern concept of world order is the theme *par excellence* of biblical theology (cf. *Problems of Old Testament Theology*, 181f.), by understanding basic New Testament theological themes like Paul's doctrine of justification, the atoning death of Jesus and his role as intermediary at creation against the background of the same presuppositions ('Schöpfung', 12ff./22ff.).

It is worth noting that in his discussion with Gese, Schmid agrees with his conversation partner over the basic methodological approach, above all in understanding the relationship between the Testaments as an ongoing process of tradition and e.g. 'also in describing it as a process of ontological transformations and developments' ('Unterwegs?' [above, 148], 79). But unlike Gese, he sees the specific Israelite elements of the Old Testament as being 'transformations of universal human presuppositions of thought and therefore as solutions – possibly specific solutions – to basic universal human problems'(88). The New Testament confession of the resurrection, from which Stuhlmacher begins, is the answer to the 'basic, universal and human question of righteousness in the totality of reality', and the whole process of tradition from Old Testament to New is to be understood as the 'extension of the ontological structures for the perception of the one total reality', which for its part tests the realities of the world against the experience that the world is God's creation. From this perspective, the many strands in the traditions are 'a decisive pointer towards the relevance of the traditions and confessions for the mastery of reality which is achieved in faith' (89f.).

U.Luck (*Welterfahrung und Glaube als Grundproblem biblischer Theologie*, ThExH 191, Munich 1976) qualifies the same basic approach more strongly in the direction of *experience of the world*: the title of one of his chapters, 'Experience of the World and Faith as a Basic Human Problem' (13) is typical. This takes up a key word which plays a not unconsiderable role in most recent theological discussion.

Thus e.g. the historian R.von Thadden in his lecture 'Erwartungen an die wissenschaftliche Theologie', given in Göttingen in 1974 to the Gesellschaft für Wissenschaftliche Theologie (in *Wissenschaftliche Theologie im Überblick*, ed. W.Lohff and F.Hahn, KVR 1402, Göttingen 1974, [71-75], 72) calls for more 'work on or thematizing of experiencable reality'; G.Ebeling (*Studium der Theologie*, UTB 446, Tübingen 1975, 25 = ET *The Study of Theology*, London 1979, 24) sees that the theological questions to be asked in the sphere of the New Testament involve 'reflecting on the coherence of the subject matter of Christian faith in the mutual critical interpenetration of traditional and contemporary experience' (cf. recently id. 'Schrift und Erfahrung als Quelle theologischer Aussagen', *ZTK* 75, 1978, 99-116); similarly, E.Otto ('Erwägungen zu den Prolegomena einer Theologie des Alten Testaments', *Kairos* 19, 1977, 53-72) sees the present understanding of reality and the mastering of life by God as the themes in the light of which Old Testament theology has to investigate the understanding of reality in the Bible; the same holds for biblical theology (61 and n.46). Conversely, and among other reasons precisely because of the necessity of incorporating one's own horizon of experience into a discipline which has been opened up hermeneutically in this way, G.Strecker ('Biblische Theologie?' [above, 155f.], 428f.) rejects the term 'biblical theology' as being too narrow. Cf. further H.Barth and T.Schramm, *Selbsterfahrung mit der Bibel*, Munich and Göttingen 1977; W.Bartholomäus, 'Zum Thema "Das Alte Testament im religiösen Lernprozess"', *TQ* 160, 1980, 29-39. Cf. recently also H.H.Schmid, 'Was heisst "Biblische Theologie"?', in *Wirkungen hermeneutischer Theologie*. FS Gerhard Ebeling, Zürich 1983, (35-50) 46f.

For Luck, the task of biblical theology is that of providing an answer to the question 'What contribution does biblical theology make to an understanding of reality?' (7ff.). Biblical theology demonstrates by means of the collection of tradition in the biblical writings that man is always already directed to faith in the experience and suffering brought to him by reality (39). Luck sees the basic dilemmas of human life in the tension between the expectation of life and the experience of the world (a tension which arises because of a lack of success in life) or, in biblical terms, in the problem of hidden righteousness (35). In the biblical tradition three ways of solving the dilemma are offered (cf. 29ff.): 1. The institutional way (justice and law as official order and the institutions required to impose it). In reality this comes to grief on the problem of imposing a comprehensive, just order in which each individual has his or her rights. Only eschatological hope opens up the prospect of a perspective of this kind. 2. The historical way (a reference to the early period of salvation history, in which salvation can be seen as the fruit of keeping God's commandments). However, the historical past, too, can no longer be brought into accord with present circumstances. 3. The 'intellectual' way, by which the individual struggles over the problem of the disparity between the righteousness he or she expects and that which is not experienced. Here too the present will not do; in the last resort only the apocalyptic hope for the new age in which righteousness prevails offers a possible way out. Thus Luck's approach, like Gese's, ends up with apocalyptic as the hidden 'centre' of the Bible; similarly, the proclamation of Jesus and early Christianity are seen against an apocalyptic background as the message of righteousness which establishes itself in forgiveness (37ff.; cf. also already id, 'Gerechtigkeit in der Welt – Gerechtigkeit Gottes',*WuD* 12, 1973, 71-89, and recently id., 'Inwiefern ist die Botschaft von Jesus Christus "Evangelium"?', *ZTK* 77, 1980, 24-41).

The suspicion has been voiced about the approach by Schmid and Luck that it could be a new form of 'natural theology' (cf. Stuhlmacher, 'Biblische Theologie' [above, 157], 59f.). The most recent criticism of Schmid by J.Halbe ('Altorientalisches Weltordnungsdenken und alttestamentliche Theologie', *ZTK* 76, 1979, 381-418) points in the same direction, though also with an extensive apparatus of arguments based on system-theory (following N.Luhmann et al.). However (with Mildenberger, 'Randbemerkungen' [above, 152], 20) one can begin from the fact that, with Schmid and Luck, too, historical contingency is taken into account and that they did not intend anthropological generalizations.

As I remarked at the beginning, the discussion of 'biblical theology' also has a strong hermeneutical element. It is more or less explicitly in the background in all the models that have been produced. There has been a vigorous dispute – though furthered on all sides with inadequate epistemological means – in this context, above all between different New Testament scholars over the relevance of the historical-critical approach to biblical theology. Since G.Ebeling in 1950 associated the historical-critical method directly with the basic Reformation principle of *sola fide* ('Die Bedeutung der historisch-kritischen Methode für die protestantische Theologie und Kirche', *ZTK* 47, 1950, 1-46 = id., *Wort und Glaube* I, 1-49, 39ff./41ff. = ET 'The Significance of the Critical Historical Method for Church and Theology in Protestantism', in *Word and Faith*, Philadelphia and London 1963, reissued London 1984, [17-61] 55ff.; cf. also E.Käsemann, 'Vom theologischen Recht historisch-kritischer Exegese', *ZTK* 64, 1967, 259-81, esp. 260f.; R.Bultmann saw his existentialist, demythologizing interpretation as a parallel to the doctrine of justification: cf. *Jesus Christ and Mythology*, New York and London 1958; id., 'Zum Problem der Entmythologisierung', *KuM* 2, 1952, [179-208] 207 = ET *Kerygma and Myth 2*. London 1962, though he did not make connections between the two) this problem remains unsolved.

In most recent times there have been intensified efforts to discuss the relationship between the historical-critical method (organized in a stereotyped system of stages of methodological development) and the claim to truth in the biblical texts. Thus W.Dietrich (*Wort und Wahrheit. Studien zur Interpretation alttestamentlicher Texte*, Neukirchen-Vluyn 1976, 9ff.) emphatically stresses: 'As a theologian, the exegete can hardly be content with establishing "what is written there"; he will have to pose to himself the theological claim of the text and also to give it new validity as something that applies to the present' (24). In his view the results of historical-critical exegesis achieved with the help of methodological stages must 'further be made to serve exegesis proper' (23). He is by no means alone in making this demand. Cf. more recently also H.Barstad, 'The Historical-Critical Method and the Problem of Old Testament Theology', *SEÅ* 45, 1980, 7-18 (although this shows no clear methodological way out of the problem of *duplex veritas* [17]); J.H.Ware, 'Rethinking the Possibility of a Biblical Theology', *PRSt* 10, 1983, 5-13; H.Riedlinger, 'Der Übergang von der geschichtlichen zur geistlichen Bibelauslegung in der christlichen Theologie', in id. (ed.), *Die historisch-kritische Methode und die heutige Suche nach einem lebendigen Verständnis der Bibel*, Munich and Zurich 1985, 89-115. J.Barr, *Does Biblical Study Still Belong to Theology?*, Oxford Inaugural Lecture 1978, begins more from praxis.

P.Stuhlmacher in particular has involved himself here; in several of the articles collected together in his *Schriftauslegung* (above, 155: 'Neues Testament und Hermeneutik – Versuch einer Bestandsaufnahme', *ZTK* 68, 1971, 121-61 = 9-49; 'Thesen zur Methodologie gegenwärtiger Exegese', [*ZNW* 63, 1972, 18-26] = 50-8; 'Historische Kritik und theologische Schriftauslegung', 59-127; cf. also 'Zur Methoden- und Sachproblematik einer interkonfessionellen Auslegung des Neuen Testamentes', *EKK*. V,4, Zurich and Neukirchen 1972, 11-55, and more recently 'Hauptprobleme und Chancen kirchlicher Schriftauslegung', *ThBeitr* 9, 1978, 53-69 [Oslo Visiting Lecture 1977]) he has discussed the theological problem of the historical-critical exegesis of scripture within the overall horizon of a biblical theology. Through all the articles mentioned runs the basic demand that while the historical-critical method must be kept as an indispensable instrument of historical research into the biblical texts (Stuhlmacher resolutely defends this standpoint against evangelical objections as well – cf. G.Maier, *Das Ende der historisch-kritischen Methode*, Wuppertal [1974] ²1975; H.Lindner, 'Widerspruch oder Vermittlung? Zum Gespräch mit G.Maier und P.Stuhlmacher über eine biblische Hermeneutik', *ThBeitr* 7, 1976, 189-97; G.Maier, 'Einer biblischen Hermeneutik entgegen? Zum Gespräch mit P.Stuhlmacher und H.Lindner', *ThBeitr* 8, 1977, 148-60; Stuhlmacher, 'Hauptprobleme', n.11; and the discussion with G.Maier, 'Zum Thema: Biblische Hermeneutik', *ThBeitr* 9, 1978, 222-34), to add to its three usual principles – criticism, analogy and correlation (Troeltsch, cf. *Problems of Old Testament Theology*, 15f.), a fourth ('perception', 'Neues Testament', 148/36, *EKK*. V 4, 48) in the context of a 'theological exegesis of scripture', in which the incorporation of the exegete into the context of the historical influence of the tradition which emanates from Holy Scripture and a dialogical relation to it (this is also the concern of W.Wink, *The Bible in Human Transformation*, Philadelphia 1973, but cf. the critical review by N.Walter, *TLZ* 103, 1978, 173-5; H.Haag, 'Neuer biblischer Fundamentalismus?', *TQ* 160, 1980, 51f.; cf. also F.Mildenberger, 'Texte – oder die ganze Schrift?', *ZTK* 66, 1969, 192-209; P.D.Hanson, *Dynamic Transcendence: The Correlation of a Confessional Heritage and Contemporary Experience in a Biblical Model of Divine Activity*, Philadelphia 1978; id., 'The Responsibilities of Biblical Theology to Communities of Faith', *ThTo* 27, 1980, 39-50; id., *The Diversity of Scripture: A Theological Interpretation*, Overtures to Biblical Theology 11, Philadelphia 1982; also P.Achtermeier, *The Inspiration of Scripture*, Philadelphia 1980, esp. 124ff., 134ff.; W.J.Abraham, *The Divine Inspiration of Holy Scripture*, Oxford 1981; id., *Divine Revelation and the Limits of Historical Criticism*, Oxford 1982) and its claim in the direction of expressing 'a hermeneutic of sharing the understanding of the biblical texts by a reflective methodology which is subject to their historical influence' ('Historische Kritik', 120; cf. 120ff.; *Vom Verstehen* [above, 156], 14, 205ff. For the general principle of 'openness towards the truth and the claim of the texts' cf. also *EKK*. V 4, 41). Later ('Hauptprobleme', 66ff.; cf. also *Vom Verstehen*, 222f.) Stuhlmacher extends this dimension in the direction of a 'meditation on the biblical texts in their claim to truth in the present'; at the same time, this considers the dogmatic tradition of the church in the light of the results of historical criticism (see below, 177). Stuhlmacher sees his concern in the context both of Reformation exegesis ('Historische Kritik' [above, 168], 71ff.; 'Evangelische Schriftauslegung' [above, 156], 169ff.) and the hermeneutical principles of R.Bultmann (here he regards the categories of the Word of God and the individual in his worth and responsibility before God as indispensable ['Neues Testament', 153/41; for Bultmann see also 'Vom Verstehen', 173ff.; but cf. also the argument between Stuhlmacher and E.Grässer, *EK* 10, 1977, 21f. – 272-4) and K.Barth ('Neues Testament', 131ff./19ff.; cf. also 'Vom Verstehen', 162ff.); however, the theological dimension of exegesis called for by Barth under the slogan 'pneumatic exegesis' (cf. *Problems of Old Testament Theology*, 13ff.) can be achieved only 'in the application of method through the historical business of textual analysis' ('Historische Kritik', 89 – similarly already O.Weber, 'Der Ort der historisch-kritischen Methode in der Selbstauslegung der Heiligen Schrift', *KiZ* 18, 1963, 134-9 = id., 'Die Treue Gottes und die Kontinuität der menschlichen Existenz', *Gesammelte Aufsätze* I, Neukirchen-Vluyn 1967, 68-81). Cf. also his deliberate adoption of the hermeneutics of A.Schlatter (P.Stuhlmacher, 'Adolf Schlatter als Bibelausleger', in *Tübinger Theologie im 20. Jahrhundert*, ZTK B 4, Tübingen 1978, 81-111 = id., *Versöhnung, Gesetz und Gerechtigkeit*, Göttingen 1981, 271-302; id., 'Adolf Schlatter 1852-1938', in *Theologen des Protestantismus des 19. und 20. Jahrhunderts* I/II, ed. M.Greschat, UTB 284/5, Stuttgart 1978, 219-40. For Schlatter's hermeneutics cf. also I.Kindt, *Der Gedanke der Einheit. Adolf Schlatters Theologie und ihre historischen Voraussetzungen*, Stuttgart 1978; there is also a more general account in H.Stroh, 'Das Erbe Adolf Schlatters für unsere Zeit', *FAB* 32, 1978, 466-74).

Quite consistently, in the context of this integrating hermeneutical approach, consisting of a 'post-critical exegesis of scripture' (thus following R.Smend ['Nachkritische Schriftauslegung', in *Parrhesia, FS K.Barth*, Zurich 1966, 215-37] 'Nachkritische Schriftauslegung' in *Was ist los mit der deutschen Theologie?*, ed. H.N.Janowski and E.Stammler, Stuttgart 1978, 59-66; cf. also Stuhlmacher, 'Hauptprobleme', 63f. and n.19), For Stuhlmacher, the overall perspective on the Bible follows from this: on the one hand, in opposition to the picture painted by the so-called history-of-religions school of the original cultural world of primitive Christianity, still influenced by R.Bultmann and his theories about gnosticism, now 'the formation of the traditions of the Old and the New Testament [appear] as closely related phenomena' ('Neues Testament', 155/43), because 'the Old Testament is the decisive breeding ground of all the essential formation of tradition in the New Testament' ('Evangelische Schriftauslegung', 176), on the other hand (following Gese, but as a more independent entity than he would suppose), the canon as a whole, which represents the result of the formation of this tradition, takes on decisive theological importance. Consideration of the early history of the canon demonstrates 'that Old and New Testament – despite the undisputed hermeneutic leadership of the latter – are always seen together in the church, so that there is not a distinctive Christian problem of either the Old Testament or the New Testament canon each by itself' ('Historische Kritik', 66), and this is also the starting point of contemporary theological exegesis: here the presupposition is both 'that the Bible, as Old and New Testament, is an inseparable *unity*, for all its tension' – in particular it is important that 'Consequently the canon of the Bible as a whole is more convincing than before by virtue of the progress of critical exegesis' and that this unity follows from a 'dominant and normative centre of scripture', namely the gospel of Christ ('Evangelische Schriftaus-legung', 175; for the slight difference from Gese at this point cf. again 'Hauptprobleme', 63f.n.18).

Stuhlmacher feels his own hermeneutical approach to be provisional ('We do not yet have a compelling new hermeneutic', 'Neues Testament', 160/48 – J.Gnilka, 'Methodik und Hermeneutik. Gedanken zur Situation der Exegese', in *Neues Testament und Kirche. FS R.Schnackenburg*, Freiburg 1974, [458-75] 469 speaks of 'a degree of perplexity in the matter of hermeneutics'). Nor is it undisputed. Granted, the anachronistic attempt of C.Hartlich to revive consistently the hermeneutics of historical positivism ('Historisch-kritische Methode in ihrer Anwendung auf Geschehnisaussagen der Hl.Schrift', *ZTK* 75, 1978, 467-84) is virtually isolated (though cf. M.Smith, 'Historical Method in the Study of Religion', in *On Method in the History of Religions*, ed. J.S.Helfer, HTh.S 8, La Haye 1968, 8-16). However, the influence of a historicist understanding of history frequently leads to thinking on two levels: there is then a separation between historical knowl-edge, which leads to the chance truths of history, and theological judgments, which have to have the form of assertions because they are grounded in an assurance behind which there is no further asking (this is put particularly clearly by M.Hengel, 'Historische Methoden und theologische Auslegung des Neuen Testaments', *KuD* 19, 1973, 85-90, esp. sections 2.4.1; 2.4.2, 87; cf. already E.Dinkler, 'Bibelautorität und Bibelkritik', *ZTK* 47, 1950, 70-93 = id., 'Signum Crucis' [above, 95], 179-203; but also F.Mildenberger, *Theorie der Theologie*, Stuttgart 1972, 83f., in whose view 'hermeneutical reflections are an addition to the historical-critical method'. For the problem cf. also J.Mejia, 'A Christian View of Bible Inspiration', in L. Boadt et al., *Biblical Studies* [above, 101], 45-74. On this cf. the standpoint of O.Eissfeldt, *Problems of Old Testament Theology*, 17f.). This dualism seems to me also to be a perspective of the most recent critical inquiry by E.Grässer ('Offene Fragen im Umkreis einer Biblischen Theologie', *ZTK* 77, 1980, 200-21) into Stuhlmacher's work (Stuhlmacher responded, ibid., 222-38, '... in verrosteten Angeln', [with rusty hinges]). There is clearly a view of the term 'historical' more characteristic of nineteenth-century hermeneutics when, for example, he asks, 'What about the necessary distinction between scripture and kerygma, understood text and word of God, historical exegesis and proclamation, professorial chair and pulpit?' (203f.), and refers to Gabler's programme (220) and A.Deissmann's comments in his 1892 probationary lecture, 'that there is still hardly any doubt about the purely historical character of New Testament theology' ('Zur Methode der Biblischen Theologie des Neuen Testaments', *ZTK* 3, 1893, 126-39 = *Das Problem der Theologie des Neuen Testaments*, ed. G.Strecker, WdF CCCXVII, Darmstadt 1975, 67-80, 126/67)(200) and accuses Stuhlmacher of giving historical work 'a dogmatic baptism' for which rather it is the case that 'in any case, historical theology has to decline another set of rules than those provided by its own methodological principles' (201).

Account does not yet seem to have been taken of this more recent development of the hermeneutics of history. G.E.Wright ('Historical Knowledge and Revelation', in *Translating and Understanding the Old Testament*, FS H.G.May, Nashville and New York 1970, [279-303], 290) clearly recognized the principle of any historical knowledge: 'Historical knowledge... is a kind of personal knowledge with which I, as a person, am involved.' A broad phalanx of literature on the hermeneutics of history from the current discussion could be cited here. However, Grässer does not call for an 'exegesis without presuppositions'; he is ready to accept H.G.Gadamer's demands for an awareness of the influence of history in the preunderstanding of the exegete (207, this awareness is otherwise understood in existentialist terms, as by Bultmann, cf. also Strecker, 'Biblische Theologie?' [above, 155f.], 442, 444).

Now if one can describe reference to Holy Scripture as the

backbone of the Christian tradition, how is Grässer's view possible that the whole of Biblical Theology as Stuhlmacher and his friends understand it would seem 'backward-looking' (206; cf. also Strecker, 'Biblische Theologie?', 426 n.2)? How can Grässer attack it as an about-face towards the 'battle-cry' uttered by Gabler '... against the dogmatic constriction by the church' – which for him had a legitimate sequel in the consistent separation of New Testament scholarship from Old Testament scholarship by Georg Lorenz Bauer (cf. *Problems of Old Testament Theology*, 4), as a renewed 'cry for help' to the dogmatic theologians (ibid.), a 'mishmash of historical research and dogmatics' (221), i.e. a new form of obscurantism?

In my view it is necessary to distinguish between Grässer's legitimate questions about specific and sometimes vague statements by Stuhlmacher (Strecker, 'Biblische Theologie?', also asks similar questions) and fundamental positions that call for a real decision. In fact remarks of Stuhlmacher's like 'those who want the text to be true in its present wording' (Stuhlmacher, 'Hauptprobleme', 61) are capable of misunderstanding, as is talk of 'linguistic models' which cannot be superseded (ibid., n.17), when he is discussing central theologumena like the vicarious death of Jesus and his resurrection (which according to Bultmann need to be demythologized). This kind of statement simply asks for Grässer to misunderstand it ('Now if these were linguistic models, they would have to be interchangable in principle', 208). Furthermore, Stuhlmacher sees the relationship between the Testaments on different levels and therefore is not clear: Grässer rightly makes the criticism that in some of his remarks Stuhlmacher designates certain Old Testament themes and structures after the fashion of the history of religions school as presuppositions for understanding for the content of New Testament proclamation in the sense of kindred perspectives, while on the other hand with Gese he begins from a traditio-historical connection between the content of the two Testaments (Grässer, 211f.). Over against the specific form of the traditio-historical model as it appears in Gese and Stuhlmacher, serious consideration needs to be paid to the question put by W.Schmithals as to whether it does not equally contain objectivizing, positivistic elements which betray modern rather than biblical thought (review of Stuhlmacher, *Schriftausle-gung*, in *RKZ* 24, 1976, [282-5] 284). F.Mildenberger, however, regards such suspicions as less justified if we note that Gese connects history with the biblical texts and the understanding of them (in faith) ('Randbemerkungen' [above, 152], 16). That must also apply to the objection made by A.H.J. Gunneweg ('Theologie des Alten Testaments oder Biblische Theologie?', *FS Würthwein* [above, 164], [39-46] 44 = id., *Sola Scriptura*, ed. P.Höffken, Göttingen 1983, [227-34] 232) that this makes every claim and promise valid now dissolve into 'past and transitory stages in the process, which is the only thing that matters'.

However, there are also central points of difference over matters of content, in which a biblical theology must take a clear position if it is to have a scientific foundation. One of these points is the question of the canon. Grässer's criticism of Stuhlmacher relates centrally to the problem of the relationship between the two Testaments as canon, when he objects to the way in which Stuhlmacher both moves back into the Old Testament from the New, in the usual way, and also builds up a series of arguments running from the Old Testament in the New, working in the opposite direction (141). To this he opposes the confession of the crucified one as the Christ of God, which is not to be derived from the Old Testament (Deut 21.23 = Gal.3.13); this confession (for Stuhlmacher, too) is *without analogy*; and more generally (with G.Klein), 'the impossibility of deriving from elsewhere the content of the earliest Christian proclamation' (219) as a whole (G.Strecker, 'Biblische Theologie' [above, 155f.], 436, has the same view; for him, 'in the perspective of the Christ event the distance between the Old Testament and the New is greater than the common factors which bind together the two Testaments'. Cf. also his definition of the history of the theology of the New Testament as a history of the criticism and dissolution of the pre-existing notion of a "biblical theology"', 'Das Problem der Theologie des Neuen Testaments', in id.[ed.], *Das Problem der Theologie des Neuen Testaments*, WdF 367, Darmstadt 1975, [1-31] = id., *Eschaton* [above, 78], [260-90] 1/260). Now Stuhlmacher would certainly also agree that the relationship between the Testaments is a dialectical one, and contains a Yes and a No (for which Grässer also refers to R.Smend, and with him to E.Haenchen, H.Conzelmann and P.Vielhauer, ibid.). However, with Grässer there is no sign of the preliminary recognition of the Old Testament as canon in the way that characterizes the 'Old Marburgers': according to Gal.1.16 the confession of Christ crucified goes back to an 'apocalypsis' for which there has been no preparation; Paul merely formulated the gospel that had been revealed to him, 'by means of pre-existing Jewish divine predicates' (218). Accordingly Grässer, very much like Gunkel (cf.218), understands the traditio-historical descent of the New Testament in a very open way: not only Judaism and the Old Testament (and in addition to that occasionally also the history of ancient Near Eastern religions), but also Gnosticism, the Hellenistic mystery religions and Stoicism also arise as factors in the tradition (Strecker, 'Biblische Theologie?', 436ff., also makes a very similar point; he refers particularly to the varied origin of the language and thought-world of the New Testament – not only from the Old Testament and Judaism but also from the Hellenistic world). This holds not only for Paul but for the whole of the New Testament: 'In the light of the absoluteness of the revelation in Christ, Old Testament Jewish and Hellenistic Gnostic ideas are endorsed by him in a *relative* way. What we have is a *twofold language...* no more and no less' (218). Dialectical theology and historical relativism are akin, as we can see in K.Barth's remark, which Grässer quotes with approval (ibid.): 'The Bible comprises the literary monuments of a Near Easter tribal religion and a cult religion of the Hellenistic period...'

Criticism of remarks made by Stuhlmacher in his Oslo Visiting Lecture is made easier, however, by the fact that there he orientated himself markedly on Paul Ricoeur's structuralist hermeneutic which in some way makes the 'text' a hypostasis (cf. 55f. – On Ricoeur cf. recently also *Vom Verstehen* [above, 156], 201-4). In fact, however, precisely at this point Stuhlmacher is particularly clearly concerned with the question of the canon and therefore he deliberately understands the exegesis for which he strives as the church's exegesis of scripture ('Hauptprobleme', 54; cf. 65); he explicitly says that he is 'following the common dogmatic tradition of the Protestant and Catholic church' (cf. also 'Hauptprobleme', 65). (In hermeneutical terms, behind this approach is the view that scripture truly discloses itself only to those who venture to exist as a community of those who share faith in Christ and as such listen to the word of scripture' ['Historische Kritik', 71].) Underlying this is the dogmatic decision of the acknowledgment of a truth-claim: as 'the originally oral and prophetic testimony of the biblical witnesses to the truth' and the 'human testimonies to origins, which as such are quite varied', the biblical texts 'have a historical and qualitative priority over all Christian witnesses of faith which are based on these texts' ('Hauptprobleme', 57). In accordance with this, 'the church has marked off the canon of biblical writings from all witness to the church's faith, and in its work the church's exegesis of the scripture sees itself punctiliously directed to this canon of Old and New Testament with which it is presented' ('Hauptprobleme', 58). Here Stuhlmacher resolutely denies that he is limiting the critical function of exegesis (cf. again 'Hauptprobleme', 68 and nn.18, 19. For this group of problems cf. also F.Beisser, 'Irrwege und Wege der historisch-kritischen Bibelwissenschaft', *NZST* 15, 1973, 192-214). For K.Barth's attitude to historical-critical method cf. recently also H.Zwanger, ' "Kritischer müssten mir die Historisch-Kritischen sein!" Hinter Barth zurück?', *EvTh* 43, 1983, 370-80.

Biblical theology (and the rejection of it) is therefore beyond question concerned with basic dogmatic decisions; to this extent the new movement supported by a few committed pioneers is in its different variations a *theological* programme. Indeed, the alleged impossibility of deriving the Christ event from elsewhere is a dogmatic thesis, although it cannot find support on the doctrine of the Trinity in the early church, in which the indissoluble connection between the redeemer and the creator is expressed (cf. John 14.6, which is usually not quoted in its entirety). In my own view biblical theology can only be tackled as an inter-disciplinary theological task (thus recently also C.Westermann, 'Aufgaben einer zukünftigen biblischen Theologie', *DtPfrBl* 81, 1981, 3-6 = id., *Erträge der Forschung [III]* [above, 145], 203-12); here the help of systematic theology cannot be dispensed with.

However, the exact way in which biblical theology is to be distinguished from dogmatic theology remains an open problem.

There is a series of proposed solutions in W.D.Jonker, 'Eksegese en Dogmatiek' in *FS E.P.Groenewald*, Pretoria 1970, (157-79) 158ff.; cf. also M.H.Woudstra, *CTJ* 1983 (above, 000). In his review ('Bijbelse theologie en dogmatiek', *VoxTh* 46, 1976, [25-36], 33) A.Geense calls the relevant section in Kraus (*Biblische Theologie* [above, 159], 391-5) 'remarkably thin'. He himself sees an additional critical task of dogmatics as being the responsibility for proclamation in the present day, but this is measured by the revelation of Christ attested in scripture (34). H.Schlier ('Biblische und dogmatische Theologie', in *Diskussion über die Bibel*, ed. L.Klein, Mainz 1963, 85-98 = id., *Besinnung auf das Neue Testament. Exegetische Aufsätze und Vorträge* II, Freiburg,

Basle and Vienna 1964, 25-34 = Strecker [ed.], *Problem* [above, 174] 425-37) thinks that biblical and dogmatic theology 'turn their faces towards each other' (32/434) in such a way that dogmatics does its thinking in the context of the tradition of the church in the light of the theological content of the Bible as expounded by biblical theology (33/435), thus arriving at the very substance (31/433). Cf. also J.Bosc, 'Exégèse et dogmatique', *RHPR* 46, 1966, 131-43. For H.Petri, 'Exegese' (above, 46), 'biblical theology must be included among the positive disciplines of theology, the essential task of which lies in establishing the didactic content of particular documents' (78). Nevertheless it becomes clear from the following survey of 'biblical theology as an understanding of faith' (80ff.) that its task goes beyond that: it must also 'arrive at a real theological understanding of what is said in the Bible' (90), and for that it needs faith which discloses the depth of understanding (88).

On this point even Stuhlmacher is more hesitant: the transition from historical criticism to 'theological exegesis of scripture' (cf. 'Historische Kritik', passim, esp. 126) is not given a clear methodological definition. Mildenberger's formula, 'Scientific theological exegesis of scripture reflects this tradition of faith that has come about, specifically in respect of its determination by the biblical texts, just as systematic theology reflects it in respect of present experience' ('Randbemerkungen' [above, 152], 26 – similarly also already O.A.Piper, 'Biblical Theology and Systematic Theology', *JBR* 25, 1957, 106-11), and stresses more the way in which something holds together aspects of which, at least, can be differentiated (cf. also 29 and n.73; similarly also already Scheffczyk, 'Auslegung' [above, 42], who stresses as an additional element – which is also valid between confessions – the fact that this exegesis takes place in the sphere of the church). R.de Vaux ('Peut-on écrire' [above, 147], 71) even remarks: 'L'opposition entre la théologie biblique et la théologie dogmatique doit disparaître parce que doit disparaître la distinction entre deux théologies.' Cf. also Manigne (*Pour une poétique de la foi. Essai sur le mystère symbolique*, CFi 493, Paris 1969, 116); 'Il n'y a, il ne peut y avoir, qu'une seule théologie, dont les sources sont toujours évangéliques et le traitement toujours dogmatique, si on entend par ce dernier terme qualifier le langage qui exprime l'intelligence de la foi.' G.Siegwalt, 'Biblische Theologie als Begriff und Vollzug', *KuD* 25, 1979, 254-72 = abbreviated version 'La théologie biblique. Concept et réalisation', *ETR* 45, 1979, 397-409, has defined biblical theology in this sense as a systematic theological discipline into which, however, exegesis is integrated. The juxtaposition of the theological disciplines can only be understood in terms of a division of work. H.J.Kraus observes: 'In all the basic questions of "biblical theology" the significance of the dogmatic premises and implications is always strictly to be taken into account.' His remark is justified, since in this respect traditio-historical researches of Old Testament scholarship are still very much in their beginnings ('Theologie als Traditionsbildung?' [above, 000], 500f./64). In this respect we must agree with H.H.Schmid that biblical theology belongs in the framework of fundamental theology ('Unterwegs?' [above, 148], 95). So it will be possible to discuss its problems successfully only in the interdisciplinary collaboration of theological specializations.

Index of Names